HIGHER GEOGRAPHY

PART I

A TEXT BOOK FOR CLASS XI (ISCE)

Dedicated to the loving and fond memory of my father-in-law Dr. (Brig) Nirendra Chandra Das Vr.C. a highy qualified physician by profession but whose immense love and zeal for academia in all it's multitudinous forms and whose constant encouragement and support proved to be one of the greatest sources of inspiration in my life.

Jayati Das

HIGHER GEOGRAPHY

PART I

A TEXT BOOK FOR CLASS XI (ISCE)

Fully covers the latest syllabus prescribed by the council for the Indian School Certificate Examination, New Delhi.

Prof. S. C. Mukhopadhyay, Ph.D, D.Sc.
Professor, Department of Geography,
Calcutta University,
Calcutta

Jayati Das Ph.D.
Lecturer in Geography
Shri Shikshayatan College,
Calcutta

RAJESH PUBLICATIONS
NEW DELHI-110 002

ISBN : 81-85891-23-0
First Edition : 1999

Price : t Edn.)
Price : Edn.)

Published by :
M. L. Gupta
Rajesh Publications,
1, Ansari Road, Darya Ganj,
New Delhi-110 002
Phone : 3274550

Lasertypesetting by :
Sanjay Gupta
Sanjay Enterprises
New Delhi-2

Printed at :
Graphic Print, Delhi-2

Preface

This book written exclusively for Standard XI, is an attempt on the authors' part to com;y with the modifications that have taken place over the years in the I.S.C.E. syllabus for Geography.

It is also an attempt at presenting a lucid and comprehensive account of the diverse range of information available, at present. Most of these information, data and material maybe found in several text books on Physical and Economic Geography, while some of the more scientific techniques mentioned can only be encountered in various journals and publication. The purpose of this book thus, has been to garner all the myriad and dissipated information within the folds of a self contained text which, it is believed, will prove to be of immense assistance and importance to the average student of Geography. A few enticing and supplementary details have also been introduced, to maintain the continuity of ideas and to stimulate a desire for delving deeper into the subject.

The maps, sketches and diagrams have also been accuratley updated to be of topical value as well as to be alluring to the aesthetic-scientific temperament and discerning nature of today's youngsters. A few satellite imageries have also been provided for a clearer cognition of the relevant topics.

It is the sincere hope on the authors' part that this modest endeavour will prove to be of enormous significance to both teachers and students alike. Betterment of the book in it's subsequent editions will always be the prime concern of the authors hereafter and any constructive and helpful suggestions towards it's attainment will be cherished and highly appreciated.

Contents

SYLLABUS (CLASS-XI)

A. Map Reading and Interpretation of Survey Maps.

Representation of geographical data in maps and diagrams. Representation of topographical features on maps. Scales and profiles. Questions may be set involving (a) grid references, converntional signs, gradients, the measurements of distance and orientation; (b) the description of relief and drainage, settlement patterns and communications.

B. Landforms and Processes

(a) Landforms resulting from folding, faulting and volcanic activity with examples chosen for study from South and South-East Asia.

(b) The Work of running water: river erosion, transportation and deposition. Landforms of river valleys including the shpae and form of the valley in the upper, middle and lower regions, waterfalls, gorges, meanders, floodplains, kevels and deltas. The causes of, and problems produced by, **Seasonal flooding.** Local Indian examples should be chosen for study wherever possible.

(c) Water resources and conservation in India with particular references to ground water, water-tables, springs, problems of water storage.

(d) Landscapes in dry climates including dunes, wadis and oases: sandy deserts; rock and stony deserts; mountain regions of aridity. All studies and examples may be selected from Iran, Baluchistan, Afghanistan, Pakistan, India.

(e) Coastal landforms and marinc processes as seen on the coastline of India; erosion and deposition, the formation of cliffs, stacks, caves, abrasion platforms, beaches, sand-bars and spits. dunes and coastal marshes, estuaries, dclta landforms and land reclamation. The problem of the coastal protection of low-lying parts of India coastline.

(f) Remote sensing in mapping/monitioring of geological structure, costal zone, land use, urban sprawl, crops, soils, wasteland, plantation, ground water, land forms, fisheries, forests, pollution.

In each section the study of local maps and photographs should be encouraged and questions may be set on the description and analysis of photographs. In any section credit will be given to work presented showing local knowledge and field-work.

C. Weather and Climate

(a) Weather study based mainly on local observation and the use of simple weather maps. Measurements of the elements of weather. The use of the maximum, wet and dry bulb, thermometers, the rain-gauge, the barometer and the wind vane. Observation and recording of the cloud type and wind force.

(b) The formation of relief, convectional and cyclonic rainfall. artificial rainfall.

(c) A study of weather types associated with the cool dry season, hot dry season and monsoon season in India.

(d) Climatic Types-the climates of the equatiorial tropical monsoon, tropical desert, Mediterranean, cool temperature, western margin, taiga and tundra climates, together with their chief annual in seasonal features of temperature, rainfall and winds.

D. Vegetation and Soils

The simple processes of soil formation; the characteristics of common soil types in India (laterites, regur soils, soils affected by salination); soil profiles of padsols, lateritic soils, alluvial soils Cause of soil ersoion in India; the problem of salination due to irrigation; methods of soil couservation.

The description of natural vegetations and factors influencing it with special reference to tropical rain forests, tropical grasslands, tropical desert vegetation and vegetation in tropical highlands and in tropical deltas. Examples may be condined to India and other parts of Asia.

E. Field-work

Field exercises based on local data, for example:

(a) The mapping of urban land use.
(b) The mapping of rural land use.
(c) A farm study.
(d) A study of port.
(c) A study of some landforms.
(f) A study of mining complex.
(g) A study of a manufacturing industry.

1

Map Reading and Interpretation of Survey Maps

Geography deals primarily with the distribution of various phenomena on the earth. These may be relief features, climatic condition, natural vegetation and other features of the environment. We also study the distribution of population and the various activities of human beings on the earth and the cultural landscapes, like settlement, roads, railway lines and others.

By such study of both natural and cultural landscapes, we try to understand the relationship between various phenomena on the earth. Maps are essential toolS for geographical studies. They are drawn to represent the earth aS a whole or parts of it on a piece of paper, Maps are easy to handle and they can be taken io the field by explorer or tourist. Maps may be drawn to show the main features of a particular distribution.

Types of Maps:-Maps are usually classified into different kinds based on the purpose for which they are used.

Topographic Maps:-Show much greater details about small areas. There maps are prepared based on a detailed survey of the areas concerned. Topographic maps are also general purpose maps as they show relief features, rivers, landuse, vegetation, settlements, roads, railway lines and administrative units and their boundaries.

Cadastral Maps:- are village maps and town maps which show individual fields and house sites. These maps contain much more detail than topographical maps. These maps form the basis for maintaining revenue records of villages and towns.

Maps are also grouped according to the particulars shown on them. Maps which show selected features only are called **Thematic maps.** A road map of India is a thematic map.

Physical Maps :- usually contain information about two relief features such as mountains, plateaus and plains, rivers, lakes, seas and other natural features only.

Scale of a Map

Maps represent the surface of the earth on a small scale on a piece of paper. Maps are drawn to a scale so that relative distances of places are correct as on the earth.

The Scale of a Map:- is the ratio or proportion between the distances of two places on the map and the actual distances between those two places on the ground. The scale of a map may be represented in three different ways. (i) **as a statement** such as 1cm to 2 km (ii) **as a Representative Fraction** (R.F) such as 1: 50,000 or (iii) as a **graphical or linear scale**.

When the scale of a map is stated as a 'statement, it is expressed in certain of measurement like kilometers or miles.

Representative Fraction:- A more useful method of representing the scale of a map is by a ratio or fraction called the Representative Fraction or R.F. This fraction is the ratio between distances on the map and the corresponding distances on the ground. The numeration of the fraction is always, I and the denominator indicates the corresponding distance on the ground.

$$\text{R.F} = \frac{\text{Distance on the map}}{\text{Distance on the ground}}$$

When the scale of a map is given as a statement it can be converted in to a Representative Fraction. When the scale of a map is 1cm to 10 km, calculate the R. F. on the map.

1cm = 10km
=10, 000 meters
=10,000+ 100 or 10,00,000 cms.

Therefore the Representative Fraction in 1:10,00,000

Graphical Scale or Linear Scale

The Graphical scale or Linear scale is a line of convenient

length divided at regular intervals and graduated in terms of distances on the ground. Using the linear scale, the distance between any two points on the map may be measured directly in terms of distance on the ground. The linear scale can be used in the units in which it is graduated. For example, when a linear scale is graduated in kilometers, it can be used for measurement in that unit only (Fig. A1).

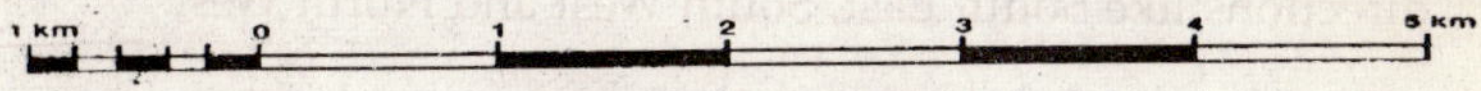

Linear scale-1:50,000

By using the same method, two linear scales are drawn below for use with maps on scales of 1:1,000,000 Fig. 18.2) and 1:4,000,000 (Fig. 18.2)

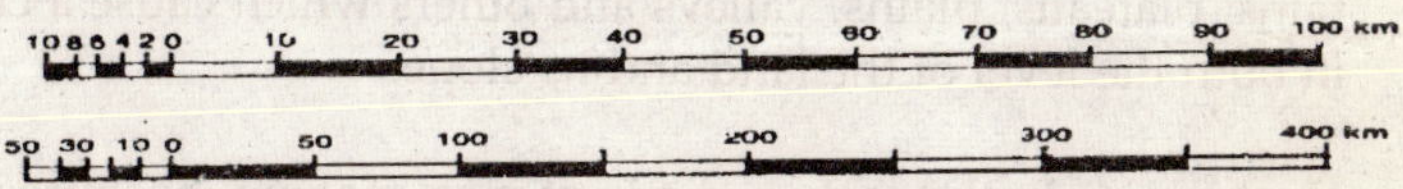

Fig . A1 ***Linear scale-1:1,000,000 & 1:4,000,000***

Measuring Distances on Maps

Distances between any two points on the map may be measured in centimetres using scale. For example, if the distance between two points A and B on the map is 4.2 cms. and the scale of the map is 1cm to 2 km, the distance between them on the ground is 4.2x2 or 8.4 km. If a linear scale is on the map, the distance may be read using the linear scale. First place a strip of paper along the line connecting A and B and mark the distance by pencil on the paper. Transfer the paper to the linear scale drawn on the map and read the actual distance in kilometres using the primary and secondary divisions.

In the case of curved lines like river, winding roads, or railwaylines, a piece of twine string may be used by carefully aligning it along the curved line connecting two points. The length of the string may be measured in centimetres using a scale and then converted to distances in kilometres based on the scale of the map.

Directions on Maps

Direction is usually indicated on a map by a North-South line with north direction represented by an arrow head. A short line perpendicular to this is drawn to show the east and west directions. On topograhic maps, the lines of longitude represent North-South lines while the latitude lines run East-West. Both distance and direction are needed to fix the location of places on a map. Therefore, direction is as important as the scale of a map. For example, if we know that Village A is located 5 km from Village B. the position of the village cannot be fixed. Village A can lie anywhere on a circle with a radius of 5 km from B. Village A can be fixed precisely only if me know its direction from B.

North, South, East and West are the main cardinal directions. North East lies, between North and East. Thus we have other directions like South East, South West and North West.

Representation of Relief Featues on Maps

The earth surface is not uniformally flat. There are mountains, plateaus, plains, valleys and others which cause a change in both the level of the land and its slope.

Hachures:- In the early periods of map making, hachures were used widely to represent the relief features. Hachures are lines drawn along the direction of maximum slope. Gentle slopes are indicated by thin lines drawn further apart. Steep slopes are shown by thick lines drawn close together. Level ground, whether in the hill tops or valley floors, is left unshaded. A number of spot heights are added to supplement hachures. Hachures are not widely used now except in mountainous areas which have not been surveyed (Fig.A2).

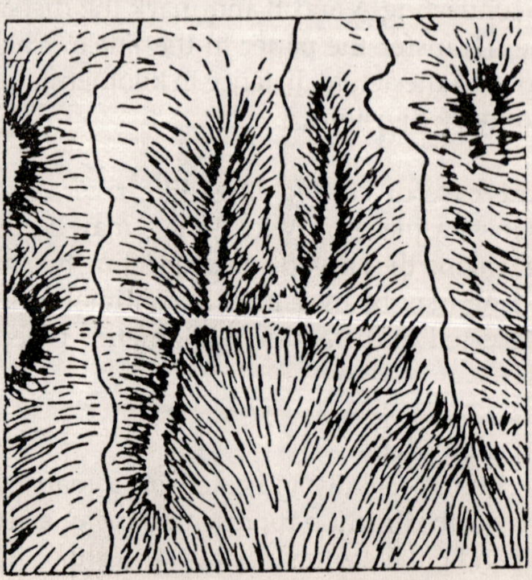

Fig . A2 ***Relief Shown by Hachures***

Hill Shading:- This is another method of representing relief features on map. In this method it is assumed that there is a source of light in the north-west direction of the area shown on the map. Mountains, hills and other relief features will cast their shadows on the slopes facing south and East. Therefore, south facing and east facing slopes are shaded on the map. Hill shading adds graphic visual effect to the map, when comibined with contours. (Fig. A3).

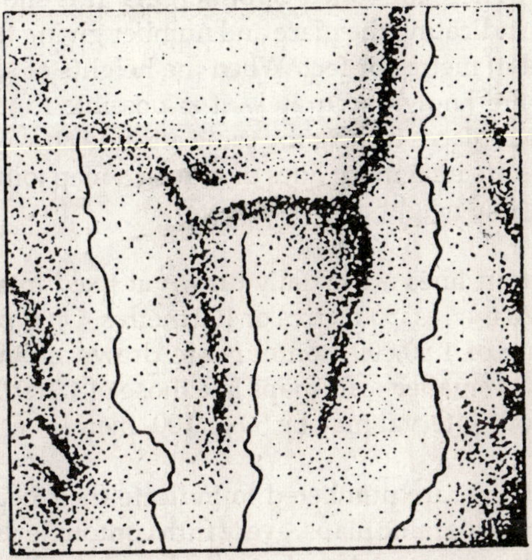

Fig . A3 ***Relief Shown by Hill-shading***

Layer Colouring:- This is a method of representing relief features on wall maps and atlas maps. Each altitude zone is shaded in a paticular colour. Heights of altitude zones are fixed arbitarily. Lowlands are shown by shades of green. Uplands are shown by shades of yellow or orange. High mountains and plateaus are shown by shades of brown or red. Snow covered areas are left white few places such as peaks of mountains are marked. A key to the colour shades adopting in given on the map. Layer colouring gives an indication of the relative heights of the land only and does not give the form of relief features or their slopes.

Layer colouring is also used to represent the depths of the sea floor. Light shades of blue are used to show shallow depths, while darker shades are used to show deeper portions of the sea floor.

Layer colouring method is not suitable for showing relief features on topographic maps.

Contours:- With the development of instruments of detailed surveying, it was possible to measure the heights of several places in a given. These, heights were marked near the points shown on the map. These are called **Spot heights.** It is shown on the map by a dot indicating the place and number giving the height above sea-level in metres or feet. When the heights of several points in an area are known accurately, it is possible to interpolate lines which join places having the same altitude above sea-level. *Contour* lines are imaginary lines drawn on a map joining places having the same height above sea-level.

Contour lines are usually drawn at fixed intervals of height such as 20 metres, 50 metres or 100 metres. On topographic maps on a scale of 1:50,000, contours are drawn at an interval of 20 metres. On smaller scale maps like those of 1:100,000 or 1:250,000 the contour interval may be 50 or 100 metres.

Contours, are numbered to indicate their height above sea-level. On topograhic maps, every fifth contour is drawn by a thick line and is numbered. Numbers may be printed by making a break in the line. Contour lines generally do not intersect on the map. In some places where they intersect, it may indicate a steep cliff or waterfall along the river.

Gradient:- The slope between two points may be expressed quantitatively as *gradient*. The gradient between two points is expressed as a ratio between the vertical interval between two points and the horizontal distance between them. In the Fig. A4 gradient between A and B

$$= \frac{\text{Vertical Interval}}{\text{Horizontal Distance}} = \frac{AO}{BO} = \frac{400}{4000} = \frac{1}{10}$$

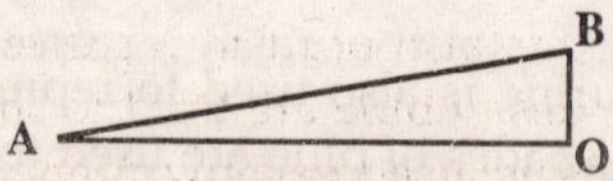

Fig. A 4 Gradient 1 in 10

The gradient between A and B is 1 in 10. This means for every 10 units of horizontal distance, there is a rise of 1 unit of height gradient is useful for the construction of roads and railway lines in hilly region.

When the gradient between two places is known it in possible to represent the slope of the land graphically.

Types of Slope

Unifom slope

Contour lines give an indication of the slope of the land as well as the elevation above sea level. Where contour lines are far apart, this represents a **gentle slope** of the land (Fig.A5). *Steep*

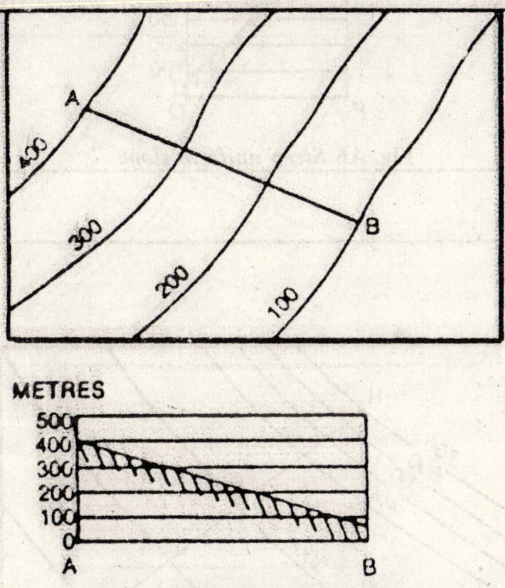

Fig. A5 ***Gentle uniform slope***

slopes are represented by a close spacing of contour lines. In places where the contour lines are spaced uniformly, it represents a regular or **unifom slope** of land (Fig. A6) The cross-section drawn below the contour diagram brings out clearly the uniform slope of the land.

Concave slope

In a concave slope, the slope of the land is gentle at low elevation and becomes steep at high elevation. The spacing of contours will be far apart at lower levels and closer at higher

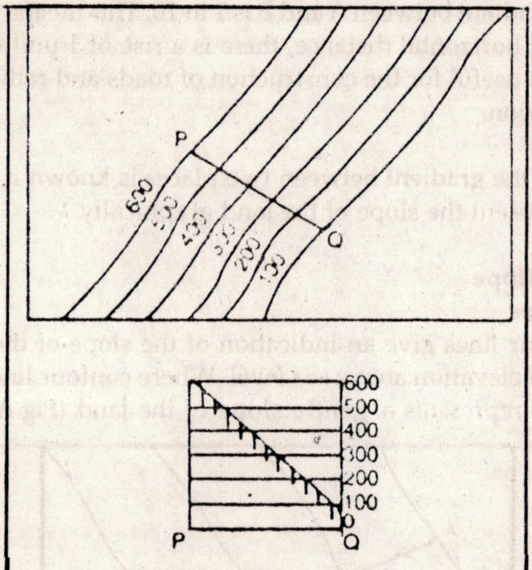

Fig. A6 *Steep uniform slope*

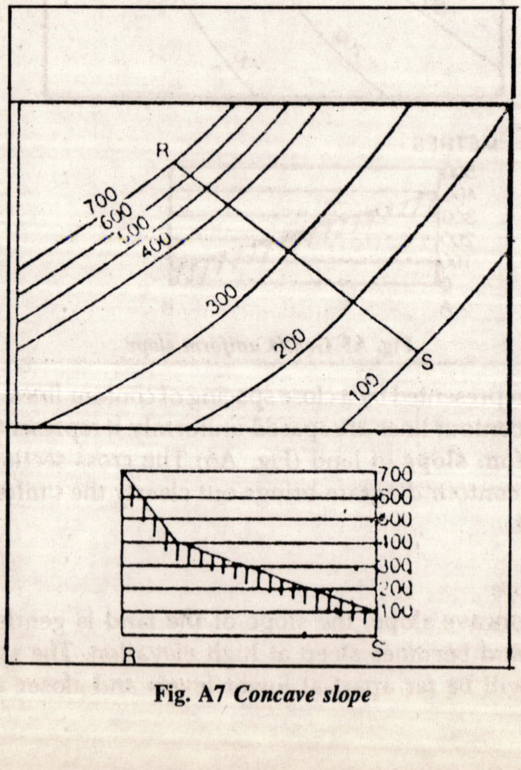

Fig. A7 *Concave slope*

levels (Fig. A7). The cross-section brings out clearly the concave slope of the land, Volcanic hills have concave slopes on all sides.

Convex slope

An example of convex slope is shown in contour diagram Fig. A8. The slope of the land is steep at low levels and gentle at high elevation. Therefore, the contours are closer at low elevations and farther apart at higher elevations. The cross-section brings out clearly the form of the convex slope. A dome mountain has convex slopes all around.

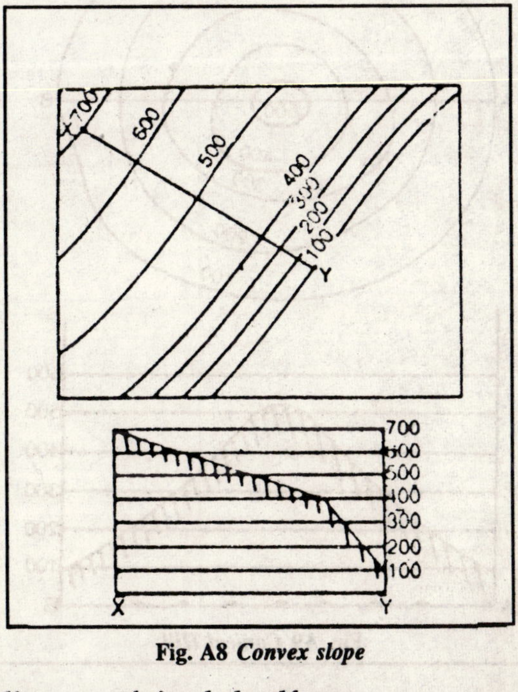

Fig. A8 ***Convex slope***

Contour diagrams of simple landforms

All landforms consist of combinations of different forms of slope described above. The different landforms are represented by varied spacing and shapes of contour lines. Familiarity with these varied forms of contour lines will enable one to interpret the map and describe the landforms found in the region.

Conical Hill

A hill is landform with a summit at a high elevation. Land slopes in all directions from the summit of the hill. Where the slopes are uniform in all directions from the summit of the hill, it is called a **Conical hill.** Contour lines are nearly equally spaced. The summit of the hill is marked by the contour line of the highest value. The contour line marking the foot of the hill has the lowest value. The cross-section brings out the uniform slope of the Conical hill (Fig. A9).

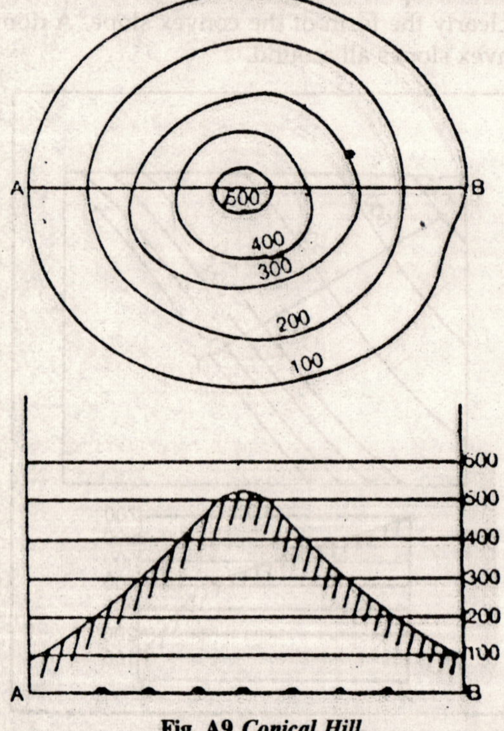

Fig. A9 ***Conical Hill***

Plateau

A **plateau** is a flat-topped highland with steep slopes on one or more sides. A plateau is also called a tableland, because it has a flat undulating surface with gentle slopes. The edges of the plateau rise steeply from the adjoining lowland. Closely spaced contour lines mark the steep slope which forms the edge of the plateau. The cross-section brings out clearly the form of the plateau (Fig. A10).

Ridge

A **ridge** is a long and narrow upland which has many peaks. A ridge is sometimes called a range of hills. The slope of the hill may be steep or gentle. The cross-section gives an idea of the form of a ridge (Fig. A11).

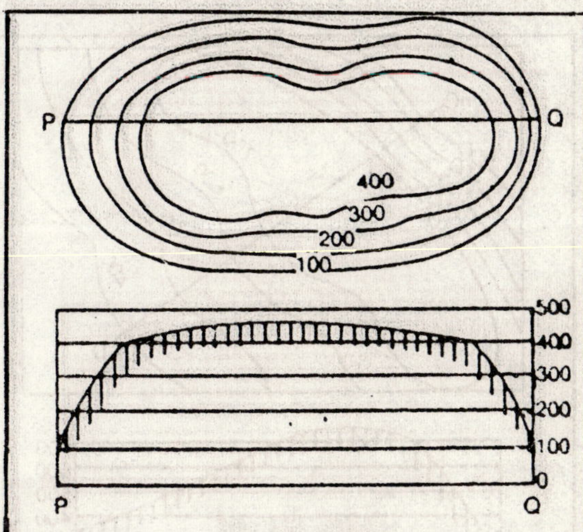

Fig. A10 *Plateau*

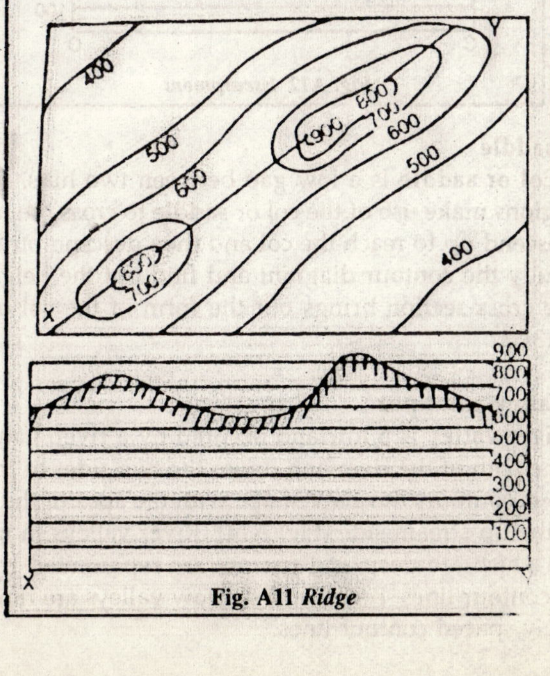

Fig. A11 *Ridge*

Escarpment

An **escarpment** has a steep slope on one side and a gentle slope on the opposite side. The steep slope is represented by closely spaced contours and gentle slope is shown by contour lines drawn far apart. The cross-section shows clearly the contrast in slopes between the two sides of an escarpment (Fig.A12).

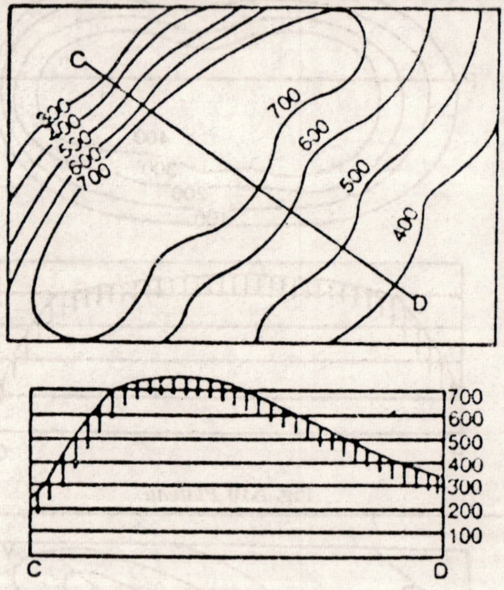

Fig. A12 ***Escarpment***

Col or saddle

A **Col or saddle** is a low gap between two hills. Routes in hilly regions make use of the col or saddle to cross the hills. One has to ascend up to reach the col and then descend on the other side. Study the contour diagram and find out the height of the col. The cross-section brings out the form of the col or saddle (Fig. A13).

River valley and Spur

A **river valley** is a lowland occured by a river. Land slopes along the path of the river and down the two sides of the valley. Therefore, contours have a V-shape with the apex of the V pointing on the up-stream side (Fig. A14). River valleys in mountain regions which are deep and narrow are represented by closely spaced contour lines. Broad and shallow valleys are represented by widely spaced contour lines.

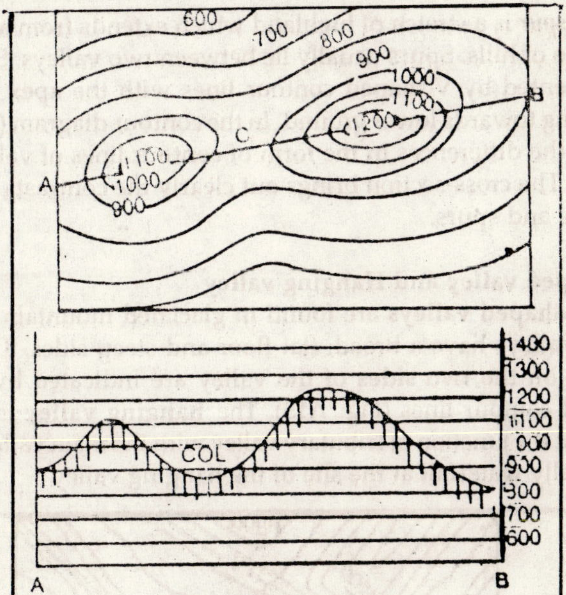

Fig. A13 ***Col or Saddle***

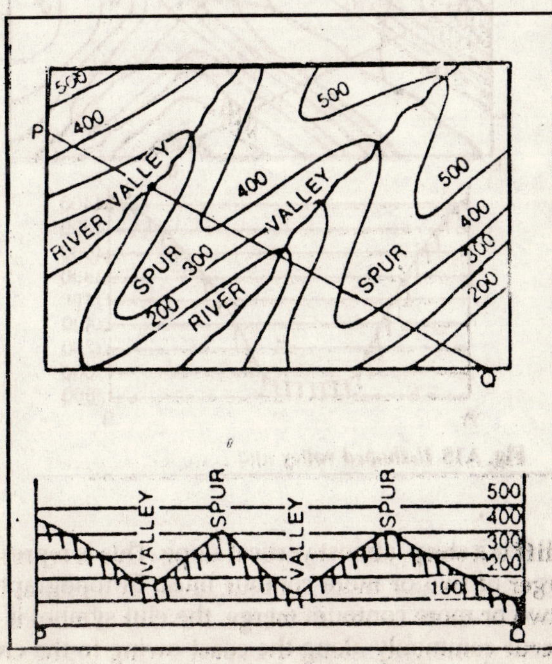

Fig. A14 ***River valley and spur***

A *spur* is a stretch of highland which extends from a ridge or a range of hills. Spurs usually lie between two valleys. Spurs are represented by V-shaped contour lines with the apex of the V pointing towards lower ground. In the contour diagram (Fig.A14) study the differences in the form of contour lines of valleys and spurs. The cross-section brings out clearly the contrasts between valleys and spurs.

U-shaped valley and Hanging valley

U-shaped valleys are found in glaciated mountain regions. Such valleys have a broad, flat floor and steep sides. The steep slopes on the two sides of the valley are indicated by closely spaced contour lines (Fig. A15). The **hanging valley** is a steep slope at the junction of tributary valley with the main valley. There is usually waterfall at the site of the hanging valley.

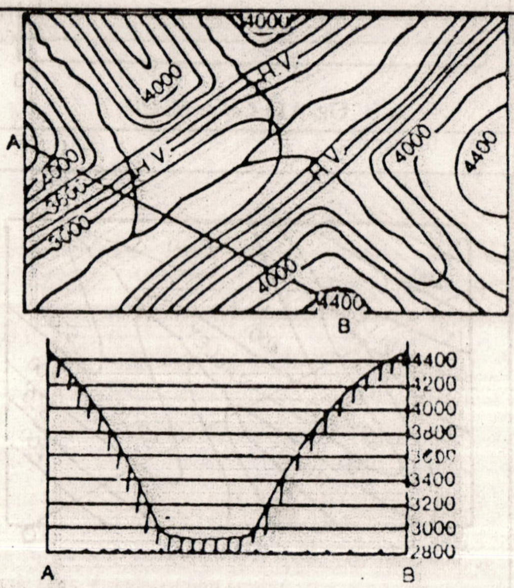

Fig. A15 ***U-shaped valley and Hanging valley (H.V.)***

Cliff

A **cliff** is a steep, almost vertical slope. This is represented by the merger of two or more contour lines. In topographic maps where two or more contours merge, the cliff symbol is marked. Cliffs occur commonly along the coast owing to the erosive action of waves. Cliffs along the coast are shown by the mergercontour lines with coast-line (Fig. A16).

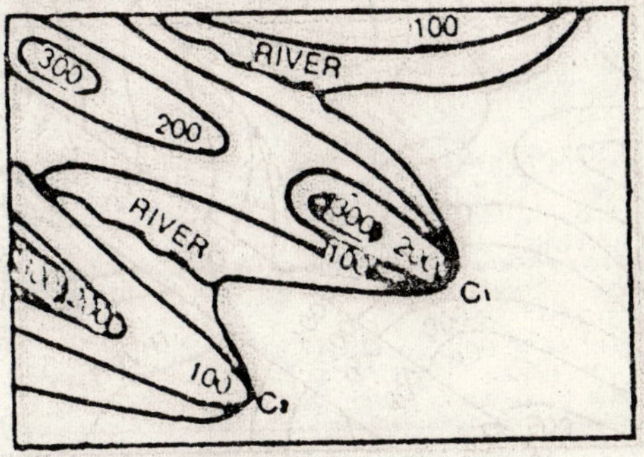

Fig. A16 *Cliffs along the coast*

Waterfall

A **Waterfall** occurs where there is a steep slope along the path of a river. Water falls vertically down the steep slope. Waterfalls are represented by the merger of two or more contours across the path of a river. The contour diagram (Fig. A17) brings out the form of the waterfall.

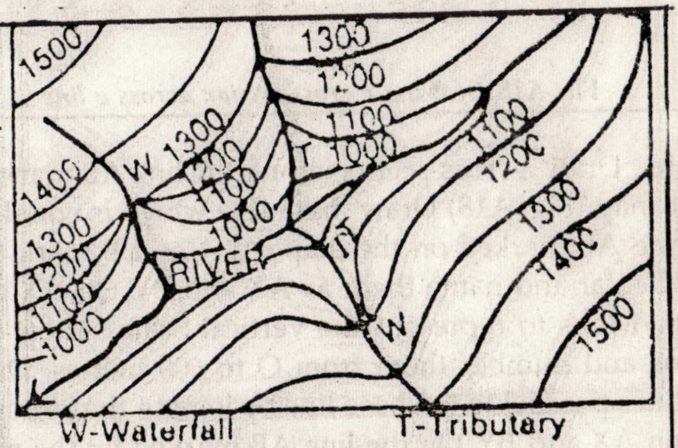

Fig. A17 *Waterfall*

Drawing a cross-section along a line

Cross sections are drawn along straight lines a won a contour map. Such cross-sections give an idea of the profile of the land along the line. Usually cross-sections are drawn with an arbitary vertical scale so that the slope of the land is brought out clearly.

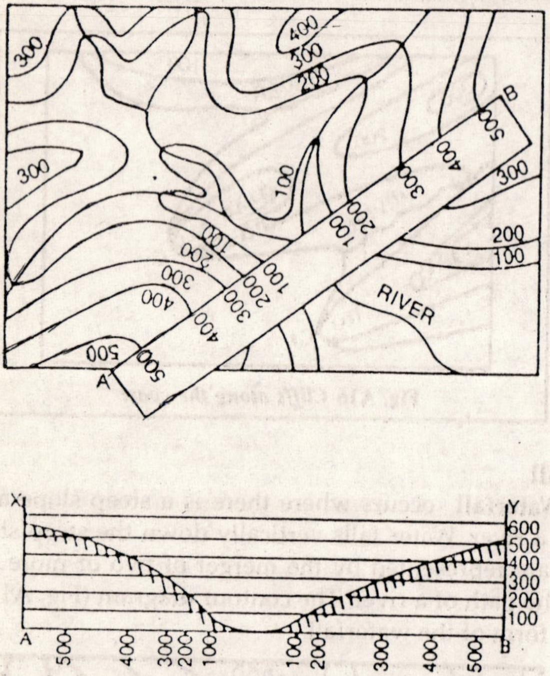

Fig. A18 ***Drawing a cross-section across a line***

Example:- Draw a cross-section along the line AB marked on the contour map (Fig. A18) Draw base line which is equal in length to the line AB marked on the map. At A and B mark two short perpendicular and name them as AX and BY. On AX and mark equal divisions to represent the vertical Scale set off 6 vertical divisions and number them from O to 600 metres. Draw horizontal lines parallel to the base line by joining the corresponding points on AX and BY. On the line AB marked on the map, lay a small strip of paper and mark the places where contour lines cross the line AB. Note the values of contour lines also near the points marked on the strip of paper. Place this paper on the base line AB and transfer these points and enter the values of the contour lines. Use the vertical scale marked on AX and BY and mark the corresponding heights of these points. Join these points by a curved line. This curved line represents the cross-section along the line AB. This cross-section gives idea about the form of the land along AB.

Survey of India Topographic Maps

The Survey of India has published topographic maps of India on different scales. These maps cover most parts of the country and form a series. India and adjacent countries series of maps are published on a scale of 1:1,000,00 (1 cm to 10 km). Each sheet of this series covers 40 of longitude. These sheets are given numbers such as 43, 44 etc. Each sheet is also given a name which refers to the most important settlement in the area shown on the map. Sheet No. 53 is also known as the Delhi sheet.

The area shown on each sheet of India and adjacent countries series is further sub-divided into 16 sheets and maps are prepared on a scale of 1:250,000. These maps are numbered as 53 A, 53B upto 53 P (Fig. A19). These sheets are called the degree sheets, because each sheet includes the area covered by 1^0 of latitude and 1^0 of longitude.

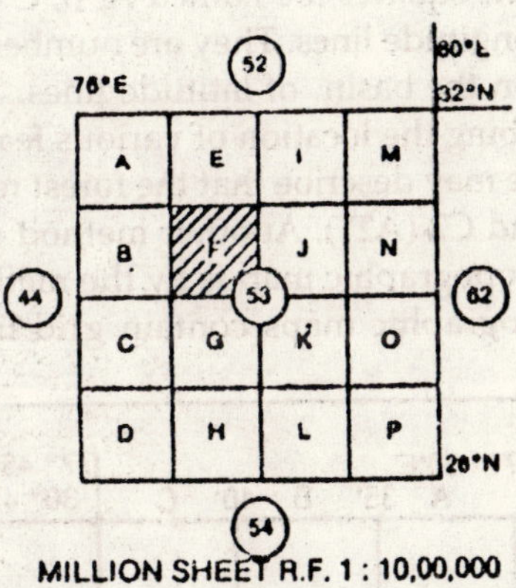

Fig. A19 ***Naming of Survey of India Topographic Maps - 53A to P***

The area shown on each degree sheet for example 53F is subdivided into 16 sheets on a scale of 1:50,000. These maps are numbered 53 f/1, 53 f/3 etc. (Fig. A20). Each sheet of this series covers 15' of latitude and 15' of longitude. These are the basic topographic maps of India and they cover most parts of the country.

Location reference

Each topograhic map on a scale of 1:50,000 is divided into

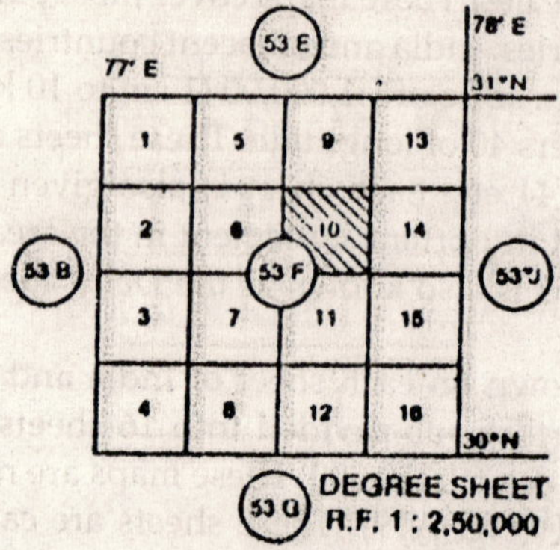

Fig. A20 ***Naming of Survey of India Topographic Maps - 53F/1 to 16***

nine squares based on the latitude and longitude lines drawen at intervals of 5'. The squares are named A, B, C from west to east, on the basis of longitude lines. They are numbered 1,2 and 3 from north to south on the basin of latitude lines. These squares are useful for describing the location of various features on the map. For example, one may describe that the forest region covers parts of squares C1 and C2 (A21). Another method of precisely locating places on a topographic map is by the method of **grid lines**. Most of the topographic maps contain grid lines which are at

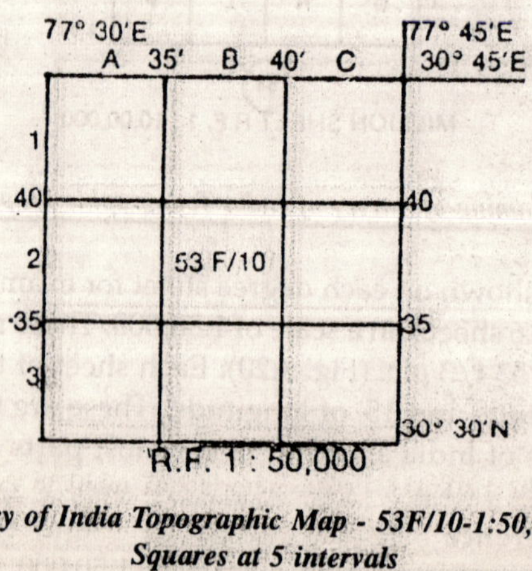

Fig. A21 ***Survey of India Topographic Map - 53F/10-1:50,000 Naming of Squares at 5 intervals***

intervals of 1000 metres or 1 km. The National Grid Reference System divides the whole area into rectangular co-ordinates by parallel north-south breath. Each 100 km square is identified by two letters such as UA, UB etc. Each 100 km squares is subdivided into squares of l km. The origin of the grid system is in the south-west corner of the map. The location of any point is fixed by noting its distance east and north of the origin of the grid. The north-south lines measure the **easting,** which the east-west lines measure **northings** of a point. when giving reference to a point easting are given first and then northings. On every map two figure easting and northings are printed along the edges of the map at intervals of 1 km. The eastings increase in value eastward, which northings increase in value north wards. This is known as **"four-figuregrid"** reference. This is adequate to locate area features which occupy some space on the map.

Point symbols like railway stations, bench marks, etc. are better located by **"Six figure grid"** reference. This is done by subdividing each 1 km. Square ten times and estimating the eastings and northings to the third digit. For example, the grid reference of point A on the map is 425623 (Fig. A22). The value of easting is 425 and that of northing is 643. Grid system is useful for locating each place accurate by a six digit number. This system is used by

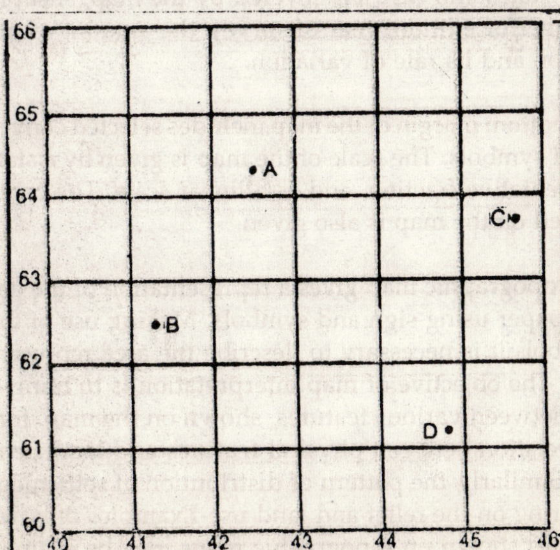

Fig. A22 ***Grid Lines Scae 1:50,000***

the Defence force for precisely locating various features in an area.

Signs and Symbols used on Topographic Maps

The topographic map contains a variety of information about physical features and cultural features. These are given by using signs and symbols in various colours so that the clarity of the map is maintained.

It is important for the map reader to make himself familiar with the conventional signs used in the map. These are provided in each toposheet in an abridged form (Fig. A23)

Boundaries

Administrative boundaries are shown by discontinuous lines with dots, dashes or crosses. International boundaries, state boundaries, boundaries of district, taluk or tehsil or pargana are shown by different types of lines. Names of administrative units like districts, taluks are written in spaced capital letters.

Marginal Information

Outside the map proper, there are margins on the four sides. The values of latitude and longitude are printed on the margins. The following details are printed on the top margin of the map. Name of states and districts covered by the map, sheet number and number or edition, year of survey, the amount of magnetic declination and its rate of variation.

The bottom margin of the map includes selected conventional signs and symbols. The scale of the map is given by a statement, as representative fraction, and as a linear scale. The contour interval used on the map is also given.

The topographic map gives a representation of the area on a sheet of paper using sign and symbols. Making use of the signs and symbols it is necessary to describe the area represented on the map. The objective of map interpretation is to bring out the relation between various features shown on the map. for example, the relation between physical features and landuse may be studied. Similarly, the pattern of distribution of settlements may have bearing on the relief and land use-Examples of how different features shown on topographic maps may be examined are given below.

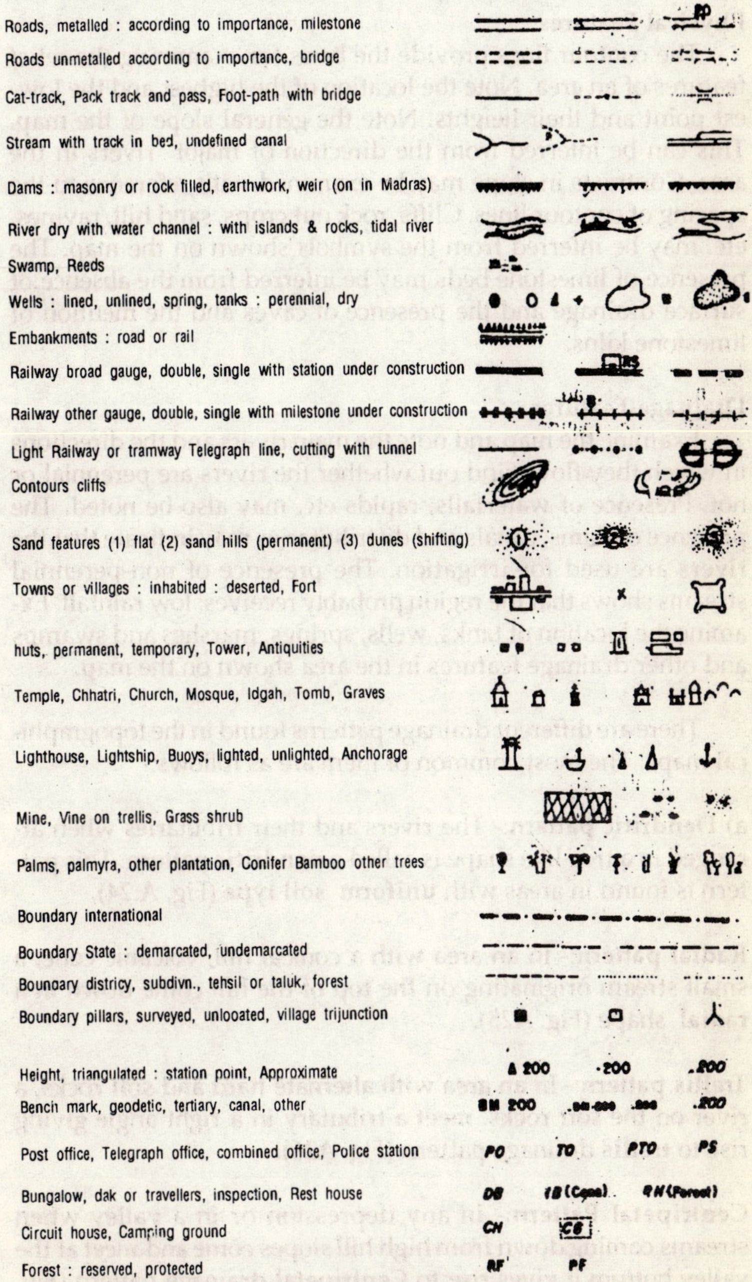

Fig. A23 *Conventional Signs*

The Conventional Signs and symbols in topographical maps are shown in standard colours. Due to some technical reasons these could not be printed in colour here.

Physical Features

The contour lines provide the basis for examining the relief features of an area. Note the location of the highest and the lowest point and their heights. Note the general slope of the map. This can be inferred from the direction of major rivers in the area. Contrasts in slope may be examined with reference to the spacing of contour lines. Cliffs, rock out crops, sand hill, ravines, etc. may be inferred from the symbols shown on the map. The presence of limestone beds may be inferred from the absence of surface drainage and the presence of caves and the mention of limestone kilns.

Drainage Features

Examine the map and note the main rivers and the directions in which they flow. Find out whether the rivers are perennial or not. Presence of waterfalls, rapids etc. may also be noted. The presence of dams, canals and distributaries may indicate that the rivers are used for irrigation. The presence of non-perennial streams shows that the region probably receives: low rainfall. Examine the location of tanks, wells, springs, marshes and swamps and other drainage features in the area shown on the map.

There are different drainage patterns found in the topographical maps. The most common of them are as follows:-

a) **Dendritic pattern**:- The rivers and their tributaries when arranged in a tree-like shape is called a **dendritic** pattern. This pattern is found in areas with **uniform soil type** (Fig. A.24).

Radial pattern:- In an area with a conical hill, volcanic cone, a small stream originating on the top of the hill come down in a **radial** shape (Fig. A25).

Trellis pattern:- In an area with alternate hard and soft rocks, a river on the soft rocks. meet a tributary in a right angle giving rise to **trellis** drainage pattern (Fig. A26).

Centripetal Pattern:- In any depression or in a valley when streams coming down from high hill slopes come and meet at the valley bottom it gives rise to **Centripetal** drainage pattern (Fig. A27). In and around a water hole or in areas with numerous sinkholes this pattern is very common.

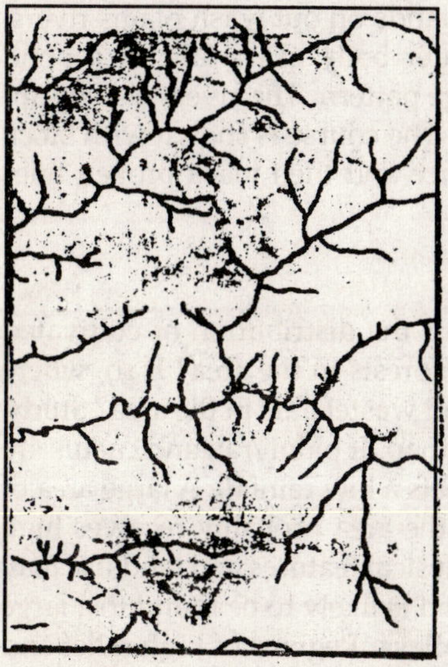

Fig. A24 *Dendritic pattern Virginia, NL, quadrangle*

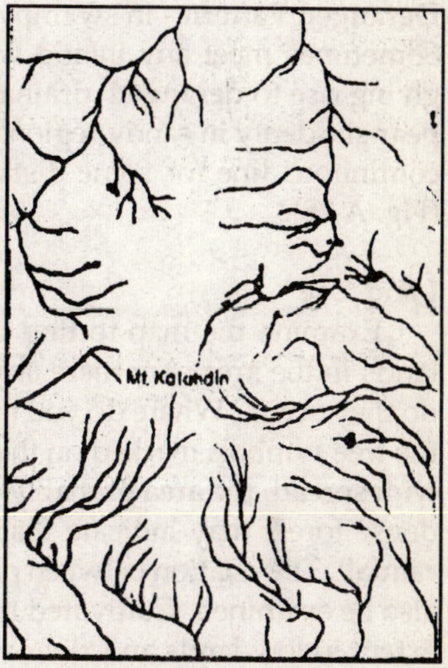

Fig. A25 *Radial pattern Kalahdin, Me, quadrangle*

Fig. A26 *Trellis pattern Monterey, Va., quadrangle*

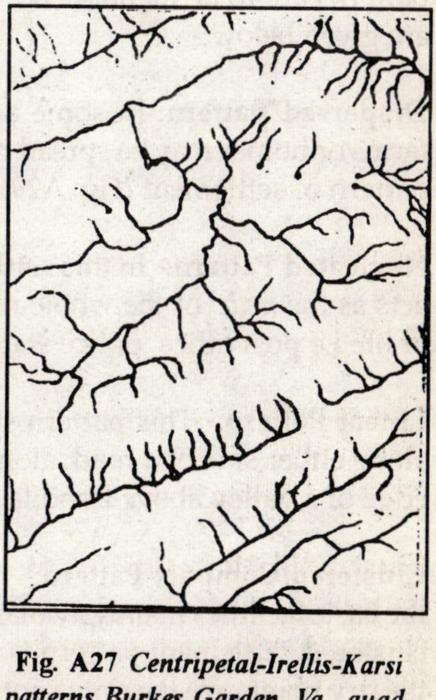

Fig. A27 *Centripetal-Irellis-Karsi patterns Burkes Garden, Va., quadrangle*

Deranged Pattern:- In swampy lands on out wash plains rivers. Sometimes meet any inland water body like a lake or a pond giving rise to **deranged** drainage pattern. The rivers also disappear suddenly in sandy regions. The course is shown with block continuous line for some distance and then black broken lines (Fig. A 28).

Land Use

Examine the map to find out the distribution of cultivated lands in the area. Are there any forests in the area? If so, where do they occur? Where do you find wastelands in the area? Study, the tree symbols marked on the map. If palmyrah and cactus are widespread, the area probably gets a low rainfall. A large area of dense forest may indicate that the area probably receives high rainfall. The relation between physical features and land use may also be examined. Cultivated land is likely to be found to a large extent in low lands and river valleys. Regions of high relief and steep slopes are likely to have forest or scrub jungle as they are not suitable for cultivation.

Settements:- Find out from the map the average distance between villages in different parts of the area. The different settlement patterns are to be mentioned . The common settlement patterns are given below:-

Dispersed pattern:-In some areas large numbers of scattered farms or homes may be spread over an area to produce **dispersed** pattern of settlement (Fig. A29).

Nucleated Pattern:- In this settlement pattern one town or a city acts as the *node* of the whole region with all the basic amenities of life i.e post office, police station, school etc. (Fig. A 30).

Linear Pattern:- This pattern shows the houses being arranged along either side of a road, along a river bank or levee, along the edge of a valley above flood level along the coast. (Fig. A 31)

Clustered/Compact Pattern:- In an agricultural field where all the basic facilities mainly availability of water is uniformly found, clustered settlement pattern is found there. In a marshy region, the dry points are the only spots where settlements can be found giving rise to a **Compact** nature. (Fig. A 32).

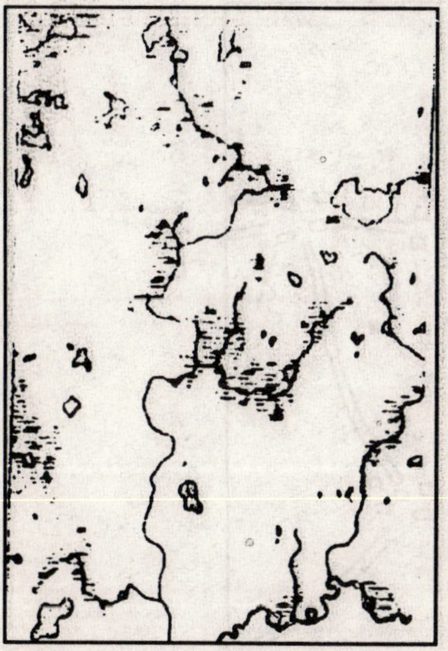

Fig. A28 *Deranged pattern Galesburg, Mich., quadrangle*

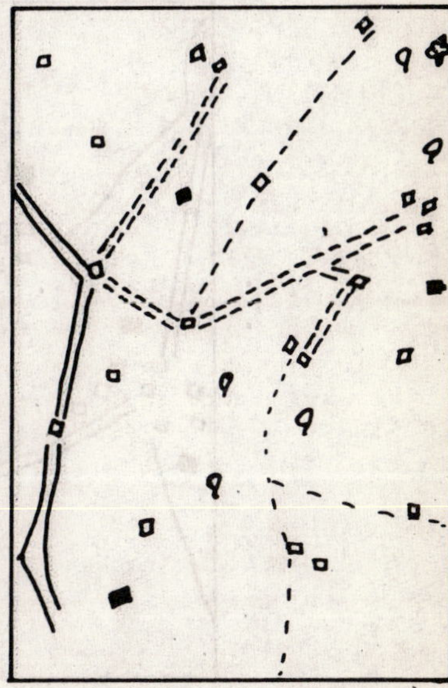

Fig. A29 *Dispersed Settlement*

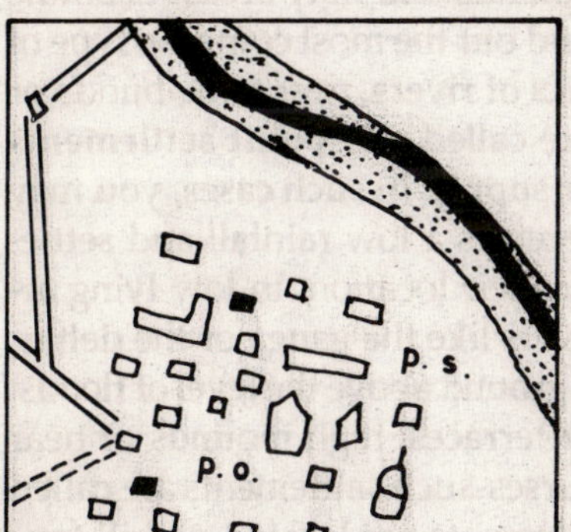

Fig. A30 *Nucleated Settlement*

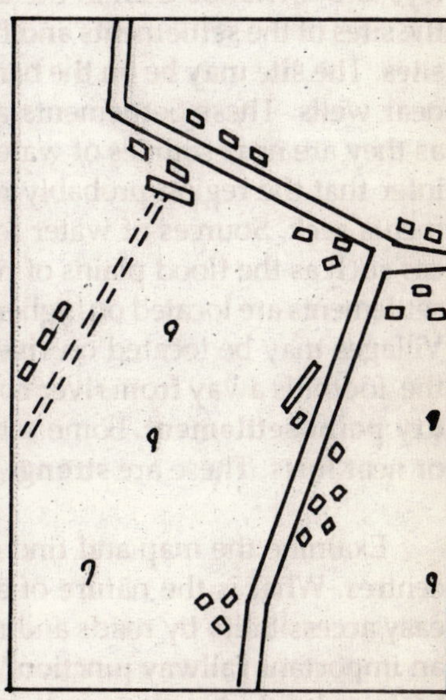

Fig. A31 *Linear Settlement*

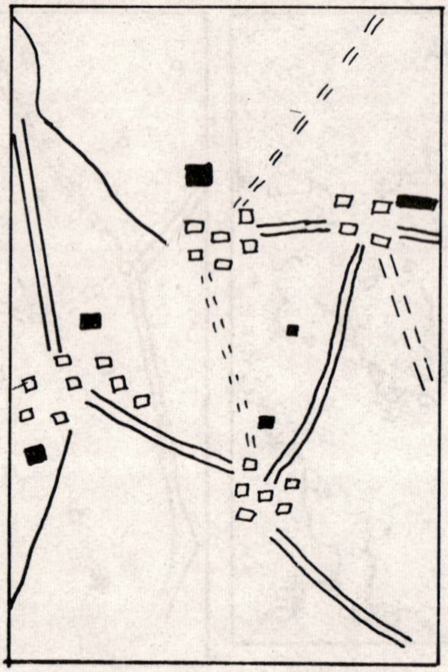

Fig. A32 ***Clustered Settlement***

Settlements are likely to be more closely spaced in the valleys and lowlands than in the uplands and hilly areas. Examine the sites of the settlements and find out the most common type of sites. The site may be on the banks of rivers, near tank, bunds or near wells. These Settlements are called **wet point settlements** as they are near sources of water supply. In such cases, you may infer that the region probably receives a low rainfall and settlements seek. Sources of water for their location. In low-lying areas such as the flood plains of rivers like the ganga or the deltas, settlements are located on higher ground above the level of floods. Villages may be located on river terraces, high mounds or near the foothills away from river courses-such settlements are called **dry point settlement.** Some settlements are located on hill tops or near forts. These are **strong** point settlements.

Examine the map and find out whether there are any urban centres. What is the nature of a site? Is it a nodal centres with easy accessibility by roads and railway lines? Is it a port town or an important railway junction? The function of the town has to be found out. Are there any industries in the periphery of the town? Can you identify the old nucleus of the town? It may be a temple, mosque, fort or a road intersection.

Find out from the map the areas where settlements are absent, Are there deserted village sites? Such sites occur in forested regions. What are the possible reasons for the desertion of sites?

Transport and Communication

Do you find railway lines in the area depicted on the topographic map? In which part of the area do you find the railway line? Is it a broad gauge or meter-gauge? Is it a single or a double track? Are there cuttings, embankments or tunnels along the railway line? What do you infer from this? Such features are likely to be found where the railway line traverses an undulating ground with depressions and uplands. Which is the most important railway station?

Study the pattern of roads in the area. Are these roads metalled or non-metalled? which settlements are not served by roads? Why is it so? How many settlements are linked by cart-track or footpaths only? Are there causeways over the rivers. Is ferry system available? In which months do they operate? What does this indicate?

Occupation of the People

The occupation of the people may be inferred indireclty from evidences regarding landuse and settlements. If the area has large tracts of cultivated land, the dominant occupations likely to be agriculture. Presence of tanks, wells or canals proves the cultivation to be of intense type with wet crops like rice and sugarcane being common. If the area has a large belt of forest, collection of fire wood, forest products like leaves, fruits or nuts is likely to be important. Where there are quarries or mines, mining is likely to provide occupation to the people. In the case of villages only along the coast, fishing is likely to be important cities are likely to provide employment in industries, trade and services, Name of some of the industries like brick kiln, textile mills, carpet factory, cement factory etc., are given in the map. In the care of towns which are headquarters of districts and taluks, large number of offices may be marked on the map. These provide employment in administration and related services.

Interpretation of Selected Topographical Maps

A few topographical sheets from the Survey of India on 1:50,000 are expected to be studied carefully at this stage. Only two sheets, i.e., 63 K/12 and 45 J/8 have been selected for this purpose. Parts of these sheets representing some regions of India e.g. the edge of the Vindhyan plateau, the part of the Gangetic plain around Mirzapur and a flood plain of the Ganga from Sheet No. 63 K.12; a portion of Aravalli hills, south of Ajmer, and Beawar town and its surroundings from Sheet No. 45 J/8 have been selected to provide examples of interpretation technique.

The Vindhyan Plateau in Mirzapur District

This portion of Sheet No. 63 K/12 (Fig. A33) represents part of Mirzapur district in Uttar Pradesh. It spreads between 25^{0}N latitudes, and 82^{0}30'E-82^{0}7'30" E longitudes. The important physical feature of the area is the plateau region, which is part of the Kaimur hills of the Vindhyas-lying a few kilometres south of this region.

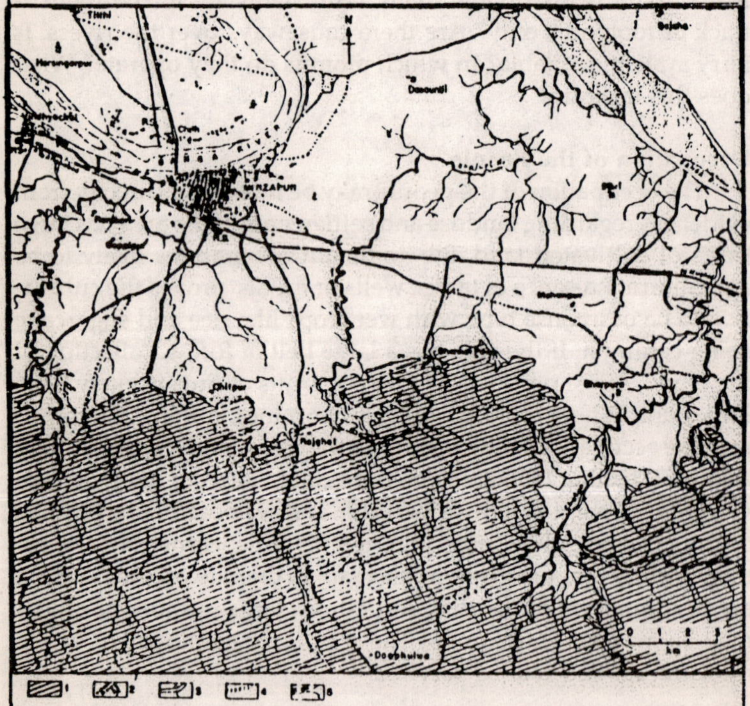

Fig. A33 *1-Plateau; 2-Settlements; 3-Metalled road; 4-Unmetalled road; 5-River.*

Note the maximum and minimum heights mentioned on this sheet. A bold contour line of 150 metres running across the region in the north and in the east is of significance in or four contours that are very close and almost parallel to it. What do they indicate? They represent a steep slope. What is the amount of fall or rise near Rajghat in the north-eastern part of the sheet? The sudden fall in the level of an elevated and fairly flat land, as marked by the closely set contours running almost parallel to one another, represents the steep edge of a plateau.

Study the land enclosed partially or wholly by the contour line of 150 metres. What type of relief does it represent? Are there any residual hills on the plateau region? if any, Describe them.

Note carefully the zigzag shape of the contours that mark the edge of the plateau. What is it due to? Is there any relationship between the rivers and the shape of the plateau? A plateau that is interspersed with deep and numerous river valleys is called a disected plateau. Would you describe this area as a disected plateau? Substantiate your answer with specific examples.

Draw a section along the line joining Majhwani village in the south-east and the temple in Chitpur village in the north. Describe the major landmarks and land forms along this line with the help of the profile drawn by you.

There are two rivers/streams in this region, one flowing in the west and the other in the east. In what direction do they flow? In what respect do they differ from each other. Note a big waterfall on the river that flows in the western part of the plateau. Name the fall and find out its height. Which is the largest tank? Find out the length of its embankment.

That vegetation do you find in this region? Which is the favoured location for vegetation in this area?

Note the major roads in this area. Study carefully the alignment of the road in the northern portion of the sheet. What is the impact of the relief of this area on the alignment of the road? Find out the length of this road in kilometres.

Note that there are no settlements in the two river valleys

referred to above. However, there are settlements along the small stream and its tributaries flowing into the tank-Tandadari Tal. How would you account for this situation? What is the main occupation of the people in this area? Also, note the power line, telephone and telegraph lines in this region.

Mirzapur : A River Town

This part of the sheet is in continuation of the previous one as it represents on adjoining areas in the north spreading between latitudes 25°'N and 25°' 10 N and longitudes 82°30'E and 82°37' 30"E. The map represents typical features of the Gangetic plain in eastern Uttar Pradesh. The location of Mirzapur, an important river town in the region, adds to the significance of this sheet.

Locate the area represented on this sheet on a small-scale map of India with the help of latitudes and longitudes mentioned here. State the location of this region in relation to the area shown on the previous sheet.

How would you describe the relief of this area? Note the value of the contour-line running along the southern margin of the sheet. Except for a few contour-lines in the south-eastern part of the region they are almost conspicuous by their absence.What does it suggest? Find out the minimum, maximum and average elevation of the entire region. How would you do it in the absence of contour-lines? In what direction is the general slope of the area? How does the relief of this region differ from that of the area shown on the previous sheet.

Observe the course of the two rivers running along the eastern and western margins of the sheet. What does it indicate as regards the relier of the region through which they flow? What technical term is used to describe the nature of such a course?

Note the ravines in the western part of the sheet. What do they suggest?

Study carefully the channel of the Ganga river along the northern margin of the sheet. Compare the two banks of this river. What difference do you notice? Which terms would you use to describe these two types of banks? Remember that the river shown on the map is only a part of a big loop. The northern bank of the river is, in fact, the inner bank of the loop. Note the sand deposites on this bank. How steep is the southern bank? This is outer bank of the loop.

Note the presence of deciduous trees in this area which give it the appearance of an open woodland.

Which are the major lines of communication that serve this area? Note the alignment of the main railway line. What does its straight course indicate? Which is the major highway of the region? See how different metalled roads converge on Mirzapur town. To what extent is the river used for transport? Where do you think is the maximum river traffic? Is there any bridge to cross the river? What kind of bridge is it? Is there any ferry service?

Note the size of the village settlements. Many of them are compact settlements of fairly large size. There are also a few permanent scattered huts. Are there temporary huts as well? Do you find any relationship between the perennial tanks and the location of big villages? Is there any correlation between the roads and the settlements?

What do you think is the major occupation of the people? What are the sources of irrigation in this region?

What factors in your opinion favour the location and growth of Mirzapur town? Why do you think that this town could not have been located on the northern bank of the river Ganga? Compare the location of Vindhyachal with that of Mirzapur. Which of the two sites is more favourable and why?

A Flood Plain of The Ganga

This portion of topo sheet No. 63 K/12 lies between latitudes 25°10' N and 25°15' N and longitudes 82°30' E. It is in continuation of the previous two plates. It represents a portion of Mirzapur district and the southern tip of Varanasi district. The meandering course of the river Ganga through its flood plain is the major geographical feature of great importance in this area.

Consult the scale and find out the length of the river course and its maximum and minimum width on these two sheets showing the river Ganga.

The complete absence of contours on this map points out the smooth topography of the region. The monotony of this homogeneous region is broken by the meandering course of the Ganga. But for a couple of isolated knolls and a small patch of ravine lands in the north-eastern part of the region, the entire area presents a smooth topography. The knolls are shown by form lines. How do the form lines differ from a contour? What special purpose do they serve?

What indicates that the river has a very low gradient? How would you account for the presence of sand deposits on the river bed and along the banks? Note that there are no sand deposits where the river is confined to a narrow channel. On the other hand, large-scale sand deposits occur where the river spreads over a broad channel. Note that the sand deposits are generally found along the inner bank of a loop where the velocity of water current is usually low as compared to what it is along the outer bank. Due to the loss of the velocity of river water its capacity to carry load also decreases leading to the deposition of sand in the river bed.

River banks are steep along the outer bank of a loop as the river water moves very fast along this bank causing lateral erosion. The banks are shelving along the inner bank of a loop.

Trees in this region may be seen in patches. In the north, there are some orchards or plantations, perhaps, mango groves.

A railway line runs along the northern margin of the sheet. One of its branches runs north-south up to the river Ganga. The name Mirzapur Ghat Railway Station suggests the importance of Mirzapur town on the opposite bank of the river. It is a metre gauge, single line track. A metalled road also runs parallel to the railway line.

Compare the settlements on the two sides of the river on this and the previous portion of the sheet. How would you explain the sparsity of settlements in the major part of this sheet? The settlements are again fairly dense in the northern part of the region. What does it indicate? How would you explain the presence of large size compact villages along the northern bank of the river whereas a large part of the area in this sheet is devoid of such large settlements.

Aravalli Hills in Ajmer District

This is a portion of topographic Sheet No. 45 J/8 (Fig.A34) spreading between latitudes 26°5' N and 26°10' N and longitudes 74°22' 30" E and 74°30' E. The map represents a part of Ajmer district in Rajasthan. A part of the Aravalli range passing through this area is the significant feature of this region. The Aravallis are one of the oldest mountains on the earth. Today, they represent only the remnats of a once lofty mountain chain.

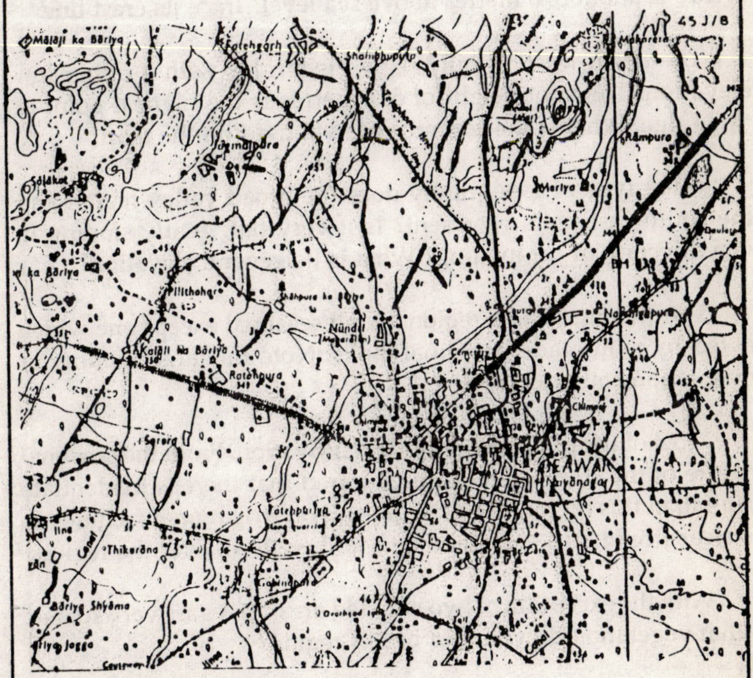

Fig. A34

Calculate the total area represented on the map. Locate this region on a map in your atlas.

Based on its relief, the region may be divided into four separate units-the north-western hilly region, the broad valley region, the elongated hilly region, and the south-east plain. All these units run parallel to one another. The broad valley region and the elongated hilly region are the important units.

Draw a cross-section along a line joining the north-western and south-eastern extremities of this portion of sheet. Name the roads, rivers and the crest of the ridges along this profile.

The extensive water divide between the streams flowing north-west and south-east is narrow and long with sharp slopes on both sides. Can you calculate how high these escapments rise above the base of the hills? The average elevation of the water divide is about 570 metres above sea level. Trace its crest line.

The north-western hilly region is a ridge with a rather low elevation. The spot height of 511 metres is the highest point of this ridge. What is the contour-interval used on the map?

What type of topography does the broad valley region and the south-east plain represent? Is it very flat, gently sloping in one direction or undulating? What is its general elevation?

The streams in this region are all seasonal except one which is fed by man-made perennial tanks. Note the large number of man-made embankments.

Most of the plain area is under cultivation. From the seasonal nature of the streams, it can be inferred that there is inadequate rainfall in this region. It has to depend on irrigational facilities as is clear from tanks, embankments and wells all over the region.

With the exception of two wooded areas, trees are very sparse. What vegetation do you find in this region?

The region is mainly served by cart tracks. How many main routes cross this region? Correlate these lines of communication with the physical features of the area.

Note the size of the settlements. They are large and compact, but clearly indicate the sparse population.

Beawar and its Surroundings

This part of the sheet lying between latitudes 26°5' N and

26°10' N and longitudes 74°15' E and 74°22' 30" E is in continuation of the previous sheet. It depicts the adjoining region in the west. Besides Ajmer district, the area shown on the map also, includes a part of Pali district of Rajasthan. Find out the distance of the city of Ajmer located north-east of this region. The nodal position of the township of Beawar (Nayanagar) is a significant feature of the area represented on the sheet.

Locate the highest and lowest points on the map. What is the difference in their elevation? Examine carefully the contour lines and spot heights given on the map. Shade lightly the land over 500 metres in height and thus locate the hilly areas on the map. Can you divide the area into different physical units? How would you describe them? Except for a few small isolated hills and knolls, the broad valley region has a smooth topography. The few hills, however, rise more than 60 metres above the surrounding region and they are more or less rounded at the top. What is the general elevation of the valley region? Where are the ravine lands in this area?

The main streams of this region are the tributaries of the Makarera river. Are these streams seasonal or perennial? Note the valleys of the streams in the hilly area. Does the spacing of contours give any idea regarding the shape of these valleys and steepness of the hills? To what extent is the hilly region dissected by streams?

Note the man-made features that aim at improving the drainage system of this area. How are the embankments shown on the map? Are thay very common in this area? The drainage pattern in the south-western part of the area presents an interesting feature. The streams radiating in all directions represent a radial pattern of drainage. The radial drainage found in this area is, of course, on a very small scale and is true only locally.

What vegetation do you find in this area? The wooded area on the western hills is limited in extent. Why is it so?

Is the region well served with modern means of communication? Discuss the influence of relief on the roads and railways in this area. What physical features are followed or avoided by a route in order to maintain the most even gradient? Draw a cross-section along a line joining Saradhana and Chang village in the western part of the region. Mark the positions of the railway line and the road on the profile.

Beawar (Nayanagar) is the only urban centre in the entire region. It draws upon the agricultural resources of the surrounding area. How far is it from its old site, i.e. Beawar Khas? Is it a major route centre? How many and how important are the routes which meet here? How big is the settlement? Compare the sites of Beawar Khas and Bewar (Nayanagar).

Except Beawar (Nayanagar), the settlements are rural in character. These rural settlements are of two types-the scattered huts and the compact villages. Study carefully the general pattern of the distribution of population. Is it dense or sparse?

2

Landforms and Process

(a) Landforms resulting from folding, faulting and volcanic activity.

Crustal Structure and Movement

The Earth is made up of a series of concentric rock zones namely, the *crust, mantle, outer core* and *inner core* (Fig. B.1a). The crust is the main concern here. It varies greatly in thickness and

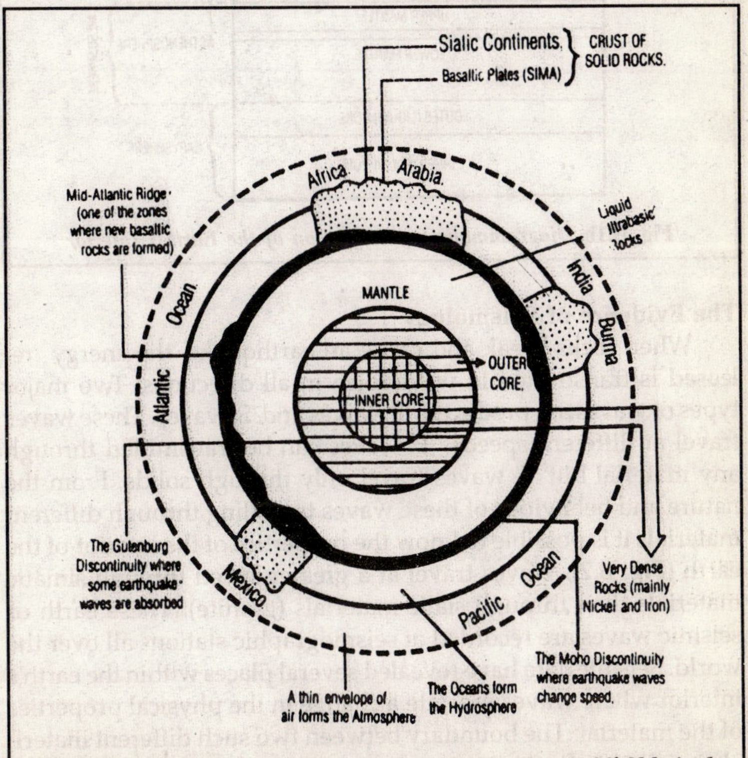

Fig. B.1a *Structure of the eart through a cross section at 20⁰ N latitude*

composition, beneath the oceans it is as little as 5 km thick in places, but under some mountain ranges it extends to depths of 70 km. Rocks in the crust fall into two main groups. The ocean basins are predominately underlain by basaltic rocks, containing much iron and magnesium, and having densities of between 2.8 and 3.0 (water=1.0). In contrast the rocks that make up the continents are lighter in colour and weight (densities of c. 2.7) and are rich in silicon and aluminium. Below the crust lie the denser rocks of the *mantle.* The upper part of the *mantle,* to depths of about 100 km, is solid and together with the crust forms a relatively rigid unit known as the *lithosphere.* At depths between 100 and 250 km, the *mantle* is partially molten and capable of slow flowage; this is the *asthesnosphere* (Fig. B.1b).

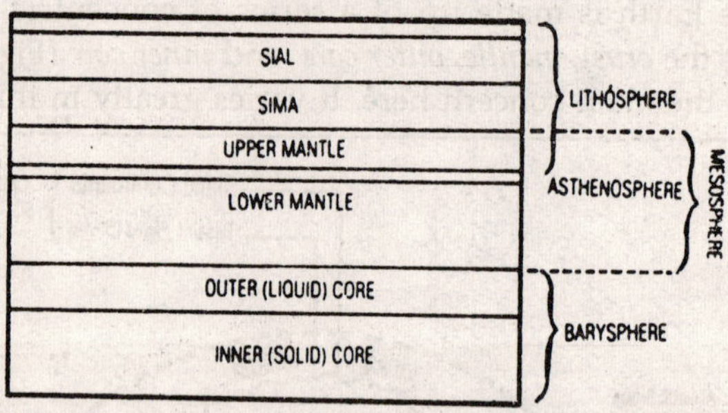

Fig. B.1b ***Diagrammatic representation of the Earth's Interior***

The Evidence of Seismology

When rocks break and cause an earthquake, the energy released is transmitted in wave form in all directions. Two major types of waves are produced, 'P' waves and 'S' waves. These waves travel at different speeds. 'P' waves can be transmitted through any material but 'S' waves travel only through solids. From the nature and behaviour of these waves travelling through different materials it is possible to know the properties of the interior of the earth (Fig. B.2). Waves travel at a greater speed through simatic materials than through sialic materials (granite). These earth or seismic waves are recorded at seismographic stations all over the world. Seismic data have revealed several places within the earth's interior where waves indicate a change in the physical properties of the material. The boundary between two such different materials is called a **discontinuity.**

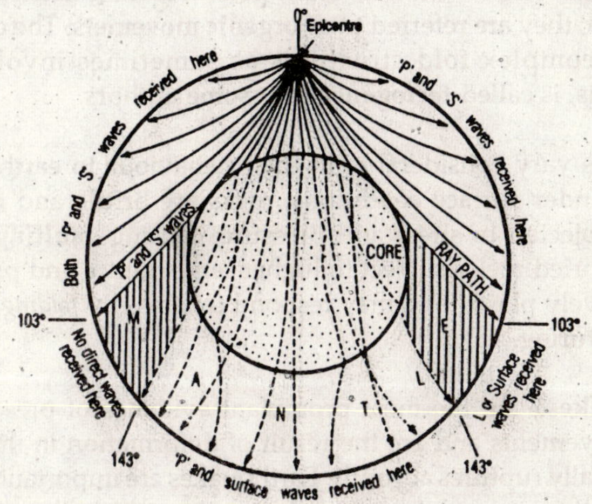

Fig. B2 ***A diagrammatic representation of Earthwaves P, S and L through the Earth***

Crustal Plates

It is now almost universally accepted by earth scientists that parts of the crust are capable of moving horizontally round the globe, causing the continents slowly to change position in relation to each other. This idea was originally synthesised under the term **Continental drift** by A. Wegener in 1915. In the last 15 years, however, new discoveries have confirmed his general ideas and have led ultimately to a body of theory which we now call **plate tectonics.**

The basic principle of plate tectonics is very, simple: the lithosphere is broken into several sections or plates. Each plate is capable of moving over the asthesnosphere, carrying oceanic and continental crust alike. Each plate moves as a single independent body. At the mid-oceanic ridges in the Pacific Atlantic and Indian oceans, plate boundaries are characterised by the creation of new crust from below, and in the process called **Sea-floor spreading,** the plates migrate slowly away from these central ridges.

At the plate boundaries, major tectonic landforms are created. The areas of collision may be made up of three elements: deep trenches on the ocean floor, some up to 11 km deep, marking areas of plate subduction into the mantle; are-like rows of volcanic responsible for the formation of the great fold mountain ranges of the world, they are referred to as **orgenic** movemets. The creation of very complex fold structures as sometimes involved in orogenesis, is called **tectogenesis** by some authors.

Rocks vary considerably in their behaviour to earth movements. Under surface conditions, rocks are brittle and fracture when subjected to stress and pressure, causing **faulting.** More deeply buried rocks, subject to higher temperature and pressure, are relatively plastic and may respond to stress by *folding* rather than fracturing.

Earthquakes:- are the most prominant evidence of present-day earth movements and are the result of deformation in the crust, which finally ruptures abruptly. Earthquakes are important in land form studies because they can trigger off catastrophic events in erosion processes.

MAJOR TECTONIC LANDFORMS

Mountain Chains

Examination of a relief map of the world will reveal a number of major mountain chains arranged in long linear arcs in lands; and mountain ranges, where the plates appear to be crumpling and thickening. All plate margins, inclnding the mid-oceanic ridge systems, are frequently areas of considerable earthquake activity and volcanism (Fig. B.3).

Earth Movements

Movements of the crustal plates cause pressure and tensions to build up on rocks, in many cases leading to deformation of the land surface. The general term **diastsophism is sometines** applied to the bending, folding, warping and fracturing of the crust.

On a broad scale, earth movements may be divided into two types. **Epeirogenic** movements are those invloving forces acting along a radius from the earth's centre to the surface, and are aharacterisd by large-scale uplift or submergence of land areas. The movements involved are often so slow and widespread that no obvious folding or fracturing is produced in the rocks.

The second type of earth movements are those generated by forces acting at a tangent to the surface of the earth, as primarily

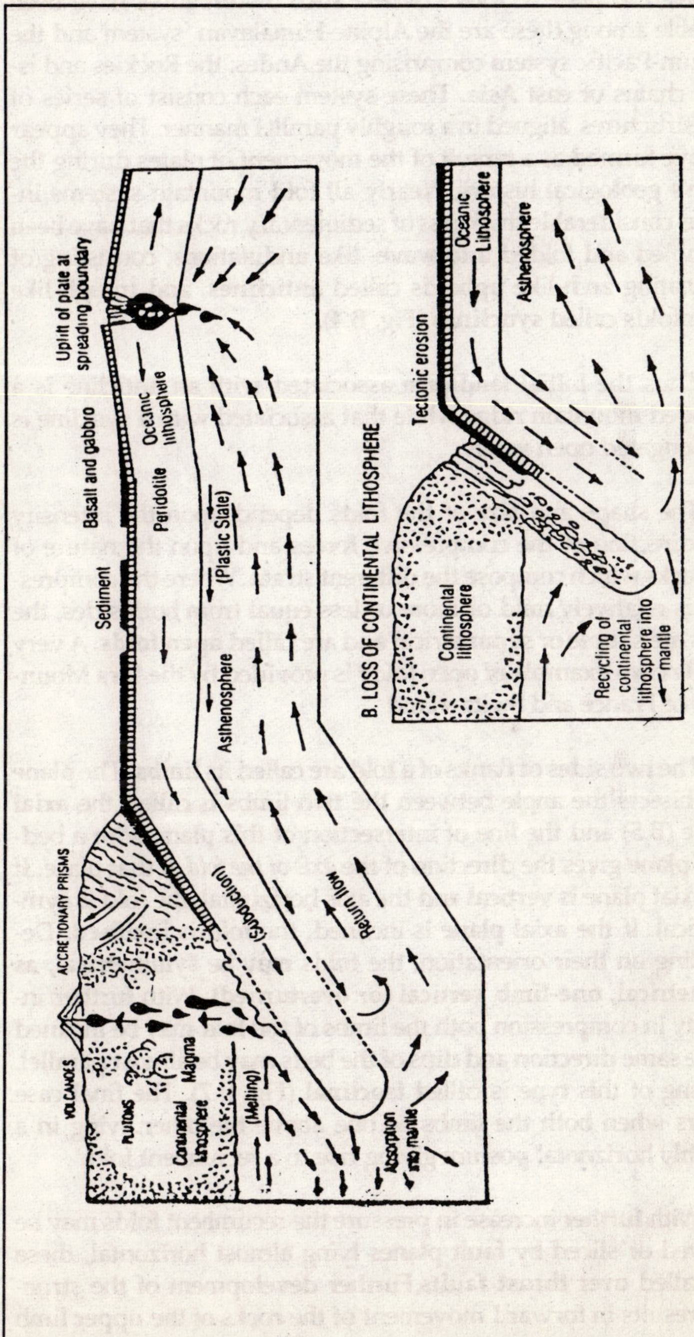

Fig. B3 Subduction and volcanism in plate tectonics

involved in plate tectonics, where such disturbances have been Notable among these are the Alpine-Himalayan system and the Circum-Pacific system comprising the Andes, the Rockies and island chains of east Asia. These system each consist of series of fold structures aligned in a roughly parallel manner. They appear to have formed as a rersult of the movement of plates during the earth's geological history, Nearly all fold mountain systems involve considerable thickness of sedimentary rocks that have been crumpled and folded into wave- like undulations, consisting of alternating arch-like upholds called **anticlines**, and trough-like downfolds called **synclines** (Fig. B.4).

Thus the initial landform associated with an anticline is a rounded mountain ridge while that associated with a syncline is an elongated open valley.

The shape and size of the folds depend upon the intensity and direction of the compressive forces and upon the nature of the rocks which compose the different strata. Where the compression is relatively mild or more or less equal from both sides, the folds are simple or symmetrical and are called **open folds.** A very well known example of open folds is provided by the Jura Mountains of France and Switzerland.

The two sides of flanks of a fold are called its **limbs.** The plane that bisects the angle between the two limbs is called the **axial plane** (B.5) and the line of intersection of this plane with a bedding plane gives the direction of the *axis of the fold* at that place. If the axial plane is vertical and the axis horizontal, the fold is symmetrical. If the axial plane is inclined, the fold is **inclined.** Depending on their orientation, the folds may be **symmetrical, as ymmetrical, one-limb vertical (or overturned).** With further intensity in compression both the limbs of the fold may be inclined in the same direction and dips of the beds may be almost parallel. Folding of this type is called **isoclinal** (Fig. B.7). The final case occurs when both the limbs lie one above the other, lying in a roughly horizontal posture giving rise to a recumbent fold.

With further increase in pressure the recumbent folds may be sheared or sliced by fault planes lying almost horizontal, these are called **over thrust faults**,Further development of the structure results in forward movement of the rocks of the upper limb

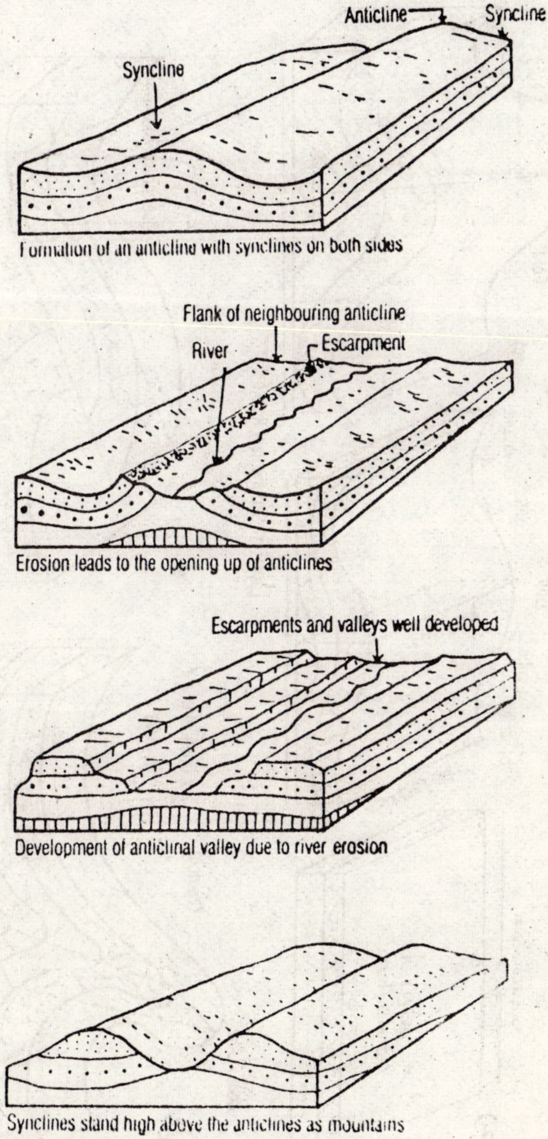

Fig. B.4 ***Folds and Rivers - Inversion of Relief***

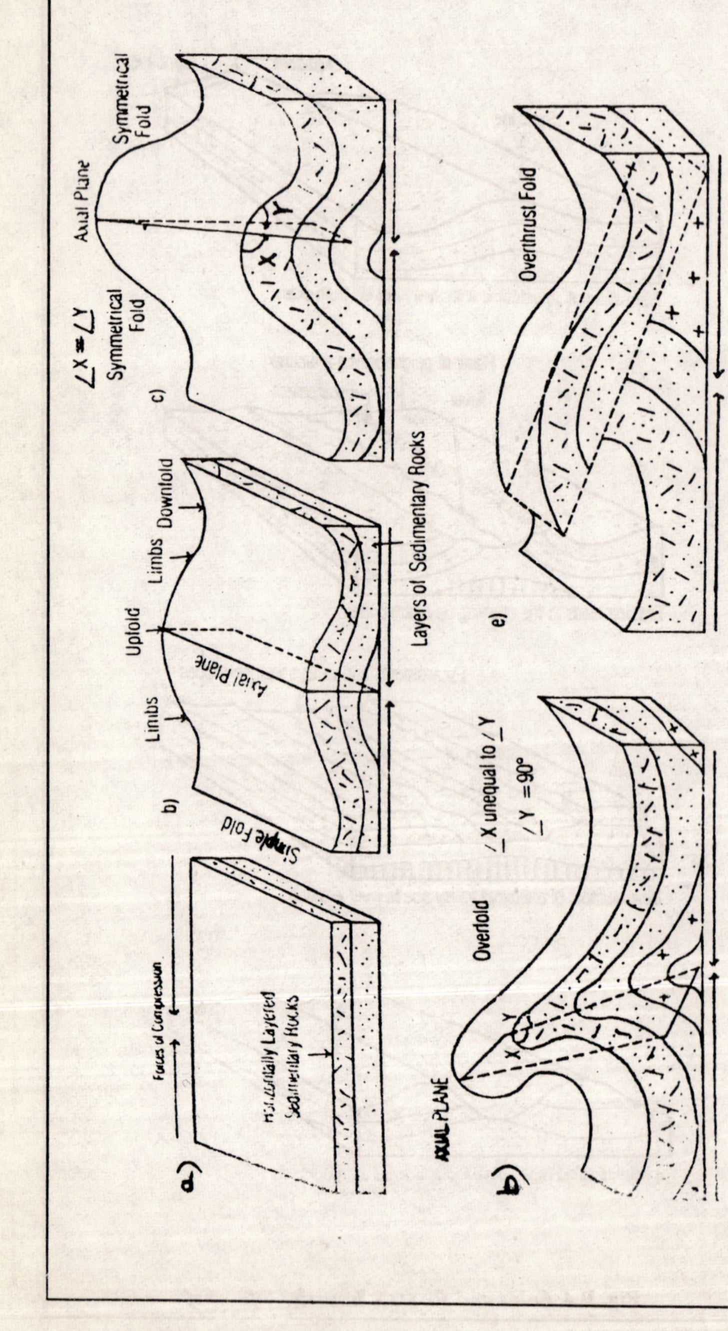

Fig.B.5 *Nature of fold mountains*

along plane of shearing. The plane of shearing is a thrust plane and the structure an **overthrust fold** (Fig. B.5). The sheet of rocks that has moved forward along the thrust plane and may be hishly contorted in the process is called a *nappe* (Fig. B.6). In the swiss Alps examples of complex nappe structure are revealed along steep mountain side, though glacial action has removed much of the nappe structure with more intense folding the beds tend to become stretched or pulled out and this finally culminates in fracture. In the Alps, the under limb of recumbent anticlines is generally found to be attenuated by stretching, or, if fracture has super vened, a thrust or "slide" takes its place, the upper block moving forward over the lower for great distances (Fig. B.7).

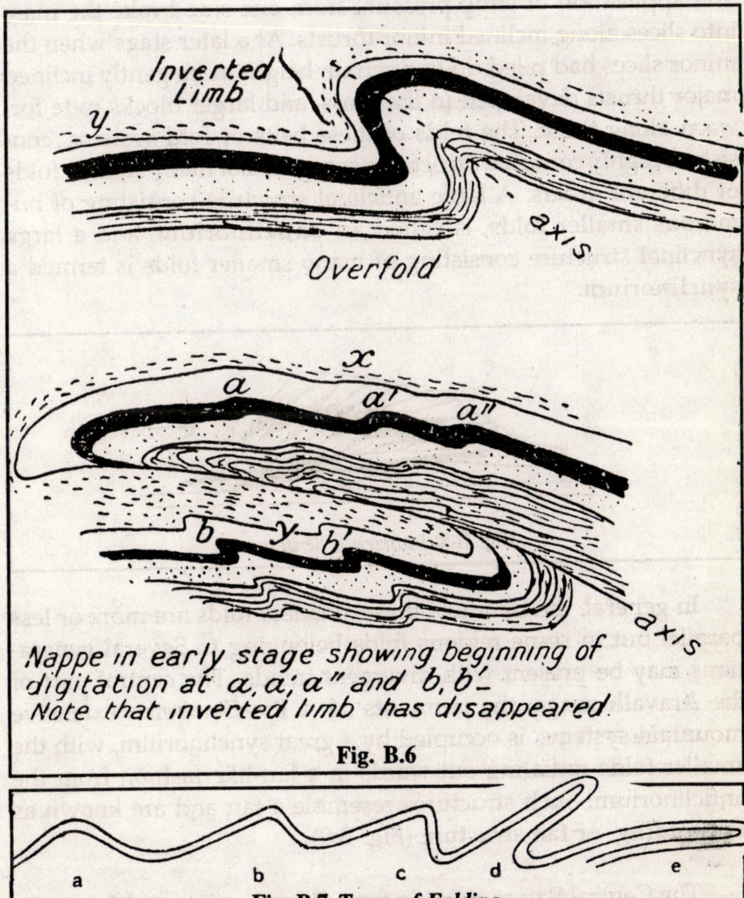

Fig. B.6

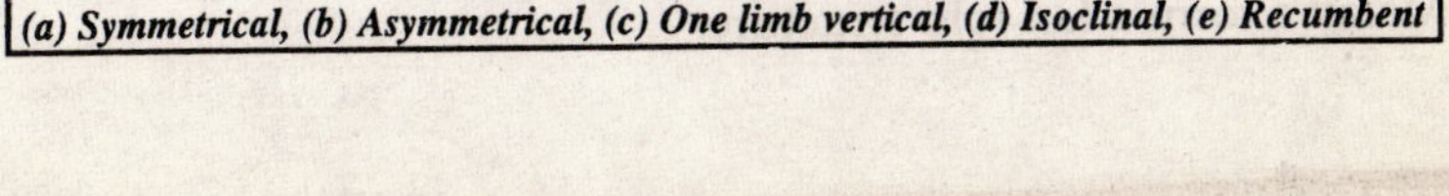

Fig. B.7 ***Types of Folding***

(a) Symmetrical, (b) Asymmetrical, (c) One limb vertical, (d) Isoclinal, (e) Recumbent

The Himalayas are not only marked by complex folds but contain over thrust and nappes of great dimensions. The Garhwal and Krol nappes are exposed in the sub-Himalayas of Uttar Pradesh. In Kashmir beyond the Murree thrust is a zone of nappes in which Palaeozoic and Mesozoic rocks have travelled some distances from their original sites of deposition.

Another mode of crustal shortening by thrust faulting is illustrated in the "imbricate structure" of the North-West Highlands of Scotland. (Fig. B.8) Here evidence of recumbent folding is absent, the rocks being disposed in great slices separated by thrust planes, with each slice broken by minor thrust faults more steeply inclined. The application of stroy pressure from one side broke the mass into slices along inclined minor thrusts. At a later stage when the minor slices had piled up to a certain height more gently inclined major thrusts developed in the mass, and larger blocks rode forward along these. The folds of these belts or fold systems, consists of highly complex. Structures composed of many smaller folds of different orders. A large anticlinal structure consisting of numerous smaller folds, is called an **anticlinorium**, and a large synclinal structure consisting of many smaller folds is termed a **synclinorium.**

Fig. B.8 ***Imbricate Structure***

In general, the trends of these smallers folds are more or less parallel but in some regions folds belonging to Several generations may be present with divergent trends. The central part of the Aravalli range, the remnants of a Pre-Cambrian extensive mountain systems, is occupied by a great synclinorium, with the smaller folds radiating out wards in a fan-like fashion from the anticlinorium. Such structures resemble a fan and are known as **fan folding or fan structure** (Fig. B.9).

The Central Range running from Patani in Siam to Malacca in Malay a form a fan fold structure.

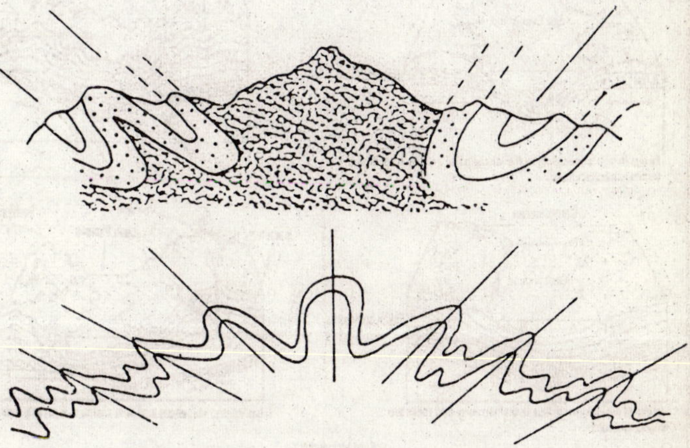

Fig. B.9 *Fan Folding*

Many of the world's largest mountain chains exist beneath the sea. Some of these are revealed as **island arcs**, as in the South East. Asian islands in Pacific Ocean. The mountain system which builds up the massif in Indo-Malayan mountain system. Associated with them are deep oceanic **trenches** on the convex sides of the arc. The ocean deep marks the site of the downward plunging of the lower plate into the mantle. These sites are known as the Subduction zones. Melting of rocks here in the mantle give rise to surface volcanic activity which is the basis of the island . The mid-oceanic ridges from the longest mountain chains. The mid-Altantic ridge rises 3 km above the flour of the Atlantic; it is Connected with the Indian Ocean ridge, and there with the Pacific-Antarctic ridge, resulting in a continuous system some 40,000 km in length (Fig. B.10).

BLOCK MOUNTAINS, BASINS AND RIFTS

The morphological results of large-scale warping and faulting are no less spectacular than those produced by orogenic movements. Recent faulting is often dearly defined in the relief. Faults are fractures in rock along which the adjacent rock surfaces have been relativaly displaced. Some faults may be quite small and their displacements may be measured in centimetres while others may be kilometres. long with displacemet in trace of a fault on the

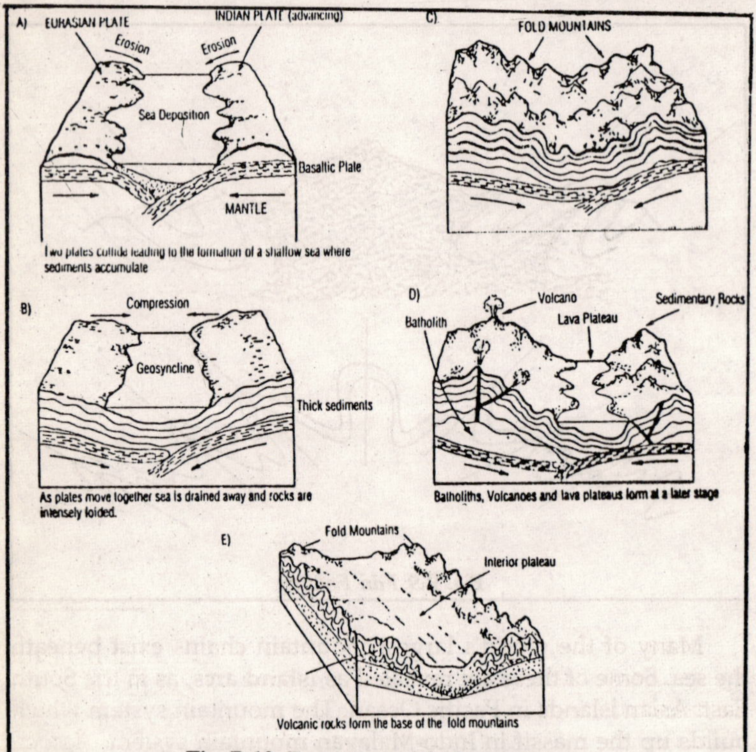

Fig. B.10 ***Formation of fold mountains***

earth's surface is known as **fault line** (Fig. B.11). When the faults are of great horizontal extent, the surface trace or the fault line can some times be followed on the ground for many kilometres. Its position may be indicated by an escarpment or scarp. If the escarpment is the direct result of movement along the fault, it is called a **fault Scarp** (Fig. B.11). On the other hand, a scarp produced by differential erosion of the rocks along an ancient fault is known as **fault-line Scarp.**

In other words, a fault scarp is of tectonic origin while a fault-line scarp is a structurally controlled erosional feature. A fault scarp is thus a relativley fresh feature and can be best seen in regions of recent earthquakes and active faulting.

The Earthquake of 1995 in Latoor region of Maharashtra has given rise to fault-line scarps.

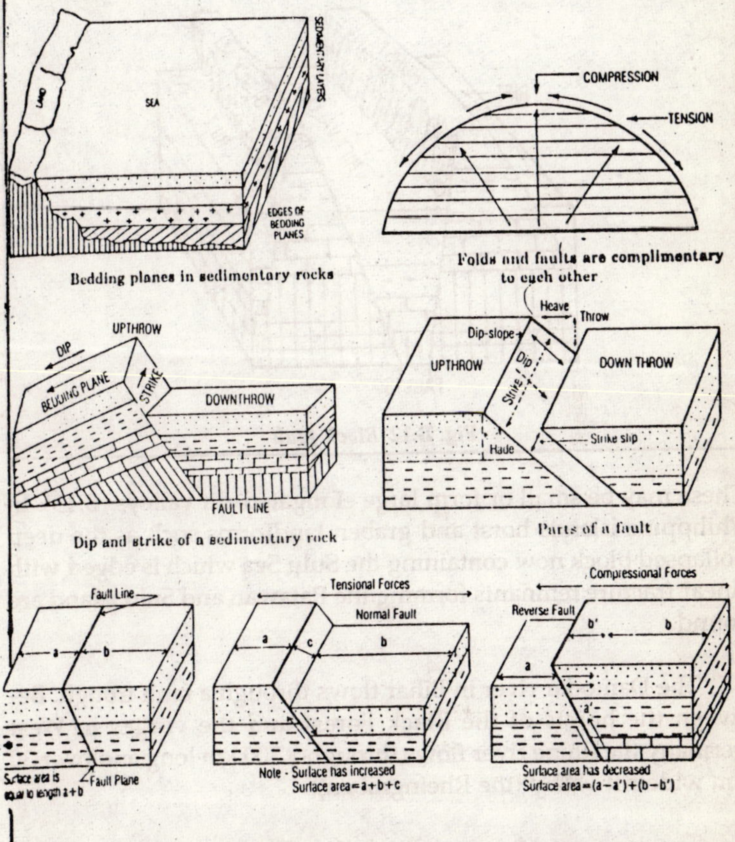

Fig. B.11 ***Faults formed by tension and compression***

Large tracts of land broken up by faults of great vertical displacement may form **block mountains** Separated by intervening basins.

The Vindhya and Satpura of India are two examples of block mountains Separated by Narmada river (Fig. B.12). The Basin and Range country of western North America is of this nature, a mosaic of sub-parallel faults and differentially uplifted and tilted blocks. Within the individual blocks, the attitude of the strata does not necessarily reflect the most recent earth movements, and may be highly contorted from a previous episode. An uplifted block may alternatively be called a *horst;* a dropped block is a *graben.*

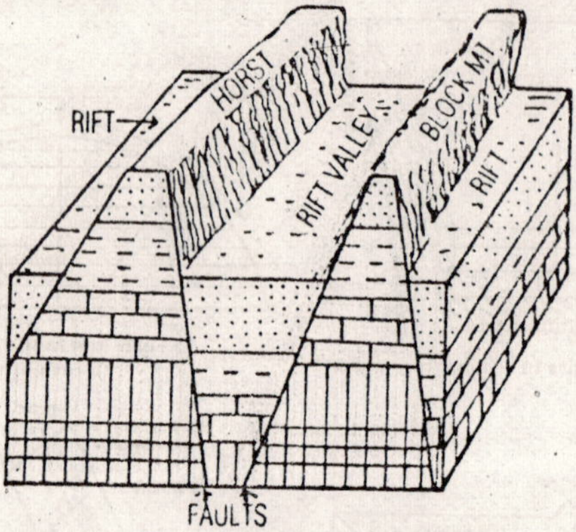

Fig. B.12 *Block fault*

These may be small or form large elongated rift valleys (B.13). In Philippine islands horst and graben landforms such as the deep collapsed block now containing the Sulu Sea which is edged with linear fracture remnants forming the Palawan and Sulu island are found.

The Damodar river in Bihar flows through a fault trough. Between the horsts of the Black Forest and the vorges in West germany the Rhine river flows through a 300 km long and over 30 km wide rift valley (the Rheingraben).

The most notable example of rift valleys is found in East Africa where the great Rift valley is made up of several grabenas, above which tilted horsts produce a linear mountainous topography.

Sometimes a rift valley may result from the forcing down of a central block along reverse faults caused by fracturing of the strata under lateral pressure. Such valleys formed by compression are called **Ramp valleys**. The Brahmaputra Valley of NE India is an example of rarup valley formed due to compression between the uplifted Himalayas in the north pressing against the horst of shillong plateau in the south.

For our purposes, three types of faults may be distinguished.

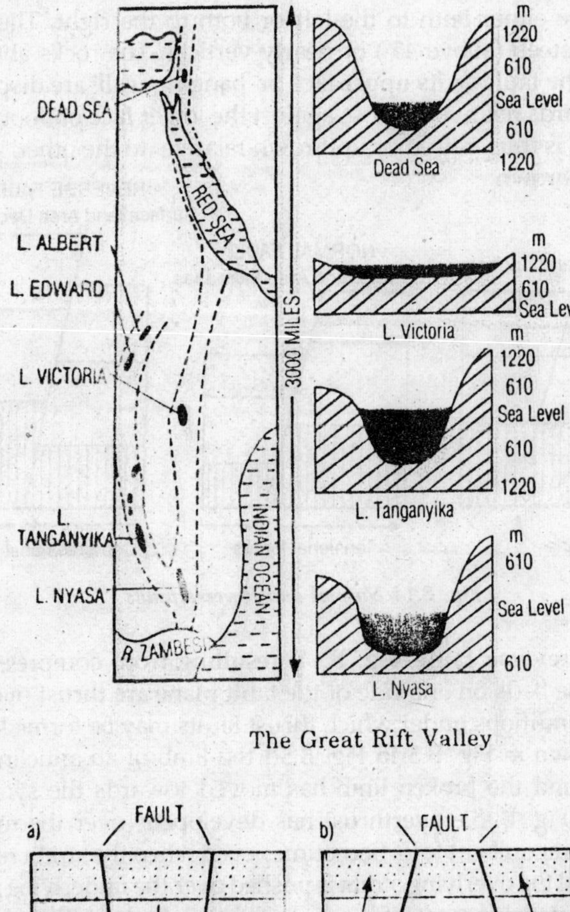

The Great Rift Valley

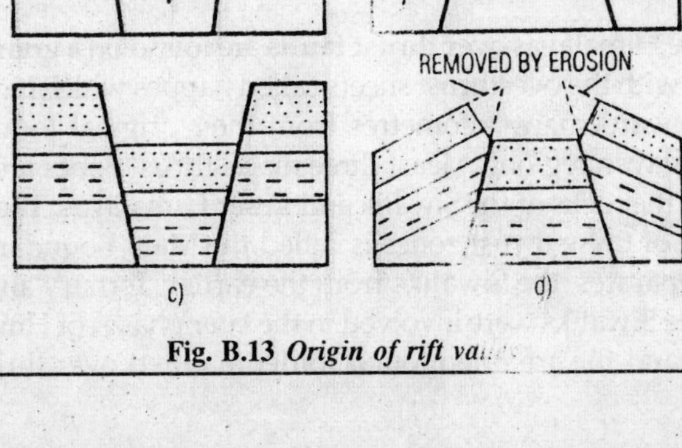

Fig. B.13 *Origin of rift val*

In a **normal fault** (Fig. B.14), usually the result of tentional forces, the inclination of the fault plane and the direction of down throw are either both to the left or both to the right. The fault plane is steep (above 45^0) or nearly vertical. The rocks abutting against the fault on its upper face or 'hanging wall' are displaced down wards relative to those against the lower face or 'foot way'. One side is thus raised or upthrown relative to the other, which is downthrown.

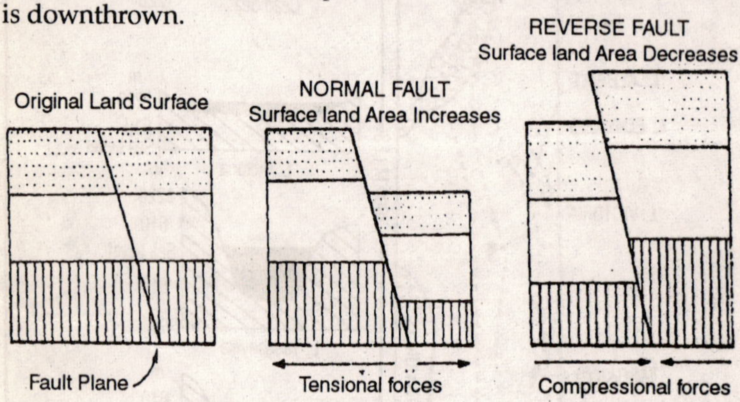

Fig. B.14 *Normal and Reverse faults*

In a **reverse fault** (Fig. B.14) resulting from compressional forces, the beds on one side of the fault plane are thrust over the other. Conditions under which thrust faults may be formed have been shown in Fig. B.5 In Fig. B.5d the limb of an anticline has broken, and the broken limb has moved towards the synclinal beds. In Fig. B. 5.e overthrust has developed over the middle limb of a recumbent fold. Sometimes even when the strata remain horizontal the overlying strata is pushed over the underlying strata after the development of a **compressional fault**. A **thrust fault** (Fig. B.5e) is developed which cuts across the folded layers.

In the Himalayas over **thrust faults** are found on a grand scale, together with the overthrust sheets called nappes which have travelled. forward many kilometres from their original location. In the Himalayan region, at least three major thrust zones are recognised in the rocks of the Siwalik and Leser Himalayas. The southern most of these thrust zones is called the Main Boundary Fault which separates, the Siwaliks from the earlier. Tertiary and older rocks. The Siwaliks were involved in the later phases of Himalayan orogeny and the are often found folded, faulted over thrust and lying at steep angles against other formations.

When overthrust, there order of **superposition**. There has been so much of movement that even within the Siwaliks the older strata are found thrust over younger strata.

A **tear or lateral fault** (B.15) is on in which rocks are displaced horizontally along a line of fracture, with little or not vertical movement. The amount of vertical displacement, if any, on a fault is referred to as the **throw** of the fault the amount of lateral displacenent is known as the **heave.** The best known example of tear fault is the great San Andreas fault of california, nearly 1200 kms long, which can be followed from the gulf of california to north of San Francisco with parallel or interlacing faults.

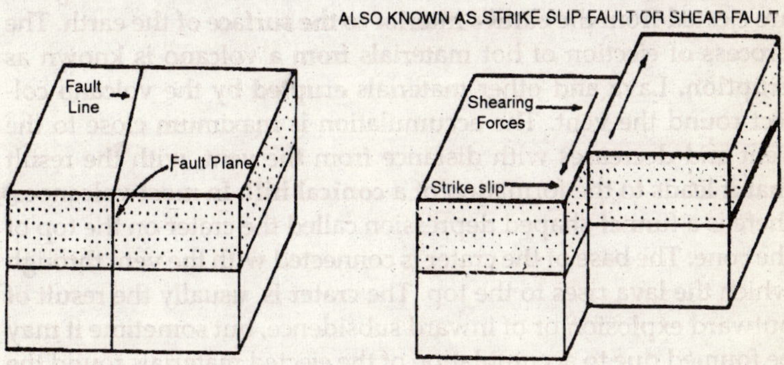

Fig. B.15 *Tear fault*

SIGNIFICANE OF FAULTS

It should be noted that faults do not produce only earthquakes. Along the fault planes the rocks are usually fractured. This permits **ore-forming solutions** to rise along the fault planes. Many important ore bodies are thus found here. Petroleum too finds its way along fault planes or it may became trapped in porous beds that have heen faulted against impervious shale beds.

VULCANICITY AND ITS RELATED LANDFORMS.

The term 'vulcanicity' covers all those processes in which molten rock material or magma into the crust or is poured out on its surface, there to solidıfy as a crystalline or semicrystalline rock.

Volcanic activity produces dramatic and strikingly beautiful landforms in a relatively short period of time.

The volcanic landforms may form in any latitude or climate but have similar, distinctive and symmetrical appearance. In course of time they are modified by the climatically controlled processes.

With the help new techniques it is possible to know the exact dating of erupting rocks. By measuring the amount of rock eroded from a dated vlocanic landscape, it is now possible to measure the absolute rate of landscape, modification and to reconstruct the original volcanic features.

The Nature of Volcanoes

A volcano (Fig. B.16) is defined as a deep vent in the earth's crust through which molten rocks or hot lava, ash and hot gases are ejected from the earth's interior to the surface of the earth. The process of ejection of hot materials from a volcano is known as **eruption.** Lava and other materials erupted by the volcano collect round the vent. The accumulation is maximum close to the vent and decreases with distance from the vent, with the result that it leads to the formation of a **conical hill.** In most volcanoes, there is a funnel-shaped depression called the crater on the top of the cone. The base of the crater is connected with the vent through which the lava rises to the top. The crater is usually the result of outward explosion or of inward subsidence, but sometime it may be foumed due to accumulation of the ejected materials round the Vent.

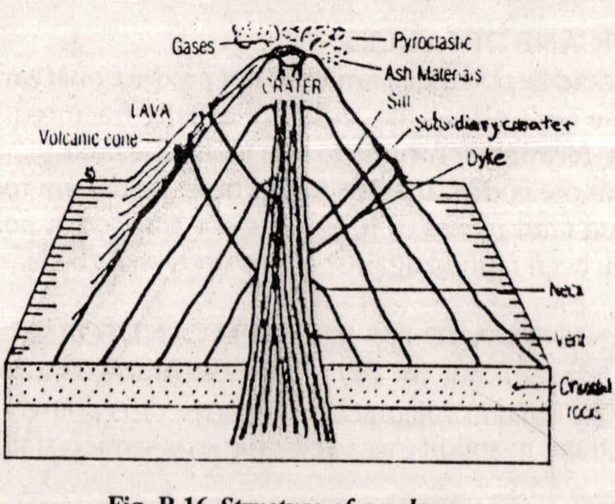

Fig. B.16 ***Structure of a volcano***

Frequency of Eruption

In some volcanoes the eruption continues uninterruptedly for a long time, but in most volcanoes it is discontinuos. In some volcanoes the period of rest or quiet is fairly long and these are extremely dangerous. Based on the frequency of eruption the volcanoes are divided into extinct, dormant and active.

Volcanoes in which the eruption has completely stopped and is not likely to recur are called **extinct.** Popa mountains in Burma. Examples of extinct volcanoes are also found in Mauritius, Malagassy and Several other islands of Indian Ocean. Volcanoes which have been quiescent for a long time but in which there is a possibility of eruption are called **dormant** volcanoes. Krakatoa of Indonesia is a dormant volcanoe. It was quiet for nearly 200 years and then suddenly erupted in 1883 which continued for several months. The eruption was so violent that nearly two-thirds of the island of Krakatoa disappeared.

The volcanoes which continue to erupt periodically are called **active** Volcanoes. Mona Loa in the Hawaii Islands, Etna in Sicily, Meon in Phillipines, Merup in Indonesia are active volcanoes.

Products of Volcanic Eruption

The products of volcanic eruption may be either solid, liquidor gaseous.

The solid rock fragments of different sizes which are ejected with the eruption are together called **pyroclasts.** When the volcanic eruption is explosive, a lot of rock fragments are thrown in to the air which fall down near the vent or the adjacent areas. The pyroclastic materials are sometimes collectively colled **tephra.** It consists of fragments of different sizes and shapes they have been given different names according to their size. The largest angular rock fragments are called **blocks or breccia.** When the molten lava is thrown into the atmosphere and its bigger drops solidify before falling down, they assume round, oval or pear-shaped forms. The solid rounded materials are **volcanic bombs.** when their sizes resembles peas, they are called **lapillis.** When they have a vesiculer structure, they are referred to as **pumise or cinders.** When the volcanic material consists of sand size and finer tephra, it is called **volcanic ash** and when materials are still thinner, they are called **volcanic dust.**

The most important product of the volcanic eruption, is of course the liquid lava. Its temperature is usually between 900⁰ to 1200⁰ C. The lava containing a higher percentage of silica is called **acid lava**, while lava with a lower percentage of silica is called **basic lava**. Acid lavas have an high melting point and are usually very viscous. Basic lavas melt at a lower temperature and are generally very liquid.

Some times the surface of a solidified lava is smooth; but more often it is very rough. If the lava is viscous, the surface becomes ropy like that of a stream of flowing pitch. Frequently too, both in acid and basic lavas, escaping gases make the upper layers of the stream vesicular or full of little holes, like a piece of bread. The fragments of the the crust, if they are vesicular, are known as **Scoriae.**

Of the volcanic gases by for the most important is steam. Lot of steam is ejected with the eruption and its condensation usually results in heavy rainfall. Besides steam (60 to 90%), other volcanic gases include Carbon dioxide, nitrogen and sulphur dioxide, and there are very small quantities of hydrogen, carbon monoxide sulphur and chlorine as well.

Volcanic Land Forms

Volcanic landscapes consist of assemblages of very distinctive landforms built largely by accumulations of solidified lava and of fragmentary volcanic products.

The constructional volcanic landforms may be said to fall into two broad categories (a) Coves and fields of coves, domes and related features, (b) volcanic, plateaus and plains.

Basaltic lava forms: Domes, Shield volcanoes and Lava Plateaus

Basalt domes and shield volcanoes (Fig. B.17) are formed as a result of emission from localized vents. Basalt emerges from fissures rather than pipe-like vents. The basaltic domes built of sucessive flow filed around a central vent are called **exogenous domes** (B.18) to distinguish them from **endogenous domes** of very viscous acid lava which may rise upward into a crater but be too stiff to flow out, resulting in a skinned over or bulbous protrusion of lava from the vent (Fig. B.19).

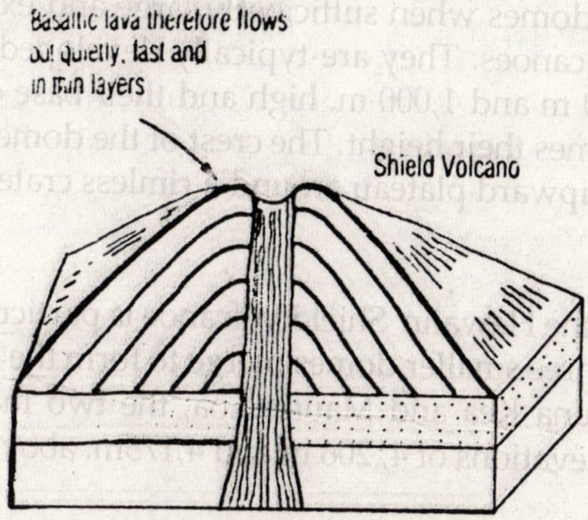

Fig. B.17 *Lava cones of the thin lavas*

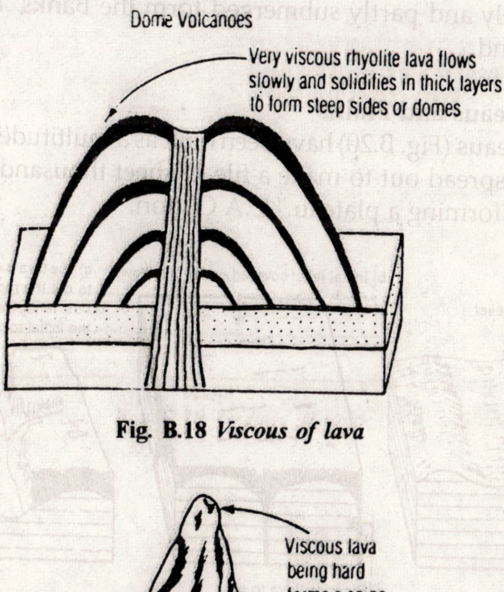

Fig. B.18 *Viscous of lava*

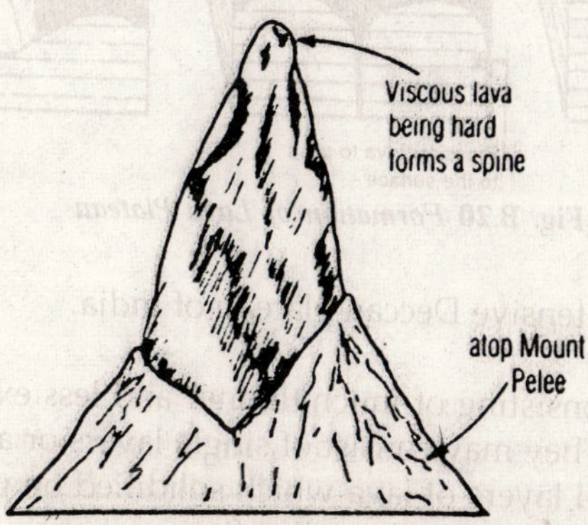

Fig. B.19 *Spine formed of viscous lava*

Exogenous domes when sufficiently large and extensive become shield volcanoes. They are typically developed in Iceland are between 100 m and 1,000 m. high and their base diameter is about twenty times their height. The crest of the dome becomes a broad, convex-upward plateau around a rimless crater or a summit caldera.

The size of the Hawaiin Shield volcanoe is particularly large- two large and three smaller domes merge to form the large island of Hawaii. Mauna Kea and Mauna Loa, the two major shields have summit elevations of 4, 206 m and 4,175m. above sea-Level.

Among islands of Pacific Ocean, there are basalt domes in all stages of dissection by erosion. Two overlapping domes, dissected sub-maturely and partly submerged form the Banks Peninsula, New Zealand.

Basalt Plateaus and Plains

Basalt Plateaus (Fig. B.20) have been built as a multitude of sources have been spread out to make a file of sheet thousands of meter thick, then forming a plateau." C.A Cotton.

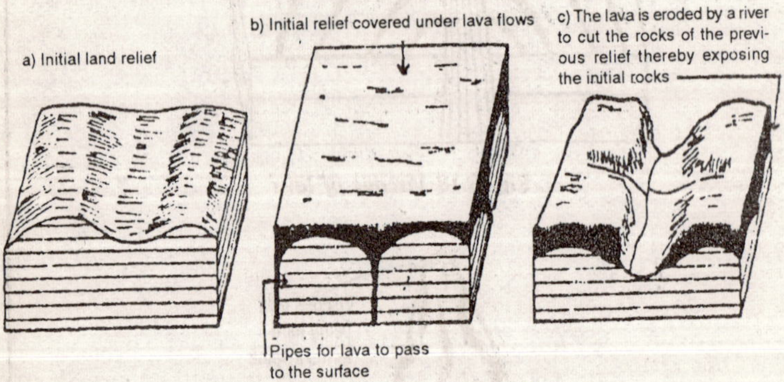

Fig. B.20 ***Formation of Lava Plateau***

The most extensive Deccan plateau of India.

Basalt plains consisting of much thinner and less extensive files of lava sheets. They may consist of single layers or at the most a few super posed layers of iava which solidified on gentle slopes or after running, down on the valley floors.

Andestic Volcanic Forms

These are characterised by great cones and cone clusters with surrounding plains built up by deposits of shower. Andestic is lava of intermediate compositon with medium silica content.

Cones consisting entirely, or almost entirely, of fragmental material, are known as **ash or cindercones** (Fig. B.21).

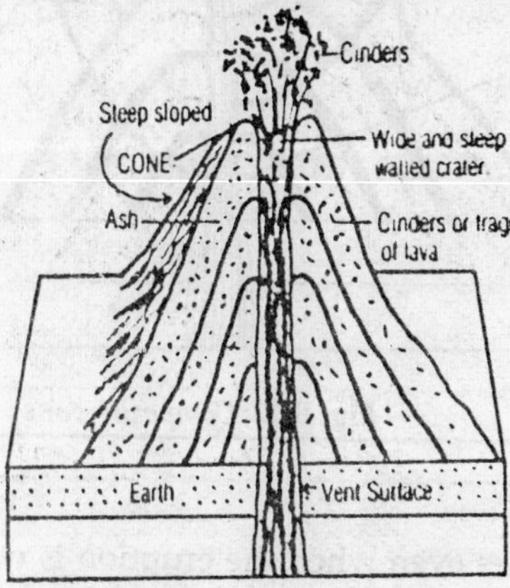

Fig. B.21 ***Ash and Cinder cone***

In shape they often almost perfect cones, but the cone spreads out towards the base so that in profile the sides are curved instead of straight.

Volcanic eruptions, however, are not always explosive. In some volcanoes, called **lava volcanoes**, the lava rises slowly and is poured out quietly.

If the lava is acid and viscous it behaves like a mass of paste squeezed through an opening, and the dome is very convex, with steep sides and often without a crater (Fig. B.19).

If the lava is basic and fluid, if flows readily and for great distances. The diameter of the volcano is great but the slope of its sides is gentle, and the form is that of a very flat dome. The crater is simply the hollow left when the lava in the pipe subsides.

When the cones have a layered structure with alternating ash and lava they are described as **strato volcanoes or composite vol-**

canoes (Fig. B.22). Meyon in the Philippines is an ideal example.

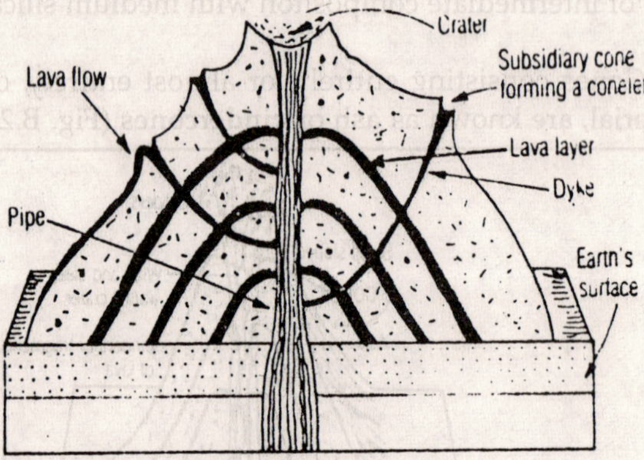

Fig. B.22 ***Composite cone***

Acid domes

Sometimes even when the eruption is not explosive and the lave wells up and overflows quietly, the lava may be acid and not basic. Where the lava is acid it is viscous and pasty and cannot flow far from the vent giving rise to an inverted bowl structure called **Acid-Cumulo Dome.** Reunion Island, north of Madagascar in the Indian Ocean is an example.

Sometimes the lava solidifies as soon as it comes out of the vent and then a vertical dome may be formed in the crater it self. Such domes are called **plug domes or volcanic necks.**

The Batak Highlands of Sumatra forms an acid dome.

Volcanic Craters and Calderas

We come across primarily two kinds of topographic depressions in the volcanic regions. These are **craters** and **calderas** Craters are smaller depressions, while the Caldera covers a wider area. Just above the volcanic vent there is usually a rounded bowl or funnel-shaped depression which is called a **Crater** (Fig. B.16) It is formed as a result of either the blowing up of the rocks from the violent or due to collapse of the rocks near the vent mouth. Sometimes the materials which come out of the vent are deposited around its mouth and form a circular ring with a depression in the middle. Such Craters are called *Ring Craters* or *Crater Rings*, as found around Anak Krakataur volcano in the East Indies.

The **Caldera** (Fig. B.23) is an extensive rounded volcanic depression whose diameter is many times greater than that of a crater. It is formed either due to the blowing off of the top of the volcanic cone through violent explosion or the collapse of the overlying rocks due to lack of support after a considerable amount of lava has been ejected from the lava reservoir. On the top of the Barisan Highlands in north-west Sumatra there is a huge caldera, having an area of nearly 1,000 sq. kilometre in a section of which Lake Toba is situated. The Lonar Lake in Barar, Madhya Pradesh,

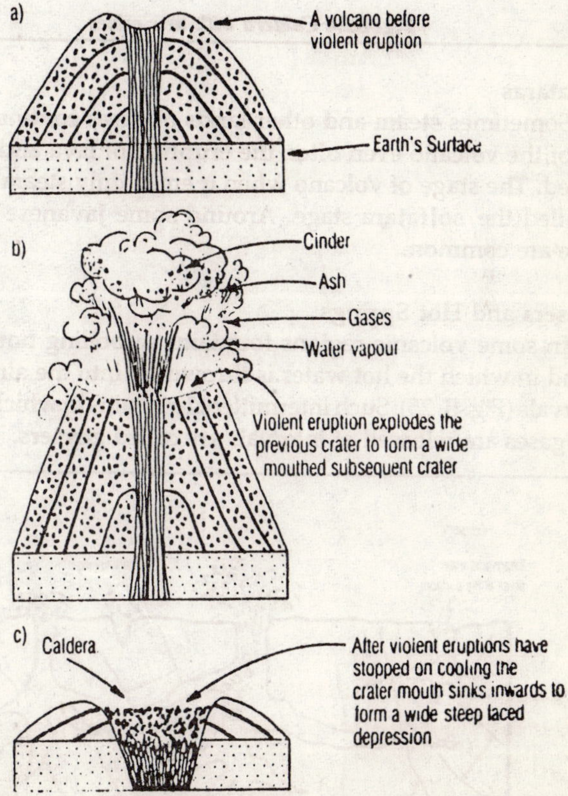

Fig. B.23 ***Formation of a caldera***

India is located in a circular caldera which is surrounded on all sides by high steeply sloping hills (B.24).

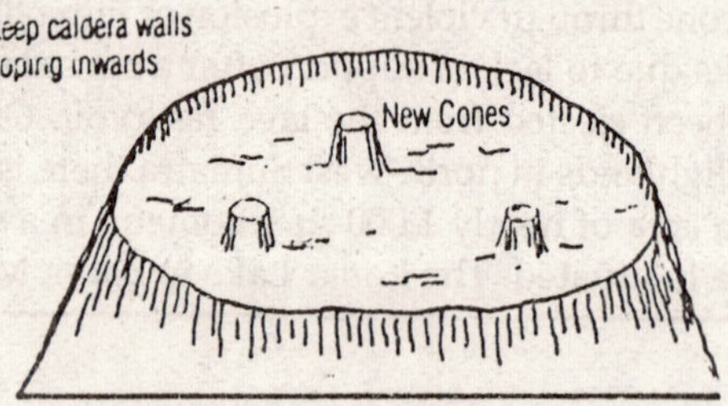

Fig. B.24 ***Caldera with new cones***

Solfataras

Sometimes steam and other kinds of gases continue to come out of the volcano even often the eruption of lava and ashes has ceased. The stage of volcano when it emits only steam and gases is called the **solfatara** stage. Around some Javanese Volcanoes these are common.

Geysers and Hot Springs

In some volcanic regions fountains of boiling hot water are found in which the hot water is thrown off into the air at regular intervals (Fig. B. 25). Such intermittent fountains in which hot water ang gases are released at intervals are called **geysers.** The mouth

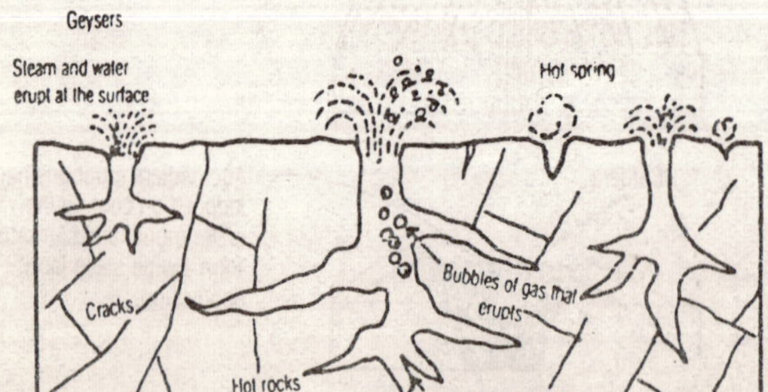

Fig. B.25 ***Hot Springs and Geysers***

of the geyser is connected with the hot interior by a pipe. In the interior of the pipe the water is heated and is changed into steam after reaching a certain temperature. The steam forces the hot water to ascend along the pipe which when forced up comes out on the surface in the form of a fountain (Fig. B.26). A famous geyser in Yellow Stone Park is the Old Faithful.

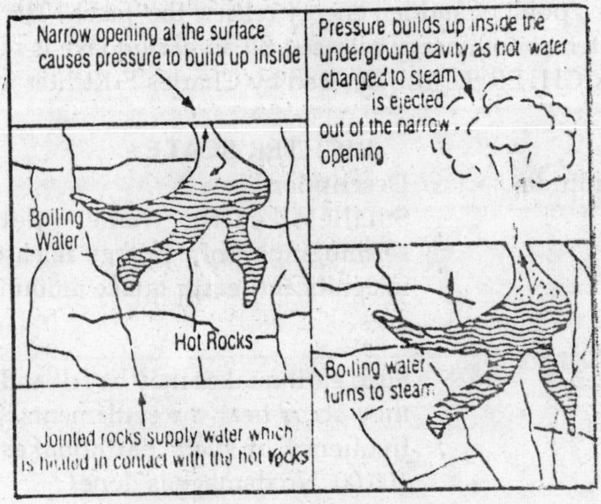

Fig. B.26 ***Formation of a geyser***

Sometimes the water does not rise into a geyser but hot water flows continuously from a spring such **hot Springs** are quite common in volcanic regions (Fig. B.27). Hot spring are common in the volcanic belt of Indian Ocean which passes through Andaman, Sumatra, Java, Bali, Sunda and Myanmar.

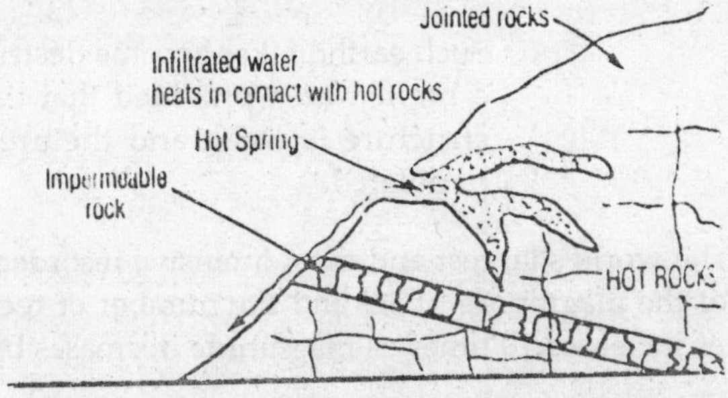

Fig. B.27 ***Formation of a hot spring***

Earthquake

An earthquake is a major demonstration of the power of the tectonic forces caused by endogenetic thermal conditions of the interior of the earth. 'An earthquake is a motion of the ground surface, ranging from a faint tremor to a wild motion capable of shaking buildings a part and causing gaping fissures to open in the ground. The earthquake is a form of energy of wave motions transmitted to the surface layer of the earth in widening circles from a point of sudden energy release the 'focus'. The magnitude or intensity of energy released by an earthquake is measured by the RICHTER SCALE devised by Charles F. Richter in 1935.

RICHTER SCALE

Magnitude	Description
0	Smallest earth tremer detected by seismograph only. Energy released by such insignificant earth quake amounts to $3x10^{12}$ ergs.
2.5 to 3.0	Such earthquakes may be felt and detected if they occur near the settlements. The annual frequency of such earthquakes is around 100,00. No damage is done.
4.5	Local damage is done.
5.0	The quakes of this magnitude equal in energy to ordinary atomic bomb. The atomic bomb hurled on Hiroshima (Japan) during Second world war equalled to the magnitude of 5.7 on Richter Scale. The energy released from such earthquakes equals $8x10^{20}$ ergs.
6.0	Such earthquakes become destructive within a limited area provided that the geological structure is weak and the area is heavily populated.

'The world's largest and most intensive recorded earthquake was of the magnitude of 8.9 and the number of recorded earth-quakes increases 10 times as magnitude decreases by one'.

The place of the origin of an earthquake is called FOCUS which is always widden inside the earth but the depth of which varies from place to place. The deepest earthquake may have its focus at a depth of even 700 km below the ground surface but some of the major Himalayan earthquakes, such as the Bihar-Nepal earthquake of August 21, 1988, have their focus around 20-30 km deep. The place on the ground surface, which is perpendicular to the buried 'focus' or 'hypocentre', recording the seismic waves for the time is called EPICENTRE (Fig. B.28). The Seismic waves move away from the source of the earthquake (focus or hypocentre) in the form of (i) Primary or Pressure waves (P waves), (ii) Secondary, shear or Transverse waves (S waves) and (iii) Long waves or surface waves (L waves). These seismic waves are recorded with the help of an instrument called SEISMOGRAPH or SEISMOMETER at the epi-centre.

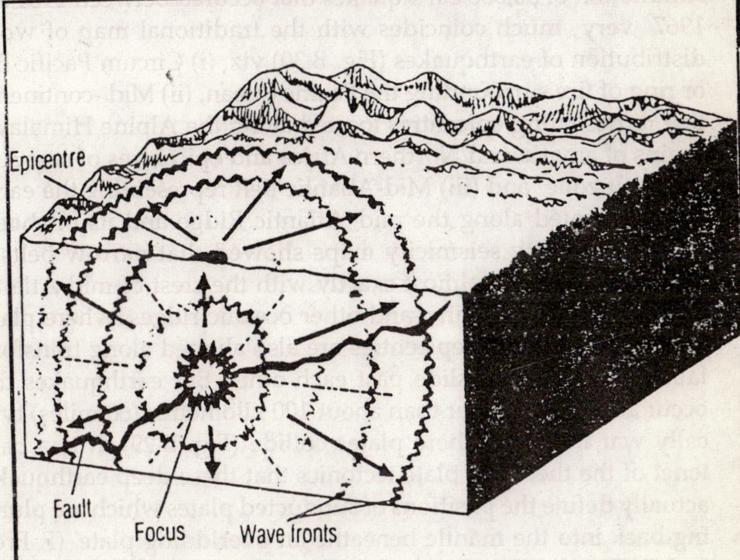

Fig. B.28 ***Focus and epicentre of an earthquake***

CAUSES OF EARTHQUAKES

Earthquakes are caused due to disequilibrium in any part of the crust of the earth. A number of causes have been assigned to cause disequilibrium in the earth's crust such as volcanic eruptions, faulting and folding, upwearping and down werping. hydrostatic pressure of man made water bodies like reservoirs and lakes, and of late the plate movements.

Recently PLATE TECTONIC THEORY has been accepted as the most plansible explanation of earthquakes. As per theory of the plate tectonics the crust of the earth is composed of solid and moving plates having either continental crust or oceanic crust or even both-continental-oceanic crust. The earth's must consists of major plates (Eurasian plate, American plate, African plate, Indian plate, Pacific plate and Antarctic plate) and 20 minor plates. These plates are constantly moving in relation to each-other due to thermal connective currents originating deep within the earth. Thus all the tectonic events take place along the margins of plates.

DISTRIBUTION OF EARTHQUAKES

The world map of the distribution of earthquakes prepared by the seismologists on the basis of computer analysis and simultation of 30,000 earthquakes that occured between 1961 and 1967 very much coincides with the traditional map of world distribution of earthquakes (Fig. B.30) viz. (i) Circum Pacific Belt or ring of fire surrounding the Pacific Ocean, (ii) Mid -continental Belt representing epicentres located along the Alpine Himalayan chains of amasia and Northern Africa and epicentres of east African fault zone and (iii) Mid-Atlantic Belt representing the earthquakes located along the mid_Atlantic Ridge and its offshoots. The high-quality seismicity maps showed that narrow belts of epicentres coincide almost exactly with the crest of mid-Atlantic (Ridge), the east Pacific, and other oceanic ridges, where plates separate Earthquake epicentres are also aligned along transform faults, where plates slide past each other. But earthquakes that occur at depths greater than about 100 kilometres (60 miles) typically war margins where plates collide (Fig. B.29). It is a basic tenet of the theory of plate tectonics that these deep earthquakes actually define the positions of subducted plates which are plunging back into the mantle beneathe an overidding plate' (F. Press and R. Siwer, 1978). It may be pointed out that the occurence of earthquakes along the plate margins (boundaries) are well explained on the basis of this revolutionary theory for eg. the earthquakes of New Marid (Missomi, USA 1812), Charleston, South Carolina (USA, 1886), Boston, Massachussets (USA, 1755), Tang Shan (China, 1976), Koyna (December 11, 1967, India) etc. are few examples of intraplate earthquakes. Similarly 'the seismicity of the Indian shield as revealed from kutch (1819), Koyna (1967), Bhadrachalan (1969) and Broach (1970) cannot be explained easily by plate tectonics since they occured far away from the plate

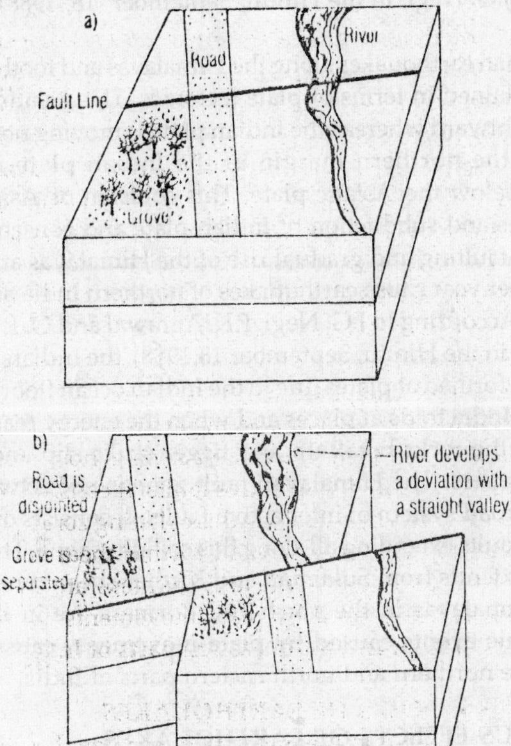

Fig. B.29 ***Earthquake in association with faults***

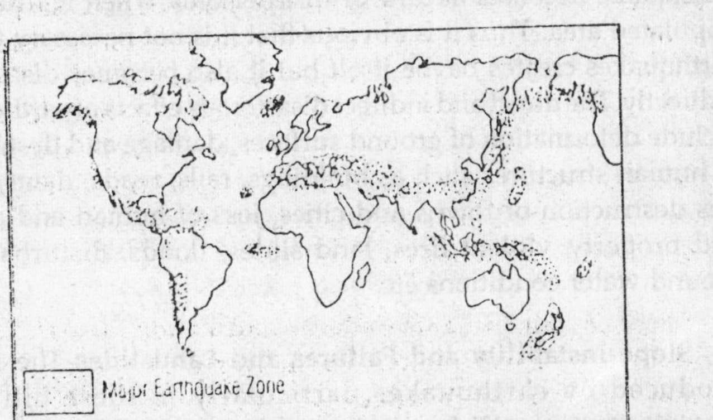

Fig. B.30 ***Major earthquake belts of the world***

boundary' (J.G. Negi, in the Hindu, September 18, 1988).

The Indian earthquakes along the Himalayas and foothill zones may be explained in terms of plate tectonics. The Asiatic plate is moving souhtward whereas the Indian plate is moving northward and hence the northern margin of the Indian plate is being subducted below the Asiatic plate. This collision of Asiatic and Indian plates and subduction of Indian plate and consequenting folding and faulting and gradual rise of the Himalayas at the rate of 600 mm per year cause earthquakes of northern India and Tibet and Nepal. According to J.G. Negi, P.K. Agrawal and O. P. Pandey (as reported in the Hindu, September 18,1988) 'the Indian subcontinent has deformed at plates due to the Indian ocean floor spreading process. India folds at places and when the energy reaches the elastic limit the rocks break up and tigger strike slip and thrust fault earthquakes. The Himalayan fault zone is not actually one fault but a broad system of inter active faults. It consists of a complex grid of faults extending all along this colliding zone. The earthquake belt extends from Sulaiman and Kirthar shear zones in the west, the Himalayas in the north and Burmese are in the east. These tectonic events caused by plate movements cause earthquakes in the northern and north eastern parts of India.

HAZARDOUS EFFECTS OF EARTHQUAKES

It may be restated that the intensity of earthquakes and their hazardous impacts are determined not on the basis of the magnitude of seismic intensity as determined by RICHTER Scales, An earthquake becomes hazard or disaster only when it strikes the populated area. Thus it is obvious that it is not necessary that an earthquakes creates havoe itself but it also becomes disasterous indirectly. The direct and indirect disasterous effects of earthquakes include deformation of ground surfaces, damage and destruction of human structures such as buildings, rails, roads, dams, factories destruction of towns and cities, loss of human and animal and property, violent fires, land slides, floods, disturbance in ground water conditions etc.

(i) **Slope instability and Failures and Landslides-**The shocks produced by earthquakes particularly in these billy and moutainous areas wlich are composed of weather lithologies and are tectonically sensitive and weak cause slope instability and slope failure and ultimately cause landslides and debris falls which damage settlements and transport systms on the lower slope segments.

(ii) **Damage To Human Structures-** Earthquakes inflict great damage to human structures such as buildings, roads, rails, factories, dams, bridges and thus cause heavy loss of human property. Infact, the principal damage emanating from earthquake disaster is construction failure It may be pointed out that the extent of damage done to the human structures not only depends on intensity and magnitude of earthquakes but also on the characteristics of ground, upon which the buildings are constructed and the nature of materials of which the buildings are constructed (such as stones, bridges, muds, concrete, cement, tins, nuts etc.) It may be stated that in the ground surface composed of unconsolidated geomaterials such as alluvium, colluvium, artificially filled up and and levelled up depressions, swamp deposits reclaimed through the dumping of coarse sands and city garbages the vibrations of earthquakes last longer and the amplitudes of seismic waves are greater than in the structure of consolidated materials and bed rocks. Thus the earthquakes cause more damages in the areas of unconsolidated ground than their counter parts in the regious of solid structures and bedrocks.

Two major earthquakes of Bihar (India)-Nepal Border in 1934 and 1988 explain the impact of earthquake disasters on human structures and human lines.

(iii) **Damage to the towns and Cities-**Earthquakes have thier worst effects on towns and cities because of great density population. The earth tremous of higher magnitudes shake the ground to such an extent that the large buildings collapse and men and women are buried under the large depris and rubbles of collapsed structural materials of buildings, ground water pipes are bent and damaged and thus water supply is totally disrupted, electric poles are uprooted and electric and telephone wires and cables are heavily damaged causing total disruption of electric supply and tele-communication systems, obstruction and destruction of sewer systems out of gear etc. Calcutta city was severely damaged due to severe earthquake of October 11, 1737 as thousand of buildings were severaly damaged and 3,00,000 people were killed. Nearly 2,00,000 people were killed within a period of 100 years due to earthquakes of 1688, 1693 and 1783.

(iv) **Loss of Human Lives And Property**-The destructiveness of an earthquake is determined on the basis of human casualities in terms of deaths. For example, the kangra earthquake of India in 1905 recorded 86 magnitude on Richter scale but it could cause death of only 20,000 persons whereas 1976 T'ang-shan earthquake of China measuring 7.8 to 8.1 on Richter scale cause deaths of 750,000 people.

The 1950 earthquake of Assam, India, produced barrier in the Dihang river, the tributary of the Brahmputra river, due to accumulation of huge debris caused by land slides due to earth tremors and thus caused severe floods in the upstream section similarly, the dam on subansire river were broke in and resultant flash flood submerged an area of 770 square kilometres.

The Kutch earthquake (Gujrat) of June 16,1819 generated strong tsunamis which caused very high sea waves which submerged the coastal areas and inflicted great damage to strips and country-made boats of the fishermen. The land area measuring 24 km in length was raised upwards because of tectonic movement triggered by the said earthquake which provided shelter to the stranded and marooned people.

(b) The Work of Running Water

Features Formed By River Erosion

When rain falls, part of it sinks into the ground some is evaporated back into the atmosphere and the most of as rivulets, brooks, streams and tributaries of rivers that flow into the sea. Streams are widespread features of the land. They are found everywhere except in certain desert areas or the snow-covered regions of the Arctic. Rivers may be very large like the Amazon and the Nile, most of them however are small.

A stream obtains its water directly or indirectly from rainfall or other forms of precipitation. When this water accumulate and flows into a stream, it has a force, which is the most important cause in breaking down and removal of rocks and is known as erosion by stream.

The Development of a river System- The source of a river may be a spring(like River Thames) a lake (eg. River Nile which has its headwaters in lake Superior) or a marsh (eg. River Lumi & some rivers of Sudan) Rivers are however formed in an upland region generally having its source in a glacier (eg. River Rhone (ALPS) River Ganga and River Jamuna (in glaciers in the Himalayas). Rivers begin as sheets of water known as surface runoffs but may soon develop into hills and streamlets which follow the depressions. Small sreamlets join to form a permanent big stream or rivers.

The source of a river is generally in an upland region where precipitation is heaviest and where there is a slope down which the run-off can flow. The uplands therefore form the catchment areas of rivers. A catchment area is generally in a mountain where heavy rain leads to form a river. The crest of the mountain or ridge is the divide or watershed (a natural divide which seperates two different drainage basins or river systems eg. Western Ghats) from which streams flow down the slopes on both sides to begin their journey to the oceans. The initial stream that exists as a consequence of the slope is called the **consequent stream.** As the consequent stream wears down the surface by deepening its channel down wards, it is joined by several tributaries either obliquely or at right angles depending on the alignment and the degree of resistance of the rocks.

If the rocks are composed of homogenous beds of uniform resistance to erosion, the tributaries will join the main valley obliquely as **insequent streams.** The drainage pattern so involved will be tree like in appearence and is therefore described as dendritic drainage. On the other hand if the rocks are made up of alternate layers of hard and soft rocks, the tributaries tend to follow the pattern of the rock structure. If the outcrops of the rocks occur at right angles to the main valley, the tributaries will join it at right angles as **subsequent streams** (Fig. B.31) The drainage pattern so developed will be rectangular in shape and is called **trellised drainage.**

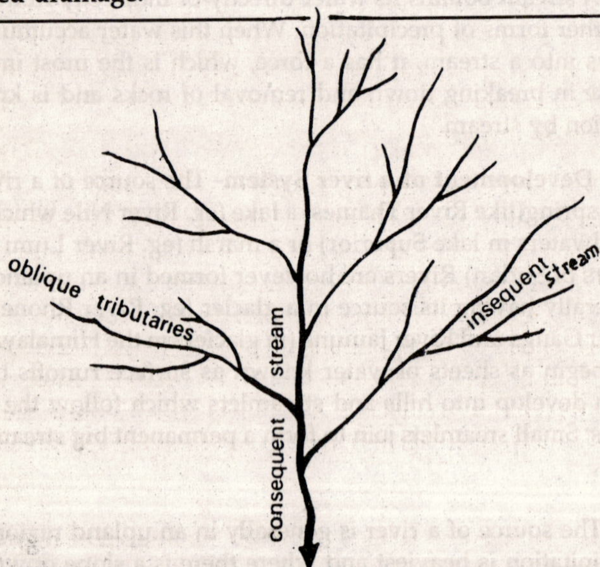

Fig. B.31 Dendritic or tree-like drainage pattern developed on homogeneous rock or beds of equal resistance

Drainager Basin-The whole area drained by the river and its tributaries.

When a river flows it carries with it eroded materials. These comprise the rivers load and may be divided into three distinct types.

1) **Materials in solution-**There are materials which are dissolved in water.

2) **Materials in Suspension**-Sandy silt and mud are carried along suspended in the water as the stream flows.

3) **The Traction Load**-This includes coarser materials such as pebbles, stones, rocks and boulders which are rolled along the river bed.

River Erosion and Transportation-In rivers erosion and transportation go on simultaneously comprising the following inter-acting processes.

1) **Corrasion or Abrasion**-This is the mechanical grinding of the rivers traction load against the bed and the bank of the river. The rock fragments are hurled against the sides of the river and also roll along the bottom of the river. It takes place in two distinct ways (i) *Lateral Corrasion*. This is the sideways erosion which widens the 'v' shaped valley. (ii) *Vertical Corrasion*. This is the downward action which deepens the river channel.

2) **Corrosion or Solution**-This is the chemical or solvent action of water (which contains Carbondioxide and oxygen) on soluble or partly soluble rocks with which the river comes into contact. For eg. Calcium Carbonate in Limestone is easily dissolved and removed in solution.

3) **Hydraulic Action**-This is the mechanical loosening and sweeping away of materials by the river water itself. Some of the water splashes against the river banks and surges into creeks and crevices. This helps to disintegrate the rocks. The water also undermines the softer rocks with which it comes into contact. It picks up the loose fragments from the banks and bed and transports them away.

4) **Attrition**-This is the wear and tear of the transported materials them-selves when they roll and slide into one another. The coarser boulders are broken down into smaller stones, the angular edges are smoothed and rounded to form pebbles. The river materials are carried further downstream to be deposited elsewhere.

Ways of Transportation- (1) **Saltation** particles being picked up and dropped. Finer silt sediments will go along with water (2) **Suspension** (3) **Solution** limestone particles.

The Course of a River- The course of a river may be divided into 3 distinct parts (1) **The upper or mountainous course** (2) **The middle or valley course** (3) **The lower or plain course** (old age) (Fig. B.32)

(1) **The Upper or Mountain Course-** (a) This begins at the source of the river near the **water-shed** which is probably the crest of a mountain range. The river is very swift as it descends the steep slopes and the predominant action of the river is vertical corrasion. The valley thus developed is deep, narrow and distinctly 'v' shaped. Downcutting takes place so rapidly that lateral corrasion

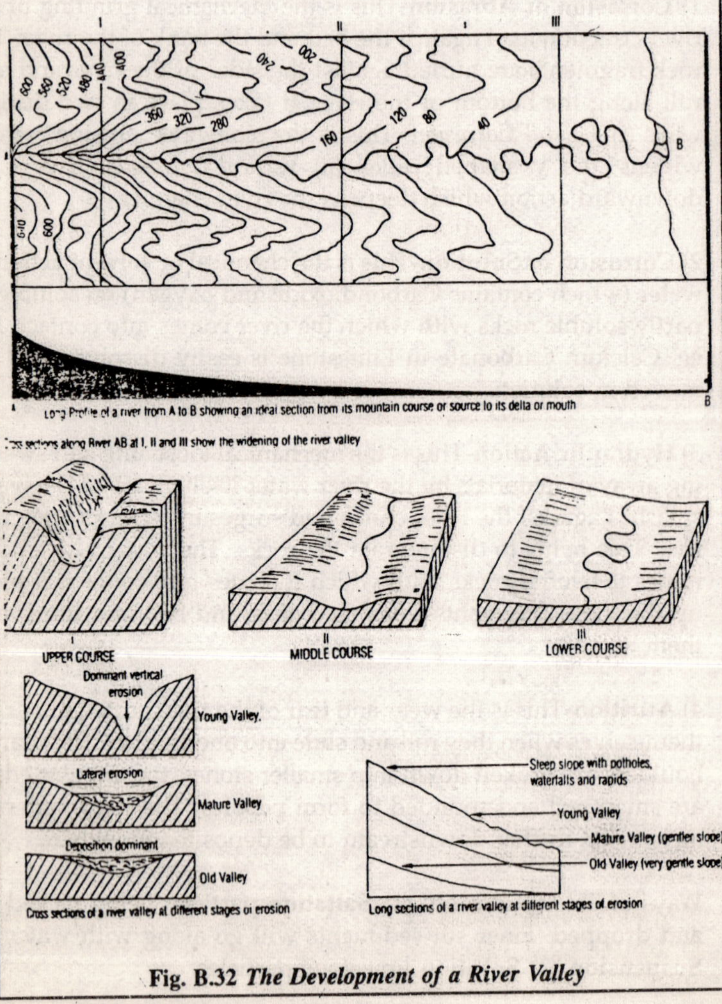

Fig. B.32 ***The Development of a River Valley***

cannot keep pace. In some cases where the rocks are very resistant, the valley is so narrow, and the sides are so steep that **gorges** (Fig. B.33) are formed eg. Indus gorge in Kashmir. In arid areas like deserts where there is little rainfall to widen the valley sides and the river cuts deep into the valley floor preciptous valleys called **canyons** are formed, the river Colorado has cut the frand **Canyon** which is about 320 kms long and in places reaches a depth of over 1000 metres.

(b) River Capture (Fig. B.34) this is also known as **river piracy** or **river beheading**. Its development is dependent on the different rate of back cutting (head ward-erosion) into a divide. The back cutting causes their sources to move further and further from their mouths. This back cutting may continue to such an extent that if

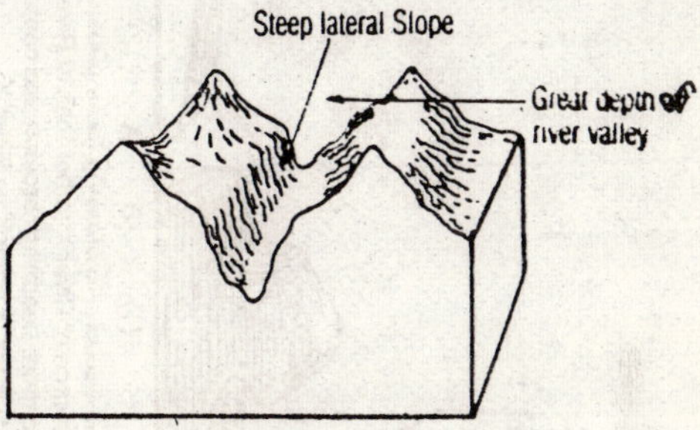

Fig. B.33 ***Gorge***

one side of the divide is of greater extent or gradient or receives more precipitation, then the river on that side may ultimately capture the headwaters of another. Its greater erosive power will succeed in enlarging its basin at the expense of the weaker stream. Ultimately the waters of the weaker stream will be diverted into that of the stronger stream. This is known as river piracy. The bend at which the piracy occurred is termed the elbow of capture' and the beheaded stream is termed the misfit. The valley below the elbow is the wind gap and may be valuable as a road or rail route. Examples of river capture-are to be found in Burma-the upper sittang has been captured by Irrawaddy in England, the Blythe and the Wansbeck are beheaded by the North Tyne.

(c) **Waterfalls** (Fig. B.35). These are liable to occur at any part of the river course, but they are most numerors in the mountain

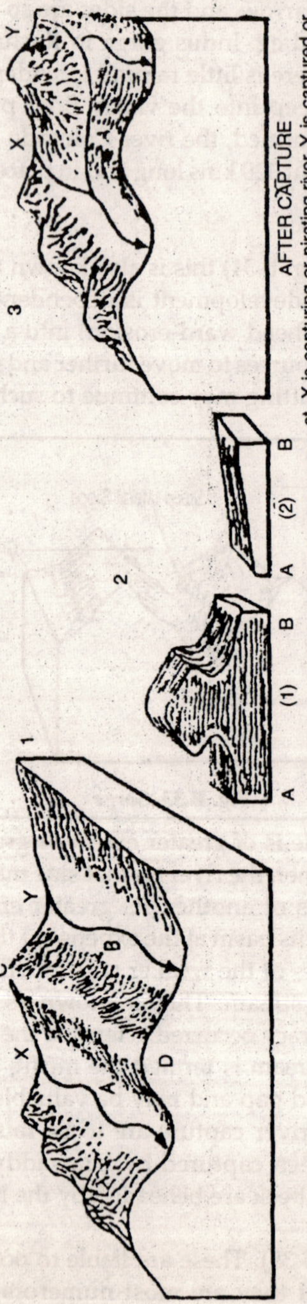

Cross section AB showing more undercutting at the source of River X rather than of River Y, leading to more headward erosion and capture of the headwaters of River Y by River X.

X is capturing or pirating river, Y is captured or pirated river, A is elbow of piracy, B is wind gap, Z is misfit or beheaded river, CD is divide watershed.

Fig. B.34 *Headward erosion*

course where changes of gradient are more abrupt and frequent. When rivers plunge down in a fall of some length they are called waterfalls. Waterfalls are formed in several ways :-

(i) When a fault line scarp caused by faulting lies across a river eg. Victoria Falls on the R. Zambezi plunging 360 feet.

(ii) When water plunges down the edge of a plateau like the river Congo which leaps for 900 feet, through a series of more than 30 rapids as Livingstone Falls.

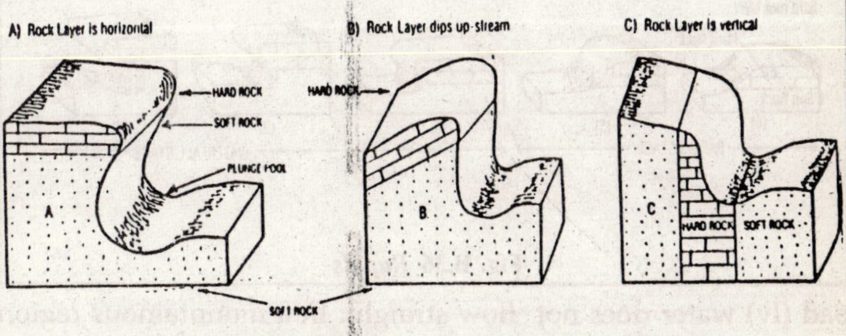

Fig. B.35 *Waterfalls caused by varying rock structures*

(iii) Glaciation produces hanging valleys where tributary streams reach the main U-shaped valley below as waterfalls eg. the Yosemite Falls of California with a total descent of 2,560 feet.

(iv) When a bar of resistant rock (often a dyke) lies transversely across a river valley eg. Niagara Falls, U.S.A. and Kaisteen Falls in Giyana.

(v) Waterfalls as a rule occur where the swirling action of water cuts away the underlying soft rocks faster than the hard rocks lying over it.

Rapids (Fig. B.36) Due to unequal resistance of hard and soft rocks traversed by a river, the outcrop of a band of hard rock may cause, a river to jump or fall downstream. Rapids are much smaller than waterfalls. Similar falls of greater dimensions are also referred to as cataracts of which there are five along the Nile that interupt smooth navigation.

(d) **Hydraulic Action**-The rivers carry pebbles and stones by the swirling motion of which hollows are widened to form depressions known as potholes (Fig. B.37).

(e) **Meanders**-The river usually starts meandering in its middle or lower courses due to (i) plain region (ii) less spread (iii) heavy

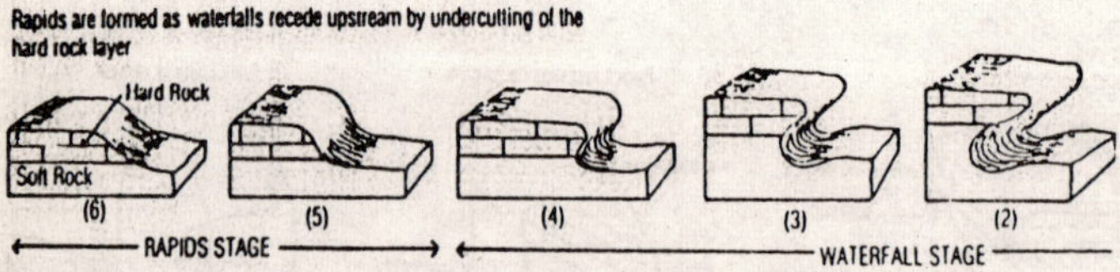

Fig. B.36 ***Rapids***

load (iv) water does not flow straight. In a mountainous region too meandering takes place when a river winds its way around outcrops of resistant rocks. Such meandering leads to the formation of interlocking spurs (Fig. B.38).

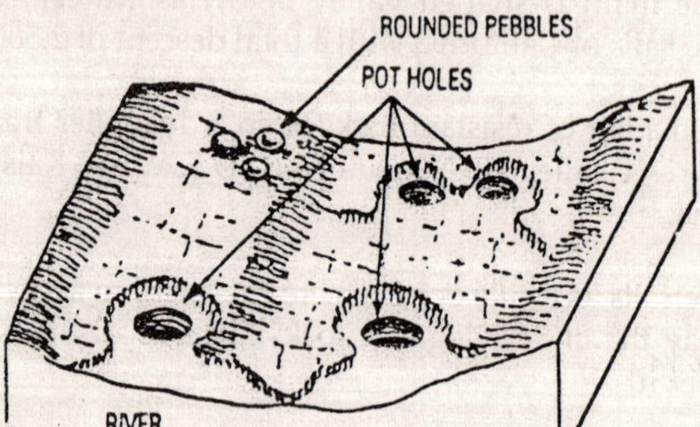

Fig. B.37

Transportation by a River-(1) Materials like calcareous rocks are carried by a river in *solution.* (2) When large stones (saltation) or rocks move in a hopping motion (3) when materials like clay and sand are carried in *suspension* (4) when large boulders are dragged along river bed it is known as *fraction.*

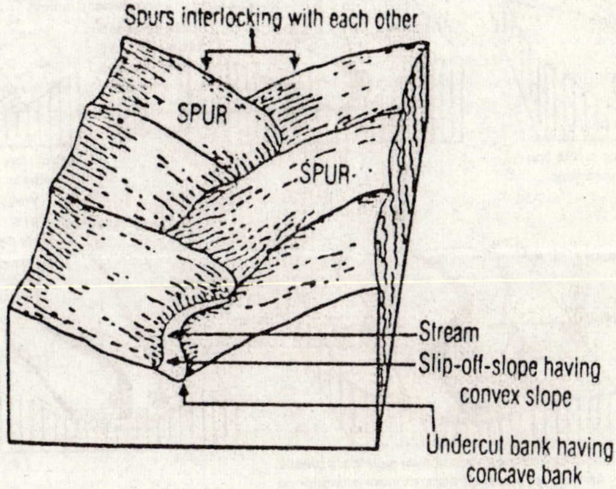

Fig. B.38 ***Interlocking spurs***

The amount of transportation depends on the volume of the river, gradient of the land, velocity of the river. It velocity of the river is doubled then transportation will be increased 64 times. If volume is doubled transportation power is also doubled.

The Middle or Valley Course- The middle course or the second stage of the river begins when it leaves the mountain and cuts into foot-hill country. Here, the volume of water increases as the catchment area also increases because of the confluence of several tributaries. The work of the river is now predominently transportaion with some deposition. At this stage, with the lower gradient, vertical carrasion, decreses while lateral corrasion increases. This causes the widening of the river valley. The river valley now forms a wide 'V'. As water exerts a great force on both the sides, many spurs are cut back and worn away. Then remains form a line of *bluffs* on each side of the valley floor. (Fig. B.39).

Here the width of the river is equal to the width of the valley. This will eventually become a flood plain when the width of the valley, is much more than the width of the river.

Now, the load of the river increases, but the load carrying capacity of the river depends upon the rate of flow. In the level

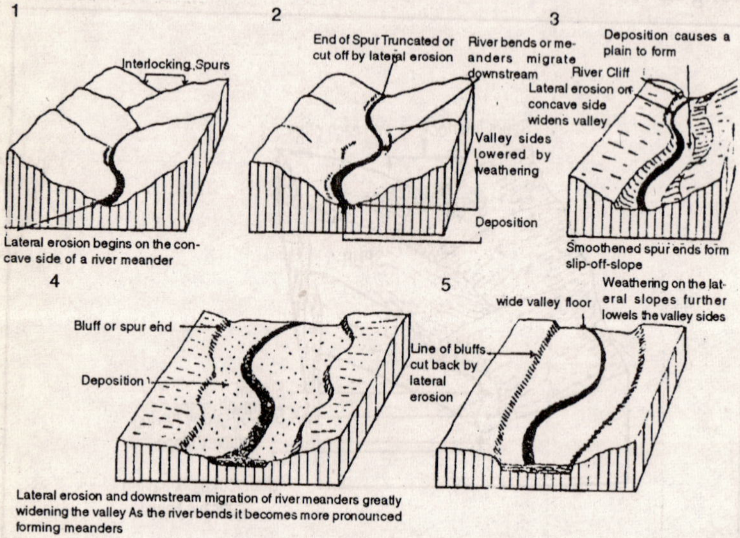

Fig. B.39 *Spur truncation, bluffs*

sketches, the rate of the flow is generally much slows. A good amount of load-especially big fragments, consisting of boulders, pebbles and sand is deposited at the foot of the hills forming a fan-like deposit called *alluvial fan*. When several such alluvial fans coalesce together they form a pied mont. or predmont plain. Such plains unlike deltas may be formed far away from the sea. At the foot of the Himalayas, the Bhaban and Terai lands make up the piedmont plain. If such type of deposition continues for a long time, a bed may build up. (Sacramento Valley in California and Bihar by Kosi).

The river practises lateral corrasion and spurs are cut away and blunted and thin debris is left behind.

Rivers in the middle and lower course carry large quantities of sediments. During annual or sporadic floods, these materials are spread over the lowlying adjacent areas. A layer of sediment is thus deposited during each flood, gradually building up a fertile flood plain. When the river flows normally its bed is raised through the accumulation of deposits and materials is also dropped on the sides forming raised bank called *levees*. It will not be long before the water level flows dangerously close to the top of the levees. In an attempt to minimise the risk of floods artificial embankments are erected on the natural levees but this allows the river to rise further. When they can no longer with strand the pressure of the flood water, the banks burst, damaging property and drowning thousands.

Sometines the river may branch out into a number of channels to bypass any obstacle even its own depositions (Fig. B.40).

It eventually joins up again to flow as a single river. The river can then be described as a braided channei or stream eg. River Ghagra and the rivers in the Sundarbans. The deposition often forms river island. India has the biggest river island named *'Mazuli.*

Some examples of **Flood plain-** In northern India on the banks

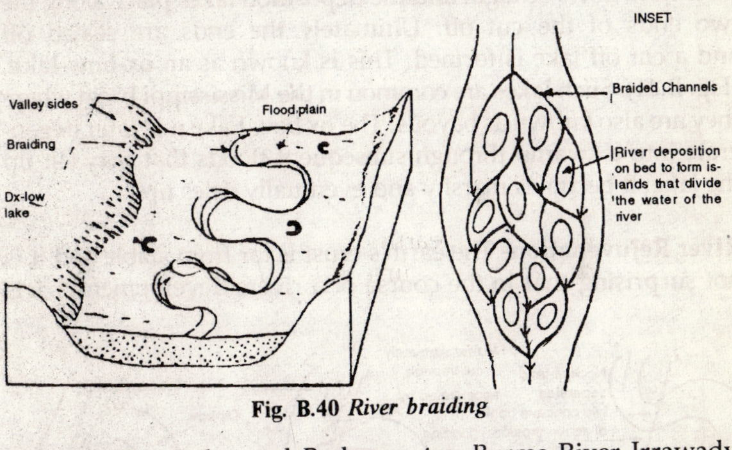

Fig. B.40 ***River braiding***

of the Ganga, Indus and Brahmaputra. Burma-River Irrawady China- River Hwang Ho, Yangtze and Mississippi, Snake-Colorado Canada-River Hudson, River Saskatchewan (River Parana and Paragway) Quinocco, Europe-River Seine, River Volga, River Danube. River Thames, River Don, River Dneiper, U.S.S.R-River Lena River Ob, River Yenisey, S. Africa-River Congo, River Nile, River Zambesi River Limpopa, River Orange etc.

India-In Bihar, some levees are as high as 8 to 12m along the river Ganga. The lowlying banks of the ganga below 50m are very poorly drained and hence a line of marshes occur parallel to the river. These are locally called chaur, or tals. The banks of the river being higher than the tals, smaller tributaries connot enter straight into the river. They flow parallel to the ganga for some distance, until they find an easy passage. Such streams like the Punpun wherever found in the world are called **Yazooc**.

An important feature of the river in the middle course is the development of **meanders or loops**. When the course of a river lies in a flat country the irregularities of the ground force the river to swing from side to side in wide bends and form meanders. (The term meander has been derived from the winding river Meanderez of Turkey). The current of the river eats into the concave side of the bend and cuts away a steep bank, while on the convex side being much slower it deposits the sediments and builds up the bank. In course of time the bends approach each other and the narrow neck is cut off because of the rapid erosion of the river. This often happens when the river is in flood. The river now flows straight and the deposition takes place along the two ends of the cut off. Ultimately the ends are sealed off and a cut off lake is formed. This is known as an **ox-bow-lake**. (Fig. B.41). Such lakes are common in the Mississippi basin where they are also known as bayous. The ox bow Lake will later degenerate into a swamp through subsequent floods that may silt up the lake. It becomes marshy and eventually dries up.

River Rejuvenation- The earth's crust is far from stable and it is not surprising that in the course of a rivers development, parts

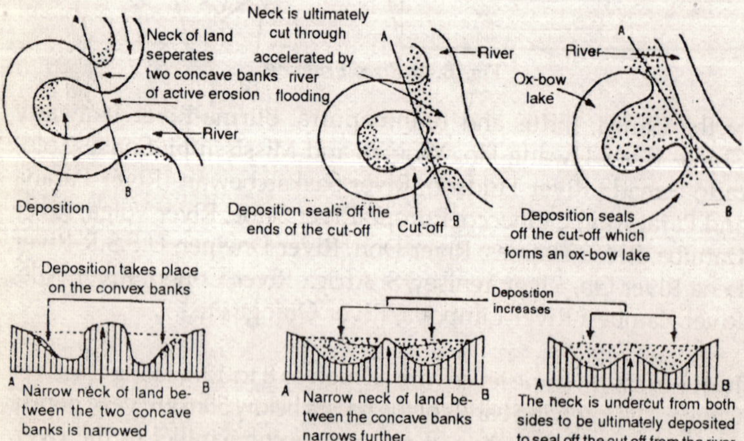

Fig. B.41 *Formation of an ox-bow lake*

may be uplifted or depressed giving rise to certain characterestics associated with rejuvenation ie. being young again.

A *Negative Movement* occurs when there is an uplift of land or a fall in sea-level. This will steepen the slope, so that active down -cutting is renewed. A fall in sea level leaves the flood plain at an increased altitude above the sea-level. The river with its renewed Vigour cuts into the former flood plain, leaving behind terraces on both sides of the river. There is also a break in the graded profile of the river, often marked by a series of rapids. This point where the old and rejuvenated profile meet is called the **Knick point** or rejuvenated head.

If rejuvenation occurs in the *upper course* the river valleys are deepened and steep sided gerges are formed. In the middle and lower course vertical corrasion replaces lateral corrasion and the existing meanders are vertically eroded by the rejuvenated stream. A distinct new inner trench is cut in the old valley and the river develops a deep valley with entrenced or **incised** meanders. The best developed *incised meanders* are those of the river Colorado, River Moselle in Germany etc., of the valley has one side steeper than the other, due to the presence of more resistant rocks it is known as an *ingrown meander*. (Fig. B.42).

The Lower or Plain Course

In the lower course the stream passes through an area of extensively low gradient or slope. The decrease of gradient causes the loss of its velocity. The increase of load in the course also makes the stream flow more slowly. As the river enters the sea, its load is checked. All these factors lead to the formation of **deltas** in the lower course near the mouth of the river. (Fig. B.43). When a river

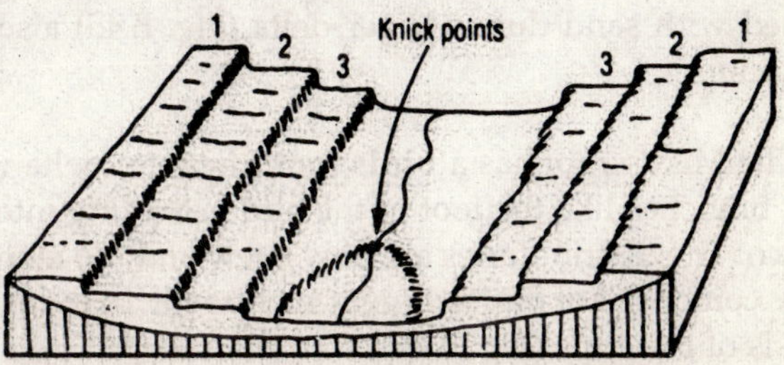

Fig. B.42 ***Rejuvenated river valley***

reaches the sea, the fine materials it has not yet dropped are deposited at its mouth forming a fan shaped alluvial area called a *delta* a word which originated from the greek letter. A which closely resembled the triangular delta of the Nile. Deltas are formed by the depositon of debris. Deltas are however not formed everywhere. Certain natural conditions are needed for the formation of deltas (1) Heavy load (2) Sluggish river (3) Flat land (4) Long plain course which results in deposition (5) Long mountainous course, so that erosion can take place and the river has a lot of load. (6) Absence of strong tides and currents or the amount of load deposited should exceed the amount of load removed by currents and waves (7) The river should not enter a lake anywhere in its course. Othewise it will form a Lacustrine Delta. (8) The sea should be shallow otherwise the load will disappear in deep water. Lacustrine deltes have been formed by the rivers Volga, Kuban and Ural before they flow into the Caspian Sea and the largest lake in the world. The **largest delta** in the **world** is the *Ganga-Brahmaputra delta* which starts near Farrakka. The channels formed when a delta is formed known as distributaries. The whole area is swampy and marshy. The height of the delta will increase by more deposition after floods. A delta is however never high as the deposits gets washed away. Deltas differ much in their size, shape, growth and importance. A number of factors such as the rate of sedimentation the depth of the river and the sea-bed, and the character of the tides, currents and waves greatly influence the eventual formation of deltas.

Types of Deltas - (Fig. B.43) The Nile, Ganga, Mekong. Hwang Ho, Po and Godavari rivers have are shaped or fan shaped **arcuate deltas** with numerous distributories (B.44a, b). The material deposited is usually gravel sand and other course materials. The Godavari delta is straighter than the Ganga delta and is lined with sand dunes Niger delta (Fig. B.45) also belongs to this group.

The Mississippi has a **birds foot** (digitate) delta with several main branches like the foot of the bird extending into the gulf of Mexico. The distributaries are only a few and the material deposited is composed of fine sediment such as silt. In India the Krishna delta is of this type (Fig. B.46)

A few rivers like the Ebro of Spain have tooth like projection

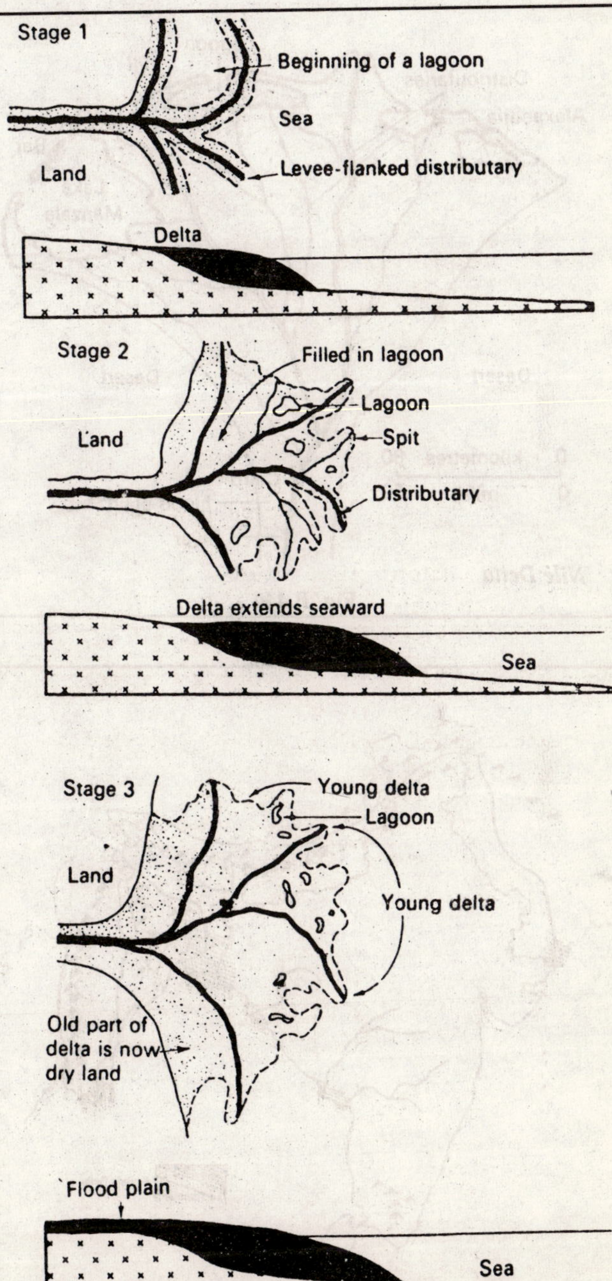
Stage 1
Beginning of a lagoon
Sea
Land
Levee-flanked distributary
Delta
Stage 2
Filled in lagoon
Lagoon
Land
Spit
Distributary
Delta extends seaward
Sea
Stage 3
Young delta
Lagoon
Land
Young delta
Old part of delta is now dry land
Flood plain
Sea

Fig. B.43

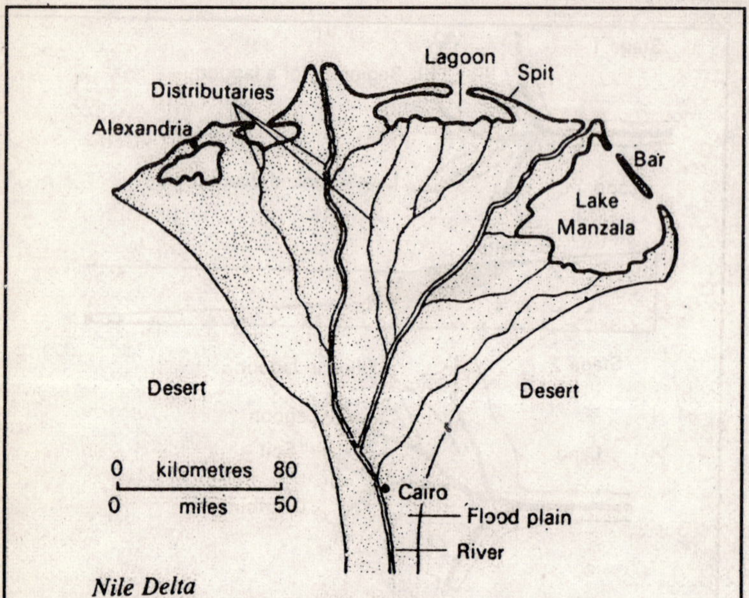

Fig. B.44a

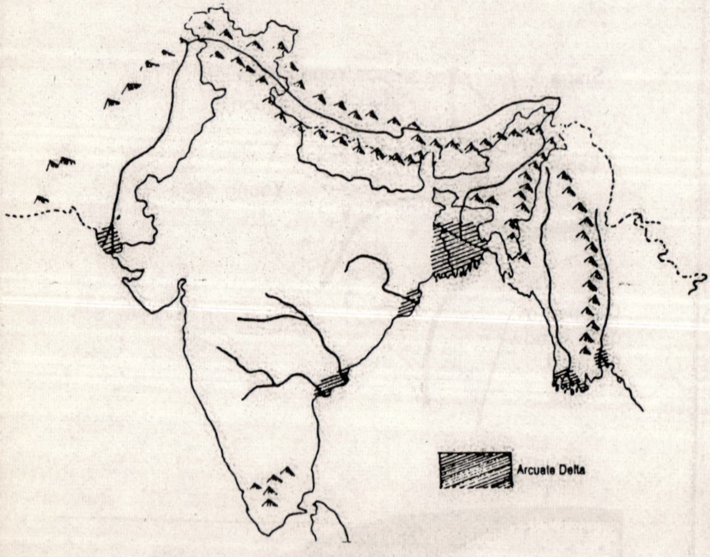

Fig. B.44b ***Arcuate deltas of the Indian Subcontinent***

Vardar Delta

Fig. B.45 *Vardar Delta*

at their mouths. These are Known as **Cuspate delta.**

Some other rivers such as the Amazon Ob and Vistula have their deltas pently submerged is coastal waters to form estuaine delta. In these deltas, there is a long narrow filling across the river mouth.

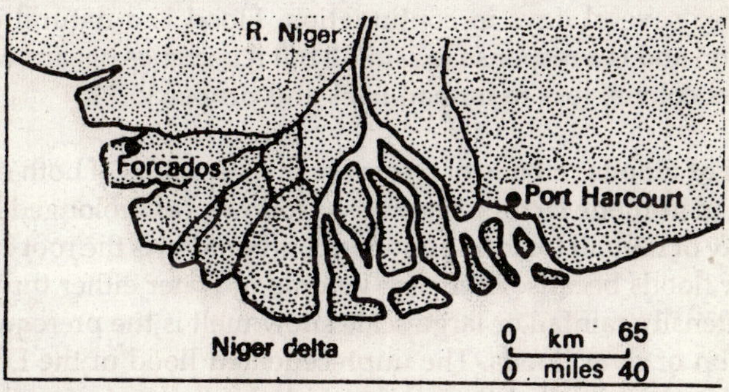

Niger Delta

Fig. B.46 *Niger Delta*

Sometimes a river does not form a delta but has an estuary at its mouth. An *estuary* may be defined as a deep inlet of water which gets narrower inland (gradually widening bay Cutting deep inland due to the scousing action of tide and currents. It is a *favourable site* for the building up of *ports* and *harbours* eg. London (Thames) Hamburg (River Elbe) Burnos Aires (Rio de la plata) and Calcutta.

Estuaries may be formed by the action of waves or it may have been a narrow valley which due to the rise of sea-level became partly wide and was filled with water to form an inlet.

The sea-level may also be referred to as the base level- Rivers try to erode all lands to this level. Vertical corrasion is carried out by rivers to bring down to the sea level, while by lateral corrasion rivers erode away lands on either side of it, so that its valley is deepened. The filling up of depressions by rivers is known as *aggradation* is also carried out by rivers to bring up lands to the sea level. (Fig. B.39).

The Causes of, and Problems Produced by Seasonal flooding.

Man has always been subject to natural disasters over which he has little control. Flooding is one of the most ubiquitous of natural hazards to affect man, mainly because he chooses to line in so many flood-prone areas.

Flood simply means inundation of extensive land area with water for several days in continuation. Flood is a natural phenomenon and is a response to rainfall but it becomes hazard when it causes colonal loss to human lives and property.

Causes of Floods- Floods of rivers are the responses of both natural and man-made factors. They are as follows. (a) Prolonged high intensity of rainfall for long period in continuation is the root cause of river floods because immense volume of water either through high intensity rainfail or large-scale snow melt is the prerequisite condition of river floods. The unprecedented flood of the Lower Damodar river in West Bengal due to torrential cyclonic rainfall of September 26-29, 1978 explains the impact of high intensity rainfall as a potent causative factor of floods.

(b) Heavy spell of rainfall in arid and semi arid areas where the rainfall is scant low and infrequent causes flash floods because such areas have poor natural drainage systems.

(c) Highly sinuous and meandering courses of the rivers obstruct the normal discharge of water and thus the velocity is reduced which delays the passage of water resulting into stagnation of water. Consequently, the meandering valleys are immediately overflown and meander belts and loops are flooded.

(d) Large-scale deforestation in the upper catchments is perhaps the most important **man-made factor** of the causes of the river floods. Deforestation effected by man for various purposes, such as extension of agricultural land, for the supply of raw materials to the factories, for domestic uses as fire woods for commercial purposes etc., increases the surface run-off and results in heavy floods.

(e) Increased surface run off also accelerates the rate of soil erosion and thus increases the sediment load of the rivers. This results in siltation of river beds which results in heavy floods. The extent of damages caused by swollen alluvial rivers and recurrent floods in the states of Uttar Pradesh, Bihar and West Bengal is increasing every year.

(f) Increasing urbanization also helps in increasing the surface run off. The extension in the pucca ground cover through the construction of building, countyards, roads, pavements etc. reduces infiltration of rain water which increases the volume and discharge of storm drains of urban areas.

(g) In India valley-side slopes of alluvial rivers are ploughed down to the channels and the farms are never irrigated. After the crops are harvested, the ploughed fields are baked hot in the scorching sunlight of Summer months with the result loose soils become extremely dry. These dried soils are soaked with water during first Summer showers and are slumped into the river bed by overland flow. This results in gradual silting of river bed. On the other hand cultivation of valley-side slopes reduces the gradient of river banks. This two processes flatten the valley and reduces the water accomodating capacity of the river valley and floods occur.

(h) Blocking of natural flow of the rivers by landslides caused by earthquakes, other natural factors cause flood. In hilly regions of West Bengal and other states land slides often cause road-blockage which hampers smooth running of human life.

(c) Water Resources and Conservation in India

In the context of the twentieth-century concern over the rate of destruction and deplation of natural resources. Man is dependent on environmental resources for food energy and also for raw materials such as water and certain minerals.

Although there is a great deal of water on this planet, much of it is saline, and fresh or usable water is one example of a resource that is exhaustible, particularly in local situations. However it can be maintained near where it is needed by proper management of the catchment area, including the building of dams and reservoirs. It may be pointed out that only one percent of the total amount of water of the hydrosphere is available to human beings and other biotic communities from various sources such as ground water, rivers, lakes, soils, atmosphere and biological system but groundwater provides the largest amount of water.

Classification of Ground Water

1) **Meteoric Water** The water which lies underground and has its source in precipitation.

2) **Juvenile Water**-The water which is trapped in the magma which is the converted form of steam.

3) **Chemical Water**-Water which is found in the crystal structures of underground minerals.

4) **Connate Water**-The water which is trapped in the sediments of underground rocks.

Ground water leads to the formation of springs, wells and artesian wells.

Permeable rocks are those which allow the water to pass through. This makes the water soak into the ground. Permeable rocks are known as porous when there is room between each grain for water to flow or seap, through it eg. gravel, sand, sandstone etc. In such a case the pores become felled with water and the whole mass becomes saturated. When the rock is hard and solid but its fissures, joints and crevices let water to pass through eg. granite limestone, chalk etc. it is known as **pervious.** Those rocks which as not allow water to pass through them freely are known as **impermeable** on **impervious rocks**, eg. gabbro, shale, slate, etc.

Below the surface of the earth there are two zones, the upper and the lower which ground water has to traverse in its downward march. The upper zone allows water to percolate further down without haulting its movement. It is also called the *zone of aeration* and the water that percolates through is called vadose (Wandering) water. Below the upper zone lies the lower zone which is called the zone of saturation. In this zone all the available pore spaces are filled up with water. These two zones are cooperated by the water table (Fig. B.47).

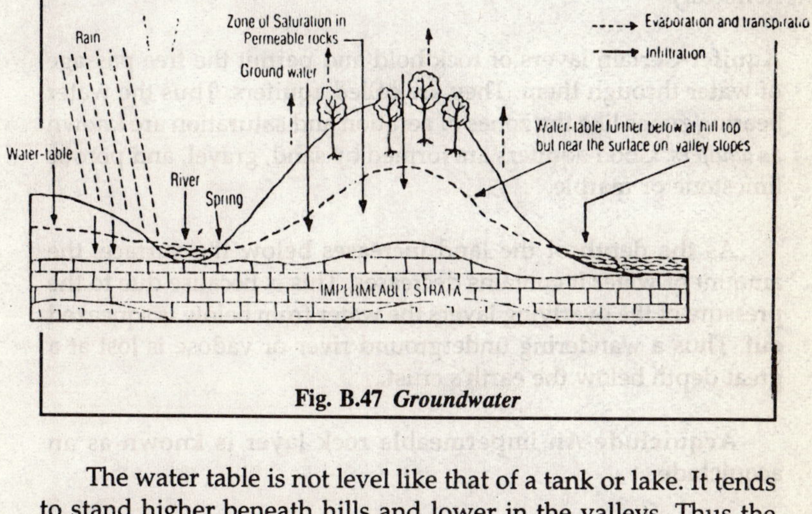

Fig. B.47 ***Groundwater***

The water table is not level like that of a tank or lake. It tends to stand higher beneath hills and lower in the valleys. Thus the water table follows the contour of the land.

The water table may be *shallow* or *deep*. (Fig. B.48). This depends on the vertical distance between the ground surface and the level at which water occurs. The water table varies from place to place and season to season. The depth of the water table depends on (1) Nature of rocks lying underground (2) The amount of rainfall or precipitation (3) The nature of precipitation (slow otherwise there will be rapid runoff) and (4) the slope of the land. Thus the water table is of a great depth where there is slow but

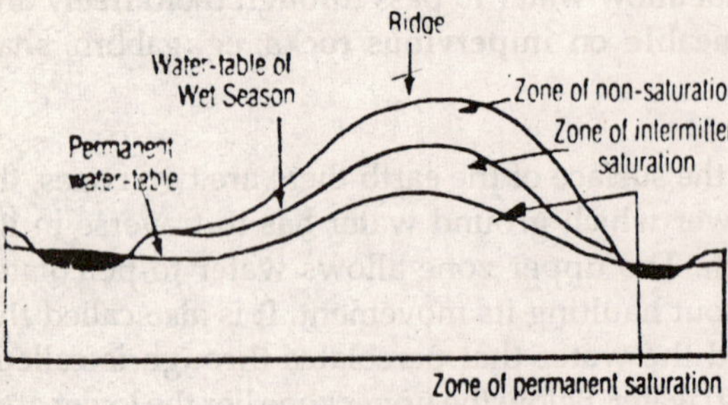

Fig. B. 48 ***Water table***

heavy rainfall on a flat land. The water table is (of a great depth) usually a few metres in depth, not more than 3 kms. below the surface. It should be near the surface if wells have to be dug economically.

Aquifer-Certain layers of rock hold and permit the free passage of water through them. They are called aquifers. Thus the water bearing zones like the zones of aeration and saturation are known as *aquifers*. Good aquifers are formed by sand, gravel, and porous limestone or marble.

As the depth of the land increases below the surface, the amount of water it contains decreases. This is because due to the pressure of the overlying layers the water from below is squeezed out. Thus a wandering underground river or vadose is lost at a great depth below the earth's crust.

Acquiclude-An impermeable rock layer is known as an acquiclude.

Wells-A well is an artificial opening in the ground that reaches below the water or penetrate, an acquifer. It the well is sunk for below the water table i.e. to the *permanent saturation level*, it will always contain water. But if it is sunk only just below the water table i.e. to the wet season saturation level it will contain water in the wet season only and will dry up in summer. The water obtained in this method is also not well filtered.

Artesion Wells-*Artesion Wells* (Fig. B.49) are found in artesian ba-

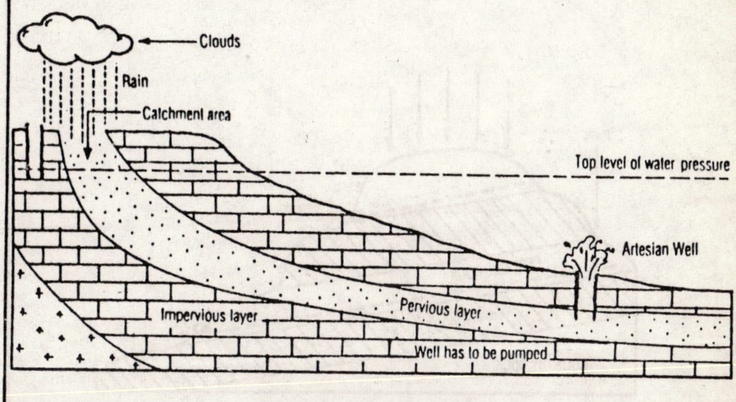

Fig. B. 49 *Artesian well*

sins where a layer of permeable rock lies between two layes of impermeable rock having a synclinal form. The ends of the rock layers are exposed on the surface at the sides of the depression. When rain falls it enters through the permeable layers where it is trapped between overlying of underlying impermeable layers. The central permeable layer, is thus an acquifer and remains well saturated. If a boring is slow done into the *acquifer* water will rise in the well under hydrostatic pressure. The jumping of water is generally not necessary. After a time, however the water does not flow out anymore and then water is needed to be pumped out. The name artesian is derived from *Artois* an old province in north-east France, where this method of boring was first adopted long ago.

The largest Arteaian Basin of the world is that of a great part of the Control lowlands in Australia extending from the gulf of conpentina lowlands in the north to the Murray-Darling basin in the south. This covers over a million square km of Queensland, part of New South Wales and south Australia. There are more than 900 artesian wells, most of which are over a kms deep. The water of these artesian wells in widely used for cattle rearing and pastural farming. The salty water is not used for human consumption.

In India, artesian wells are found in Maharashtra along the river Narmada and bordering the satpuras. Some of them are also

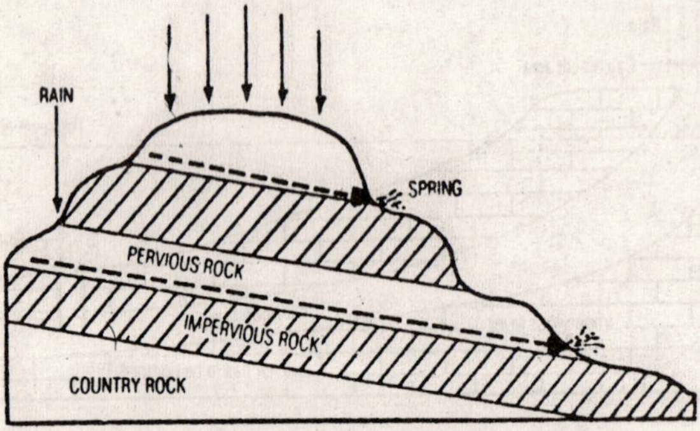

Spring formed at juncture of permeable and impermeable rocks

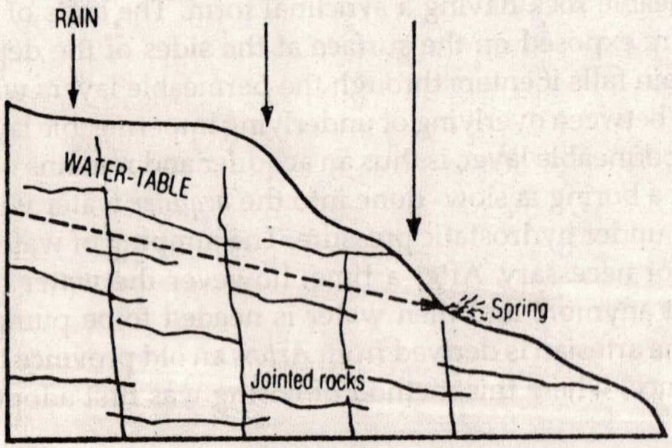

Springs in jointed rocks

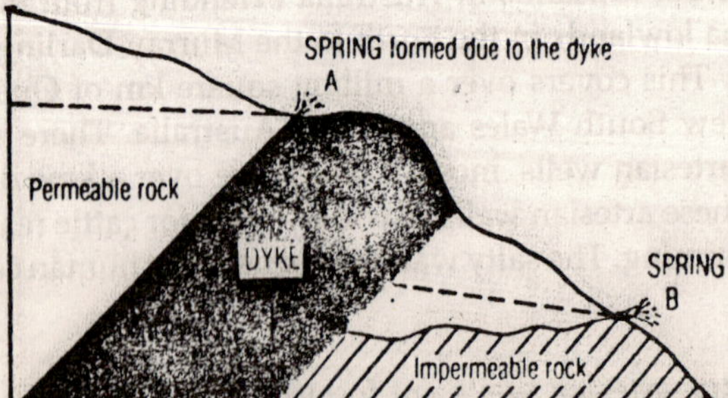

Fig. B. 50 ***Springs formed due to dykes***

found in Tamilnadu.

Spring - When water flows through a natural opening (usually on the side of a mountain) in such quantity as to make a distinct current, it is known as a *spring* (Fig. B.50) Springs occur usually at the junction of a pervious bed with an impervious bed. The water table must also intersect the surface at a point along the side.

The spring may be *permanent* or *perennial* if the water supply is continuous. This occurs when the water table is very high.

If the water supply varies form time to time it is known as *intermittent*. Here the spring may dry up when the water table becomes very low. Springs are generally formed at a level below the water table.

A step like pattern of springs occur on the valley slope where the dip of the bed coincides with the gradient of the slope and impermeable beds alternate with permeable beds. Each contact point of the permeable and impermeable beds touching the valley slope provides the site for a spring (Fig. B.50). There may be a line

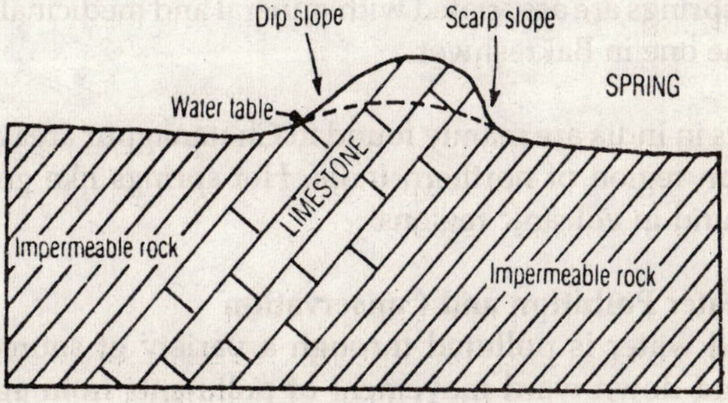

Fig. B. 51 ***Springs in limestone escarpment***

of springs at the foot of escarpments too (Fig. B.51) Springs may also be formed when a fault occurs, and an impervious rock layer lies in juxtaposition with a porous rock layer. Springs may also occur at the contact point between an impervious rock (like slate) and chalk or limestone (Fig. B.52) These springs found in limestone or chalk regions are known as Vauclusion springs from France).

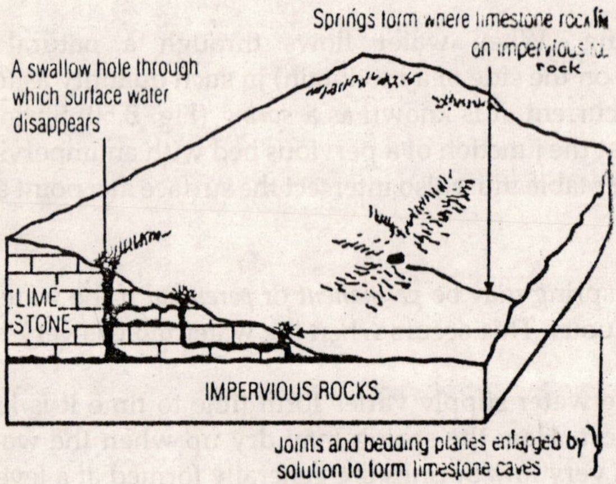

Fig. B. 52 ***Springs at the junction of limestone and impervious rocks***

Some springs are warm or hot. These hot springs get heated by their contact with hot rocks which are common in volcanic regions. Numerous hot springs are found in the Yellowstone Park of the U.S.A, Iceland, North Island and in Himachal Pradesh (Taptapani) Sita Kund (Bihar) Gangotri and Yamunotri in U.P. These hot springs are associated with mineral and medicinal properties as the one in Bakreshwer.

Springs in India are mainly found in Chotanagpur area and in the Kumaon region of northern India. Hot springs like geysers, are also found in volcanic regions.

Ground Water Pollution and Conservation

Ground water is polluted through a variety of sources e.g leaching and down ward movement of pollutants from agricultural field (such as nitrates, phosphorous, potash and several insecticides and pesticides), from industrial dumping areas, from urban and rural garbages, from earthen septic tanks and from polluted ponds and tanks.

The loose and friable sandy soils, high water table and moderate to high annual rainfall accelerate the rate of infiltration of rainwater and rapid downward movement of pollutants with percolating water and consequently high rate of pollution of ground water is the ultimate result. Generally, industrial wastes including waste water are dumped, where streams are not available in the nearby areas, into ponds or dug out tanks. The dissolved chemical pollutants are moved downward with percolating water (the process known as leaching) to meet the ground water resources and thus **ground water is polluted** which is readily reflected in the polluted water of dug wells. Similarly, pollutants are leached downward from the municipal dump sites of city garbages.

The recent incident of pollution of ground water due to toxic chemicals discharged by Patancheru industrial complex, about 30 kms away from Hyderabad city, in Medak district of Andhra Pradesh is a burning example of pollution of groundwater by human activities underground cavities caused by excessive pumping of water from ground water reserves in the cities located near the sea coast result in contamination of groundwater because of leakage of saline sea water into the cavities.

Excessive extraction of ground water for drinking purpore is a serious hazard. Metropolis of India like Calcutta where the water table has gone down due to excessive withdrawn of ground water has resulted in sinking of the city by few cms.

Conservation-of ground water requires several remedial measures involving individuals community, governments at national and international levels. There must be mass awareness and right perception at community level about various aspects of water pollution. Thus people must restrain themselves from throwing human and animal excreta and garbages into any water body. The industrials units must be obliged to treat industrial effluents before discharging them into water bodies. The municipal corporation must arrange for sewage treatment plants and government should provide adequate funds for water pollution control programmes.

The problem of water pollution has already assumed alarming proportion in many large cities and industrial complexes in India such as in Delhi, Kanpur, Varanasi, Calcutta, Bombay, Madras etc. Open earthen sewer drains, service latrines, uncovered earthen septic tanks and soak pits, improper drainage systems and frequent water logging adds to the problem of pollution.

The government of India has already taken initiative in controlling water pollution by passing the water (Prevention and Control of Pollution) Act in 1974. The government of India has constituted **Central Ganga Authority** for comprehensive planning of the cleaning of the polluted Ganga water under the jurisdiction of central Pollution Control Board. So that Ganga water after treatment can be consumed more often and thus extraction of ground water will be minimized.

(d) Arid or Desert Landforms

About a fifth of the world's land is made up of deserts, some rocky, others stony and the rest sandy. Deserts that are absolutely barren and where nothing grows at all are rare and they are better known as 'true deserts'.

All the deserts are **confined** within the 15^0 to 30^0 parallels of latitude north and south of the equator. They lie in the *trade wind belts* on the western parts of the continents where Trade winds are *Off-shore*. They are bathed by cold currents which produce a 'desicating effect' so that moisture is not easily condensed into precipitation.

Dryness or aridity is the key note. Such deserts are tropical hot deserts or 'Trade Wind deserts'. They include the great Sahara Desert; Arabian, Iranian and Thar Deserts; Kalahari, Namib, and Atacama Deserts; the Great Australian Desert and the deserts of south-west USA and northern Mexico. In the continental interiors of the mid latitudes, the deserts such as the Gobi and Turkestan are characterised by extremes of temperatures.

The Mechanism of Arid Erosion

Arid land forms- are the results of many combined factors, one reacting upon the other. Insufficient rainfall (often less than 12.5 cms) coming at most irregular periods, coupled with very high temperatures (30. 5^0c is the average) and a rapid rate of evaporation, are the *Chief causes of aridity*. Sub-arial denudation through the processes of weathering (chemical and mechanical), wind action and the work of water have combined to produce a desert landscape that is varied and distinctive.

Weathering-is the most potent factor of reducing rocks to sand in arid regions. Intense heating during the day and rapid cooling at night by radiation, set up *stresses* in the already weakend rocks so that they eventually crack. As heat penetrates rocks slowly when the outer surface of rocks is being heated by the hot sun, the inner rocks remain quite cool. The heating of the rocks causes the outer surface to expand and so prise itself off from the interior rocks, so that it peels off in successive very thin layers. Such an onion-peeling process of mechanical weathering is called **exfoliation.**

Action of winds in deserts-The wind though not the most effective agent of erosion, transportation and deposition is more efficient in arid than in humid regions.

Wind erosion is carried out in the following ways.

1. **Deflation-**This involves the lifting and blowing away of loose materials from the ground. Such unconsolidated sands and pebbles may be carried in the air or rolled along the ground depending on the grain size. Deflation results in the lowering of the land surface to form depressions called **deflation hollows.**

2. **Abrasion-**The *Sand-blasting* of rock surface by winds when they hurl sand particles against them is called **abrasion.** Abrasion is most effective at or near the base of rocks, where the amount of material the wind is able to carry is greatest.

3. **Attrition-** When wind-borne particles roll against one another in collision they wear each other away so that their sizes are greatly reduced and grains are rounded into *millet seed sand*. This process is called **attrition.**

DESERT LANDSCAPE

1. **Hamada or rocky desert-**This consists of large stretches of bare rocks, swept clear of sand and dust by the wind. The exposed rocks are thoroughly smoothed and polished. The region is bare and sterile. The best known rocky deserts are those of the Sahara Desert.

2. **Reg or stony desert-**This is composed of extensive sheets of angular pebbles and gravels which the winds are not able to blow off. Such stony deserts are much more accessible than the sandy deserts, and large herds of camels are kept there. In Libya and Egypt where the surface is mostly covered by pebbles, they are referred to as **serir;** elsewhere in Africa, stony deserts are called **reg.** Plateau of Baluchistan which lies outside the influence of monsoon consists of stony plains.

3. **Erg or Sandy desert-** This is a sea of sand which typifies the popular idea of desert scenery. Winds deposit vast stretches of undulating sand-dunes in the heart of the deserts. The intricate patterns of ripples on the dune surfaces indicate the direction of

the winds. Parts of Sahara desert. Thar desert of India, deserts of south and west Afghanistan are sandy in nature.

4. **Bad land**- The term 'badlands' was first given to an arid area in South Dakota, USA, where the hills were badly eroded by occasional rain-storms into gullies and ravines. The extent of water action on hill slopes and rock surfaces was so great that the entire region was abandoned by the inhabitants. Deserts with similar features are referred to as **badlands**. Painted Desert of Arizona, parts of Madhyapradesh along the river Chambal in India have these type of landscapes.

5. **Mountain deserts**-Some deserts are found on highlands such as plateaux and mountain ranges. Erosion has dissected the desert highlands into harsh, serrated outlines of chaotic peaks and bare ranges. Their steep slopes are cut by wadis (steep sided, often dry, valleys) and the action of frost has carved out sharp, irregular edges. In mountain deserts lowlying ground or basin surrounded by mountains is called **bolson**. In bolson the drainage is centripetal. In central Asia the Tarim Basin is a good example where the centripetal drainage flows into the **playa** lake (low level plain at the centre of bolson) of Lop Nor.

LANDFORMS OF WIND EROSION IN DESERTS

In the combined processes of abrasion, deflation and attrition, a wealth of characteristic desert land forms emerge.

1. **Rock Pedastal**- The sand blasting effect of winds against any projection rock masses wears back the softer layers so that an irregular edge is formed on the alternate bands of hard and soft rocks. Grooves and hollows are cut in the rock surfaces, carving them into fantastic and grotesque looking pillars called **rock pedastals** (Fig. B.53). Examples of such rock pedastal are seen in the western Rajasthan desert where the lower parts of granite blocks have been cut in this manner.

2. **Zeugen**- These are tabular masses which have a layer of soft rocks lying beneath a surface layer of more resistant rocks. The sculpting effects of wind abrasion wear them into a weird-looking 'ridge and landscape. Mechanical weathering initiates their formation by opening up joints of the surface rocks. Wind abrasion further 'eats' into the underlying softer layer so that deep

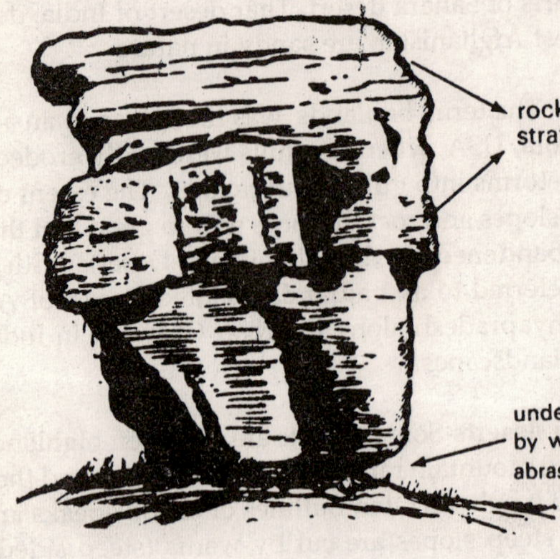

Fig. B.53

furrows are developed.

The hard rocks then stand above the furrows as ridges or **Zeugen** (Fig. B.54).

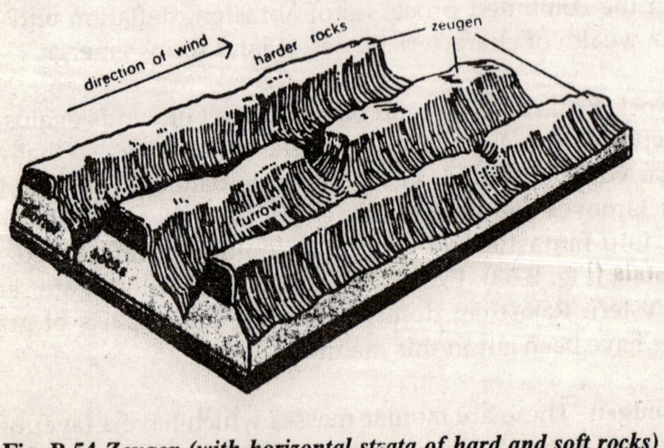

Fig. B.54 *Zeugen (with horizontal strata of hard and soft rocks)*

3. **Yardangs**- Quite similar to the 'ridge and furrow' landscape of Zeugen are the steep-sided **Yardang** (Fig. B.55) Hard and soft

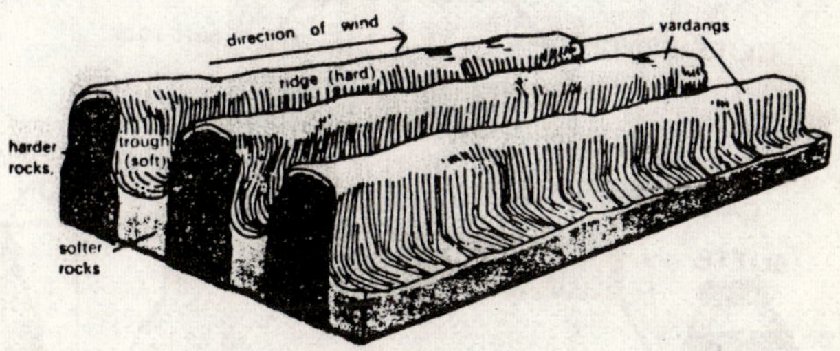

Fig. B.55 *Yardangs (with vertical bands of hard and soft rocks)*

rocks of Yardangs are vertical bands and are aligned in the direction of the prevailing winds. Wind abrasion excavates the bands of softer rocks into long, narrow corridors separating the steep-sided over-hanging ridges of hard rocks, called Yardangs. They are found in Turkestan and Central Asia.

4. **Mesas and buttes- Mesa** is a flat, table-like land mass with a very resistant horizontal top layer, and very steep sides. The hard stratum on the surface resists denudation by both wind and water, and thus protects the underlying layers of rocks from being eroded away. Mesas are found in canyon regions e.g. Arizona, or on fault blocks e.g. the table Mountain of Cape Town, South Africa.

Continued denudation through the ages may reduce mesas in area so that they become isolated flat-topped hills called **buttes** (Fig. B.56).

5. **Ventifacts or dreikanter**-These are pebbles faceted by sand-blasting. They are shaped and thoroughly polished by wind abrasion. Rock fragments, mechanically weathered from mountains and upstanding rocks, are moved by wind and smoothed on the windward side. If wind direction changes another facet develops. Such rocks have characteristic flat facets with sharp edges. Amongst the **Ventifacts** those with three wind faceted surfaces are called **dreikantes**. These wind-faceted pebbles form the desert pavement, a smooth, mosaic-like region, closely covered by numerous rock fragments and pebbles.

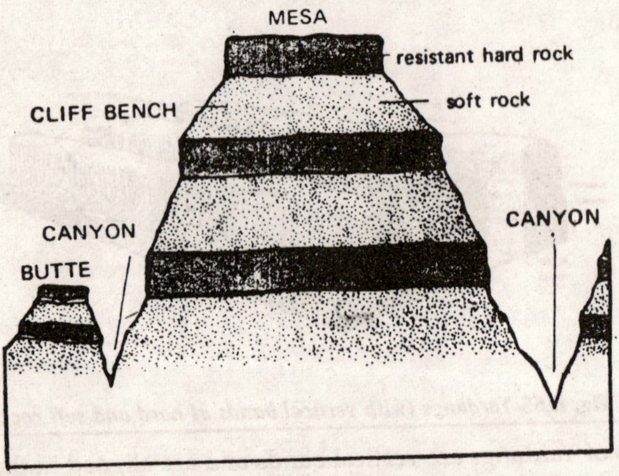

Fig. B.56 *Mesa and butte*

6. **Inselberg** -This is a german word meaning 'island-mountain'. They are *isolated residual hills* rising abruptly from the level ground. They are characterised by their very steep slopes and rounded tops. They are often composed of granite or gneiss, and are probably the relics of an original plateau which has been almost entirely eroded away. **Inselbergs** (Fig. B.57) are typical of many deserts and semi-arid landscape.

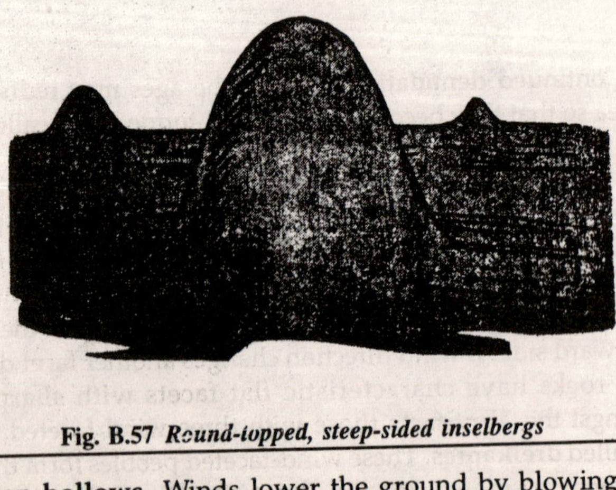

Fig. B.57 *Round-topped, steep-sided inselbergs*

Deflation hollows- Winds lower the ground by blowing away the unconsolidated materials, and small depressions may form.

Similarly minor faulting can also initiate depressions and the eddying action of on-coming winds will wear off the weaker rocks until the water table is reached. Water then seeps out forming **Oases** or Swamps, in the deflation hollows or depressions. Several such depressions are known to exist in the desert lying west of the Nile valley, of these the most well known is Quattara Depression in western Egyptian Sahara which has been excavated to nearly 134 m. below sea level. Similar but relatively shallower depressions are found also in the Kalahari and the West Australian deserts. The great plains region of the USA has thousands of small and big basins or hollows most of which appear to have been caused by deflation.

It is difficult to say why deflation begins at a particular point in preference to others. But on the process has started at a particular spot, as a result of the formation of wind eddies the hollow goes on increasing until the ground water-table is reached. The ground water-table is the base level of wind erosion and limits the depth of deflation though the water-table may be lowered as the basins develop.

LANDFORMS OF WIND DEPOSITION IN DESERTS

Materials eroded and transported by winds must come to rest some where. The finest dust travels enormous distances in the air, and may be moved completely out of the desert. The dust from the Sahara Desert is sometimes blown acress the Mediterranean to fall as '**blood rains**' in Italy or on the glaciers of Switzerland. As wind-borne materials are lifted according to their coarseness, it can be expected that the coarser sands will be too heavy to be blown out of the desert limits. They remain as **dunes** or other depositional landforms within the deserts themselves. Since they are rarely static, their **migration** pattern depends on a number of factors, the size of the particles they carry, the direction and velocity of the winds, the location and nature of the surfaces over which the particles are transported and the presence or absence of water and natural vegetation.

The following are some of the major features of wind deposition.

1. **Dunes**-Dunes are, infact, hills of sand formed by the accumulation of sand and shaped by the movement of winds. They may

be active or **live dunes**, constantly on the move, or inactive fixed dunes, rooted with vegetation. Because of their great contrast in shape, size and alignment, they have been given a long list of fanciful names, such as attached dune or head dune, tail dune, advanced dune, lateral dune, wake dune, star dune, pyramid dune, parabolic blow-out dune, hair pin dune and traverse dune.

Sand dunes are typically found in the sandy deserts like Sahara in Africa, the Gobi desert in Central Asia, the desert of Saudi Arabia, the Thar desert in India etc. Bagnold recognised only two basic dune forms, **the barchan** or the crescent-shaped traverse dune and **the seif** or the longitudinal dune.

(a) **Barchan-** These are crescent or moon-shaped dunes which occur individually or in groups. They are line dunes which advance steadily before winds that come from a particular prevailing direction.

Barchans (Fig. B.58) are initiated probably by a chance accumulation of sand at an obstacle, such as a patch of grass or a heap of rocks. They occur **traversely** to the wind, so that their horns thin out and become lower in the direction of the wind due to the reduced frictional retardation of the winds around the edges. The wind ward side is convex and gently-sloping while the leeward

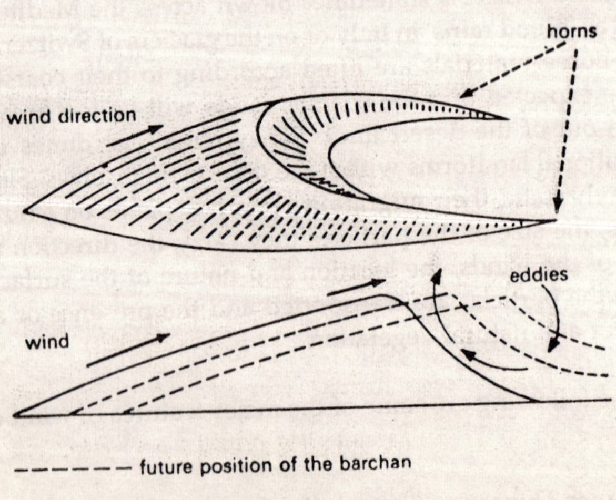

Fig. B.58 *Crescentic sand dune - barchan*

side, being sheltered, is concave and steep (the slip-face). The crest of the sand dune moves forward as more sand is accumulated by the prevailing wind. The sand is driven up the wind ward side and on reaching the crest, slips down the leeward side so that the dune advances.

The migration of the barchans may be a **threat** to desert life for they may encroach on an oasis burying palm trees or houses. Long-rooted sand-holding **trees and grasses** are therefore planted to halt the advance of the dunes thus preventing areas of fertile land from being devastated.

(b) **Seifs or longitudinal dunes- Seif** (Fig. B.59) is an Arabic word meaning 'sword'. They are long, narrow ridges of sand, often over many kilometers long lying **parallel** to the direction of the prevailing winds. The crestline of the seif rises and falls in alternate peaks and saddles in regular successions like the teeth of a monstrous saw. The dominant winds blow straight along the corridor between the lines of dunes so that they are swept clear of sand and remain smooth. The **eddies** that are set up blow towards the sides of the corridor, and, having less power, drop the sand to form the dunes. In this manner, the prevailing winds increase the length of the dunes into tapering linear ridges while the occasional cross winds tend to increase their height and width. In the egyptian desert many seifs are about 100 m. high but in southern Iran they rise to more than 200 m. These parallel dunes are also found in

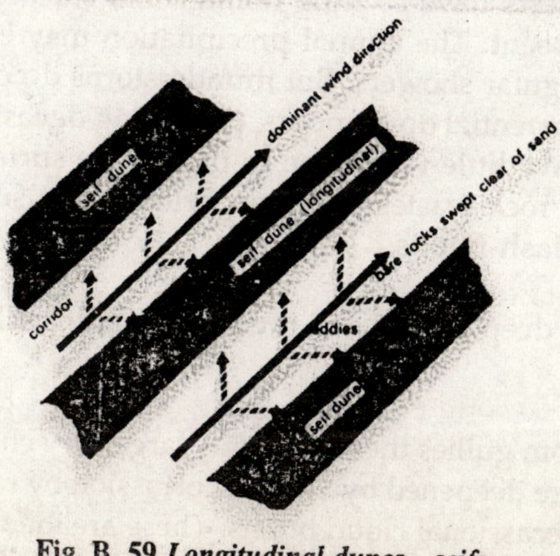

Fig. B. 59 *Longitudinal dunes - seifs*

the Libyan desert and extend continuously for 100 km or more.

The highest dune has been recorded in Algeria and is about 400 m high. It follows the line of a scarp which diverts sand flow and allows the dunes to grow in calmer pockets.

According to **Bagnold**, barchans and seifs are rarely found together. In the Thar desert of India both barchans and seifs are found but their areas are different. At places several barkhans have been joined together to form a relatively larger hill which has been divided into spurs by intervening valleys. Examples of barchan can be seen near Barmer in Jodhpur as well as in Bikaner where they are 200 to 1,000 m. in length and 180 to 600 m. in width.

2. **Loess**-The fine dust blown beyond the desert limits is deposited on neighbouring lands as **loess**. It is a yellow, friable material and is usually very fertile. Loess is in fact fine loam,rich in Lime, very coherent and extremely porous. Water sinks in readily so that the surface is always dry. Streams have cut deep valleys through the thick mantle of soft loess and badland topography may develop. The most extensive deposit is to be found in the region covering much of the Northern European plain and the Asiatic steppes, extending from France in the west to North China in the east. In China, such yellowish wind-borne dust from the Gobi Desert is called 'Hwangtu-the yellow earth.

LANDFORMS DUE TO WATER ACTION IN DESERTS

Most deserts have so little rainfall that surface drainage is practically absent. The annual precipitation may be small, and comes in irregular showers. But thunderstorms do occur and the rain falls in torrential down pours, producing devastating effects. As deserts have little vegetation to protect the surface soil, large quantities of rock wastes are transported in the sudden raging torrents, or **flash-floods**.

They cut deep **gullies** and ravines forming badland topography.

Apart from gullies there are many larger dry channels or valleys. These are deepened by vertical corrassion by raging torrents during the occassional cloud bursts. These are the **wadis** and are dry for most of the time. Wadis are *flat* and *wide floor* and *steep* and almost vertical sides. The steep side walls are primarily due to two reasons. Firstly, *abrasion* by wind is most active at the base of the mountains, and secondly, on account of *lack of rainfall* there is very little corrasion of the valley walls and stream erosion is largely vertical. The rivers are dry most of the year, with short-lived floods during heavy rains. They are wider near their mouths where the alluvial fans are deposited which gradually slope down to the plain. Wadis are common in the deserts of Baluchistan and Western Arabia.

In arid and semi-arid areas the outflowing streams from the upland regions are both short and intermittent. They drain into the lower depressions so that drainage is almost entirely **internal.** Sometimes water collected in a depression or a desert basin does not completely disappear by evaporation or seepage, and a **temporary lake** is formed which contain a high percentage of salts, because of high evaporation. The lakes and the alluvial, plains formed by them are called **playas, salinas** or **salaras** in the United States and Mexico and **shotts** in northern Africa.

The floor of the depression is made up of two features, the bajada and the pediment. The **Bajada** is a depositional feature made up of alluvial material laid down by the intermittent streams. The **Pediment** is an erosional plain formed at the base of the surrounding mountain scarps (Fig. B.60).

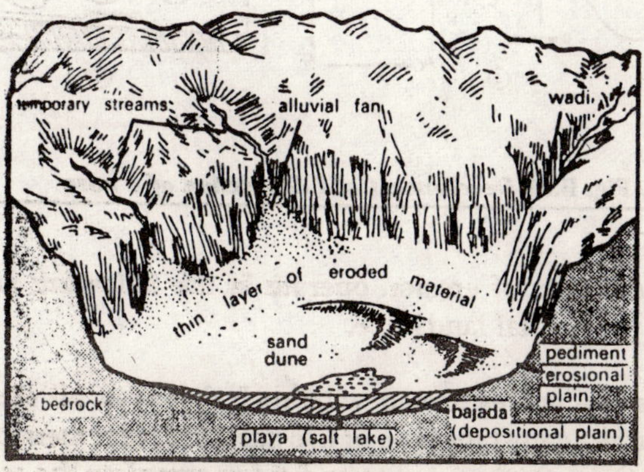

Fig. B. 60 ***Intermont desert basin***

(E) COASTAL LANDFORMS

The Action of Waves, Tides and Currents

The coastline, under the constant action of the waves, tides and currents, is undergoing changes from day to day. **Tides** affect marine erosion mainly by extending a line of erosion into a zone of erosion. This zone corresponds to the area between the low water level and the high water level. Currents help to move eroded debris and deposit it as silt, sand and gravel along the coasts.

Mechanism of Marine Erosion

The most powerful agents of marine erosion are **waves** (Fig. B.61) Their origin is due to the sweeping of winds, over the water surface, which sets a series of undulating swells surging forward. On approaching shallow water near the shores, their speed is reduced and the waves are curved or refracted against the alignment of the coast.

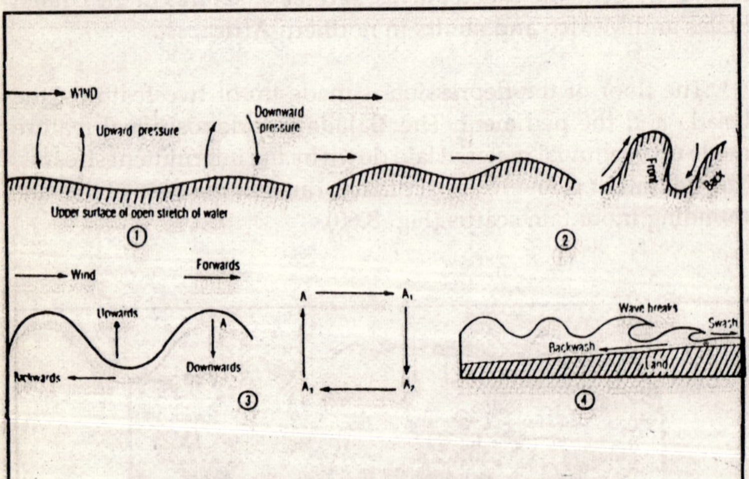

Fig. B.61 ***Development and destruction of a wave***

Marine agents of erosion operate in the following ways to transform the coastal landscape.

1. **Corrasion**- waves armed with rock debris of all sizes and shapes charge against the base of the cliffs and wear them back by corrasion. On coming currents and tides complete the work by sweeping the eroded material into the sea.

2. **Attrition**-The constantly moving waves that transport beach materials such as boulders, pebbles, shingle and fine sand also hurl these fragments against one another, until they are broken down by attrition into very small pieces. The grinding and polishing of such fragmental materials against cliff faces and against each other is largely responsible for the fine sand which form the beaches that are so typical of the seaside resorts.

3. **Hydraulic action**- Waves, in their forward surge splashing against the coast may enter joints and crevices in the rocks. The air within it is compressed. When the waves retreat the compressed air expands with explosive violence. Such actions when repeated gives rise to enlarged cracks and rock fragments are prised apart.

4. **Solvent action**- The solvent action of sea water on calcium carbonate especially on limestone coasts sets up chemical changes in the rocks and disintegration takes place.

Coastal Features of Erosion

1. **Capes and bays**- On exposed coasts, the continual action of waves on rocks of varying resistance causes the coastline to be eroded irregularly. This is particularly pronounced where hard rocks, e.g. granites and limestones occur in alternate bands with softer rocks e.g. sand and clay. The softer rocks are worn back into inlets, coves or bays and the harder ones persist as headlands, promontories or capes (Fig. B.62). Even where the coast is of one tock type regularities will be caused by variation within the rock. Very large indentations such as the Persian Gulf or the

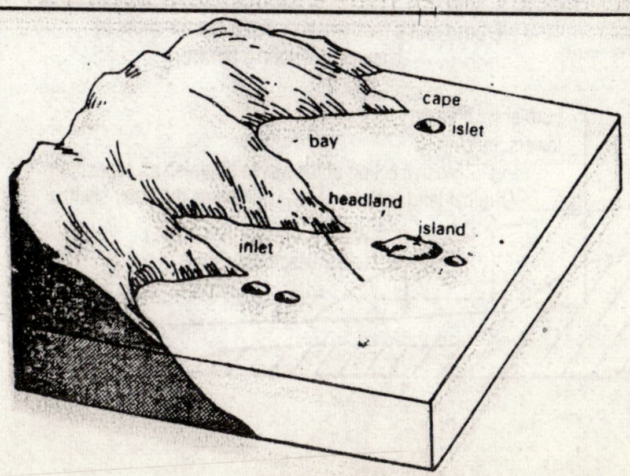

Fig. B.62

Bay of Bengal are due to other causes suchas submergence or earth movement.

2. **Cliffs and wave-cut platforms**-In quite a few places the seacliffs formed by marine erosion is a distinctive feature. Generally any steep rock face adjoining the coast forms a cliff. The rate of erosion will depend on its geological structure, that is the stratification and jointing of the rocks and their resistance to wave attack. If the beds dip seawards, large blocks of rock will be dislodged and fall into the sea. The cliff will rise in a series of 'steps' as shown in (Fig. B.63).

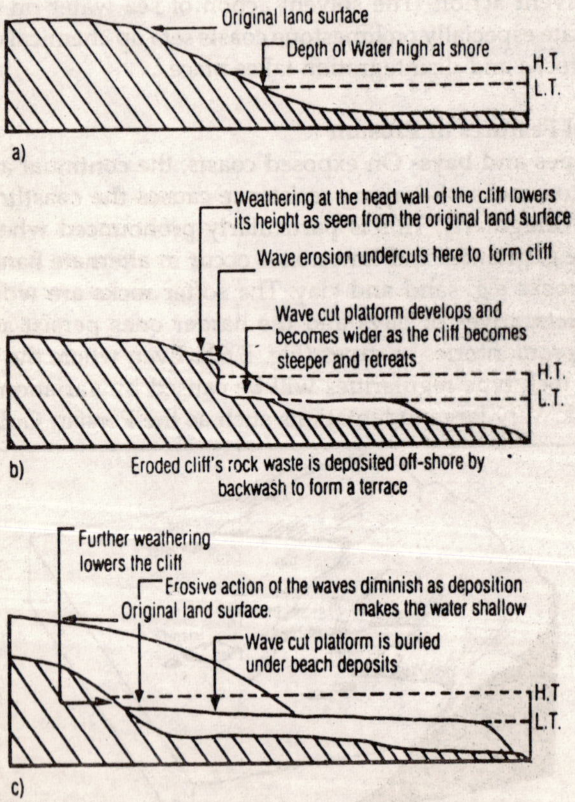

Fig. B.63 ***Development of Cliff and Wave-cut Platforms***

On the contrary, if the beds dip land wards as in (Fig. B.64) the cliff will be more resistant to wave erosion. Some of the known cliffs of Indian coast are Veraikholla Cliff, Vivekananda Rock, Cape Comorin, Bay of Bengal.

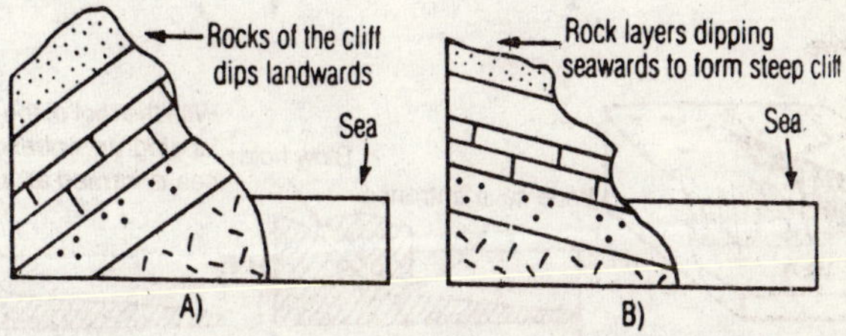

Fig. B.64 ***Sea-cliff types***

At the *base of the cliff* the sea cuts a **notch,** which gradually undermines the cliff so that it collapses. As a cliff recedes landwards under the pounding of waves, an eroded base is left behind, called a wave-cut platform. The platform, the upper part of which is exposed at low tides slopes gently seawards and its surface is strewn with rock debris from the receding cliff. The eroded materials are deposited on the *off-shore terrace.*

3. **Cave, arch stack and stump**-The narrow arms of land which project into the sea as headlands or buttresses may develop caves on either side which ultimately may join together from side to side while the upper portion of the buttress may stand like an arch.

These are known as **sea-arches** (Fig. B.65) In course of time when the arches fall down or the projecting portion of the headlands is separated from the cliff, vertices pieces of rocks may be found standing in the sea separated from the cliff. Such features are called **stacks** or sea-stacks. Good examples of sea arches and stacks are found in the Capri Islands of Italy.

In the tropics minor examples occur on limestone coasts and in association with corals as in Malaya.

It is important to remember that caves, arches, buttresses or stacks are secondary features which are formed in different stages

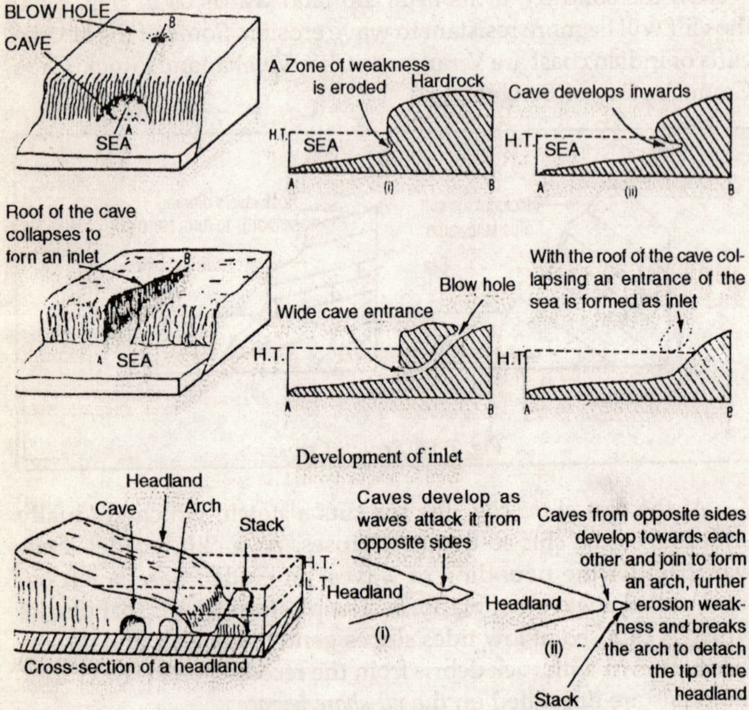

Fig. B.65 *Evolution from caves to a stack*

in the process of cliff recession. By this process the cliff continually keeps on receding towards the land and the beach platform gets extended. Eastern side of India is a fine example of a long plain of marine erosion.

Coastal Features of Deposition

Beaches- Sands and gravels loosened from the land are moved by waves to be deposited along the shore as **beaches** (B.66) This is the most dominant form of the constructive work of the sea. The eroded material is transported along the shore in several distinct ways. Where the wave-cut terraces are narrow, the undertow and littoral currents carry the debris eroded from the land out into deep water, where it is deposited, Digha beach in eastern coast of India along the Bay of Bengal is a good example.

Some beaches are like ridges with a crest and a steeper slope towards the land than the sea as found in Kovalam beach of

Trivandram, Kerala. Others are broad, sheets of sediments spread by waves and currents over the shore. They may be composed of sand, gravel or rounded pebbles as in Puri beach of Orissa.

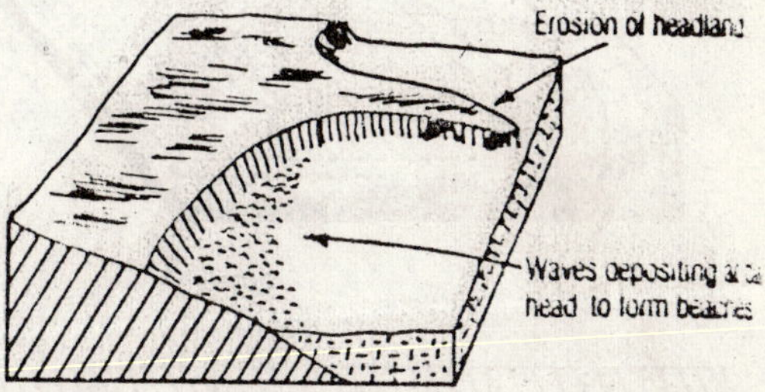

Fig. B.66 *Beaches*

The constant action of the waves automatically sorts out the shoreline deposits in a graded manner. The coarser materials (cobbles and boulders) are dropped by the waves at the top of the beach. The finer materials (pebbles and sand grain) which are carried down the beach by the backwash are dropped closer to the sea.

2. **Spits and bars**- The long shore drift continually moves debris eroded by waves and where there is an indentation in the coast, such as the mouth of a river or a bay, material may continue to be deposited across the inlet. As more materials are added, they will pile up into a ridge or embankment of shingle forming a tongue or **spit**, with one end attached to the land and the other end projecting into the sea (Fig. B.67). Oblique waves may curve the spit into a hook or recurred spit. when the ridge of shingle is formed across the mouth of a river or the entrance to a bay, it is called a **bar** good examples of bars and spits are found also on the Kerala coast in S.W. India where lagoons are usually found behind the spits.

Sometimes long and narrow embankment of sediment are deposited on both sides of the headland and wing-shaped spits are formed. Such headlands are called **winged headlands.** When the bar is deposited across the month of the bay, this is known as **bay month** or **bay bar**(Fig. B.68) Sometimes bay month bar may

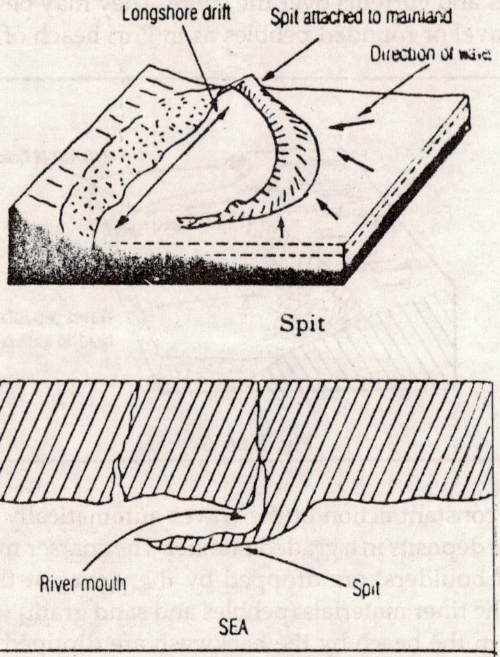

Fig. B.67 ***Spit across a river mouth***

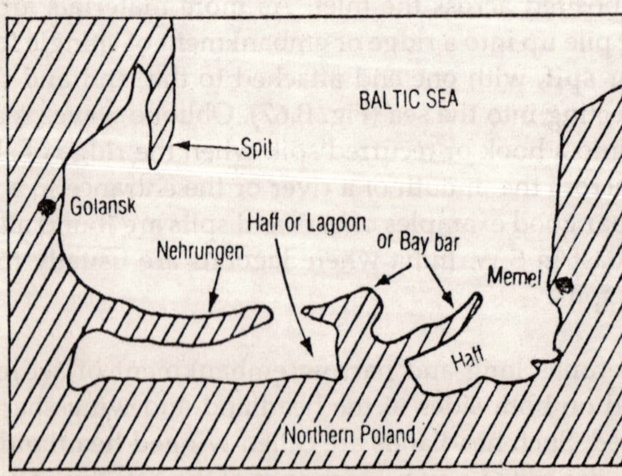

Fig. B.68 ***Nehrung or bar***

be broken in the middle by tidal or stormy waves and divided into two parts separated by an inlet in between which the lagoon connects with the sea. This feature is called **double spits**. Several good example of double spits can be seen on the western coast of India, between cananore and Mangalore. The spits are found both to the north and south of Kasaragod Harbour and harbour inlet lies in the middle-Connecting bay bars which completely cut off the water of the bay from the sea are probably not found along the Indian coast, but on a small scale between Nileshwar and Cananore on the western coast. Bars found in the off-shore areas are called **offshore bars** (Fig. B.69).

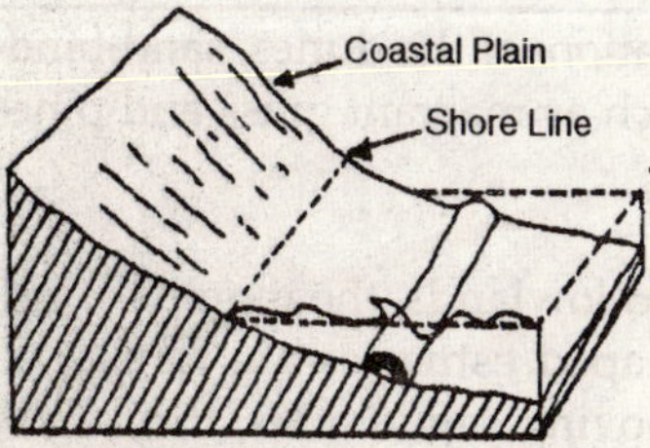

The Wave lifts up the sand deposited by the backwash and drops it again before it reaches the shore as shallow depths decrease their energy

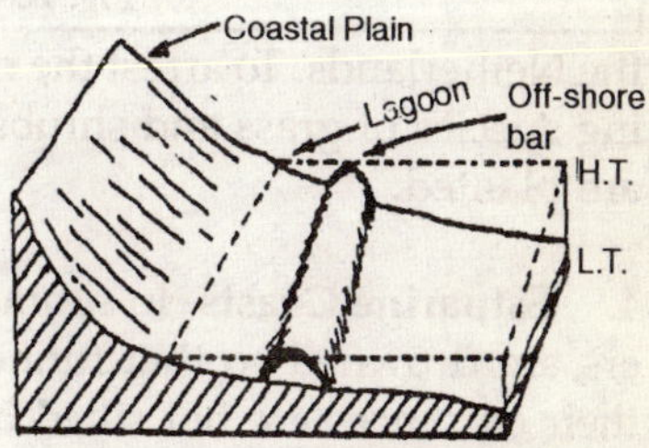

The sand bar develops by deposition of breaking waves, above the high tide level, to form a lagoon which with time gets filled up to form a marsh and then dry land

Fig. B.69 ***Development of Offshore bar***

Oblique waves may curve the spit into a **hook or recurved spit**. Good examplas of hook are found in the double spits formed near the mouth of the Shiriya river.

When the spit is so much extended that it connects two headlands or two islands or an island with the coast, then such a bar is called a connecting bar. It is often called a **tombolo** (Fig. B.70) Tombolos are found along the Indian coast near Tuticorin which joins Hare island with the coast and there is a light house on this island. On the western coast of India several examples of tied islands and tombolo can be seen between Malwan and Ratnagiri.

3. **Marine dunes and dune Belts**- With the force of on-shore winds, a large amount of coastal sand is driven land wards forming extensive **marine dunes** that stretch into **dune belts**. Their advance inland may engulf farms, roads and even entire villages. Dunes are common in the coastlands of Belgium, Denmark and

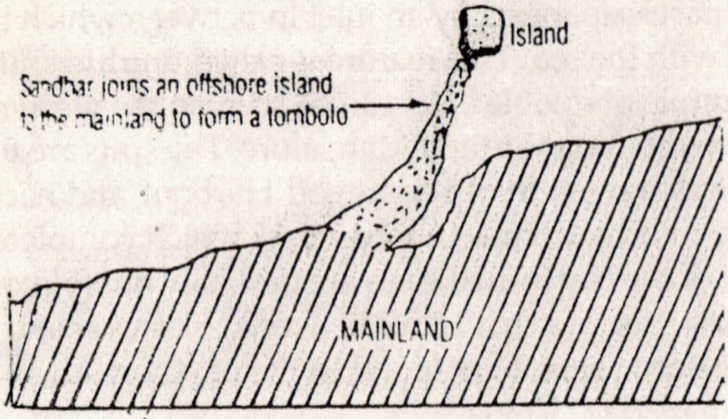

Fig. B. 70 ***Tombolo***

the Netherlands. To arrest the migration of the dunes, sand-binding species of grass and shrubs, such as marram grass and pines are planted.

4. **Estuarine Coasts-** In submerged lowlands, the mouths of rivers are drowned so that funnel-shaped estuaries are formed. If their entrances are not silted by moving sand-banks, they make excellent sites for ports e.g the estuaries of the thames, elbe and plate are the sites of such great sea ports as London, Hamburg and Buenos Aires. Tidal effects further enhance the value of the ports and even when there is a little silting, modern dredges help to keep the ports open all the time.

DELTA LANDFORMS

Tidally dominated deltaic areas of the Ganga (Sundarban coastal plain of 24 Paraganas District) is intensively studied for the representation of tidal landforms of the coastal West Bengal in Indian tropics.

Tide dominated landforms of the tropics are very sensitive to the climate.

Marshes-Vegetated inter tidal flats flooded periodically or at intervals. Inter-distributary delta plains of the Sundarban are densely colonized by mangrove vegetation. Tidal water penetrates far inland through the wider distributary channels and inundate the inter-distributary flats twice a day. Thus tidal born finer sediments are deposited in the channel banks and flat surface which provide the platform for the development of mangroves. The deltaic plain between the River Hugli and the Hariabhanga River is the part of deltaic abandonment of the Ganga-Brahmaputra. Geologists argue that in the Ganga-Brahmaputra delta, river capture has resulted from basement faulting in combination with evatic major floods. Thus capture of the Hugli River resulted in the abandonment of a large deltaic tract now occupied by a dense marshy area. (Fig. B.71)

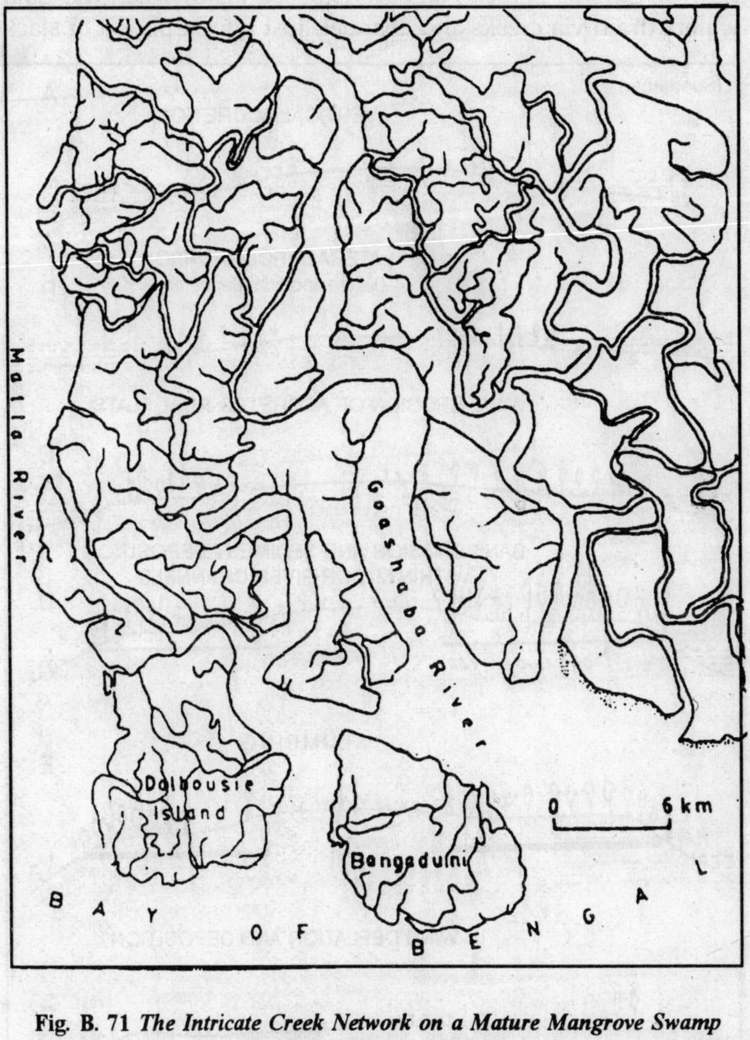

Fig. B. 71 ***The Intricate Creek Network on a Mature Mangrove Swamp Surface of the Sundarban***

Tidal Flats- Extensive tidal flats are found in the tidal settings of delta plain like sundarban. In general, tidal flats are feature less plains dissected by complex meandering tidal channels and creek systems. Massive tidal flow penetrates inland delta plains estuaries, smaller tidal channels and creeks during flood tides. Adjacent tidal flats are inundated in this stage due to tidal overflow of channel banks. Flats are exposed again when the tidal waters drain via creeks and channels just after a period of slack

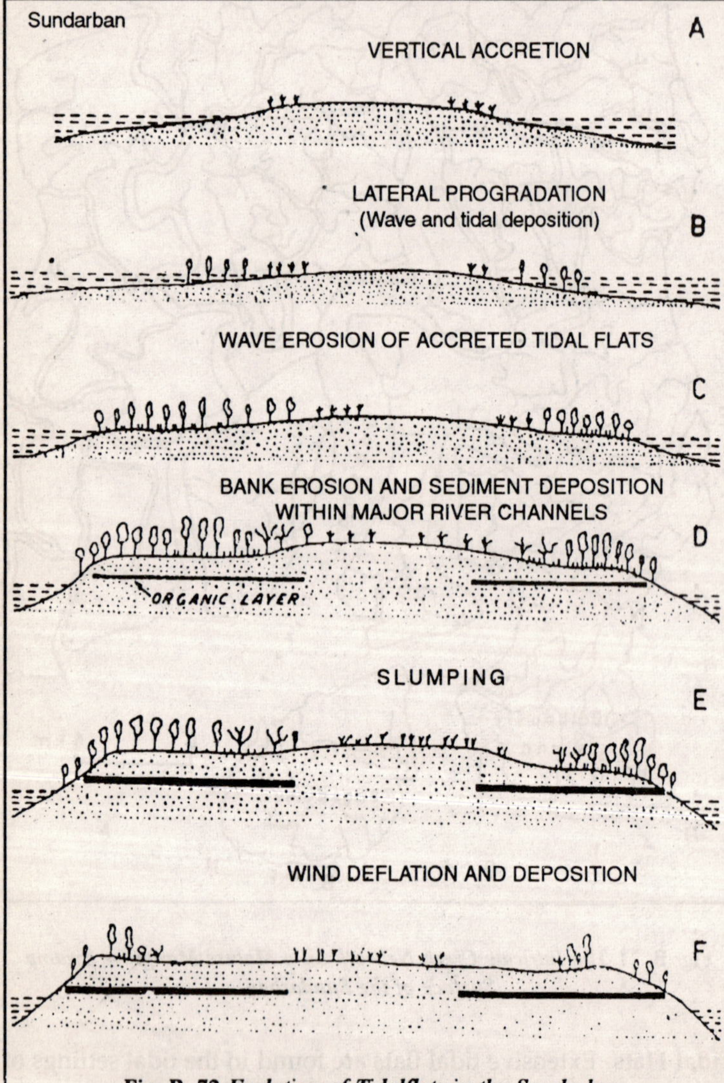

Fig. B. 72 ***Evolution of Tidalflats in the Sundarban***

water. Thus tidal currents transported sediments and suspended sediments of tidal waters are deposited on the flat surface in each high tides. (Fig. B.72).

Intricate Creek Network systems-Tidal flats of the delta plains are dissected by intricate creek network systems. The creeks are characterized by their channel patterns with point bar depositional parts on the inner banks. Creeks are active in those areas where the tidal links are not affected by man's reclamation of tidal flats. Active tidal creeks migrate laterally with the erosion and deposition of sediments and control the development of tidal flats.

Salt Pan-The small shallow pools which cover many marsh and swamp surfaces are called **Salt pans.** (Fig. B.73) The areas which were left unvegetated and the salt water which lay in these initial pools evaporated producing highly saline conditions in which no plant life can survive. Thus the salt water pools survived while the swamp surface grew up around them. Frequent salt pans are seen in the deltaic islands of the Sundarban. Salt concentrations are partly dissolved in wet seasons (peak monsoon periods) in the pans because of the high rainfall and peak freshwater discharge by the Sundarban river.

Tidal Pans-Elongated lagoons between beach ridges or sand dunes are found just behind the active shoreline of the south western Sundarban. Tidal water penetrates in the dune valleys through some high water channels in the spring. Thus the store water between two dune rows produce an elongated lagoon or **tidal pan.**

LAND RECLAMATION

The coast attracts human settlement because of its beauty, its generally equable and mild climate, the presence often of suitable flat, lowlying land suitable for agriculture, and the use of the sea for shipping and communications. As the coast is a buffer zone between land and sea, it lends itself to certain types of human activity. In general, because of the tidal influence the shore zone is not suited for permanent land uses such as agriculture, industry or settlement, apart from those that are based on marine resources, such as types of aquaculture reclamation, or 'land claim' as it is probably more accurately described, has enabled the population of many coastal areas to make increasing use of the coastal zone for agriculture, industry and settlement. Estuaries and deltas have

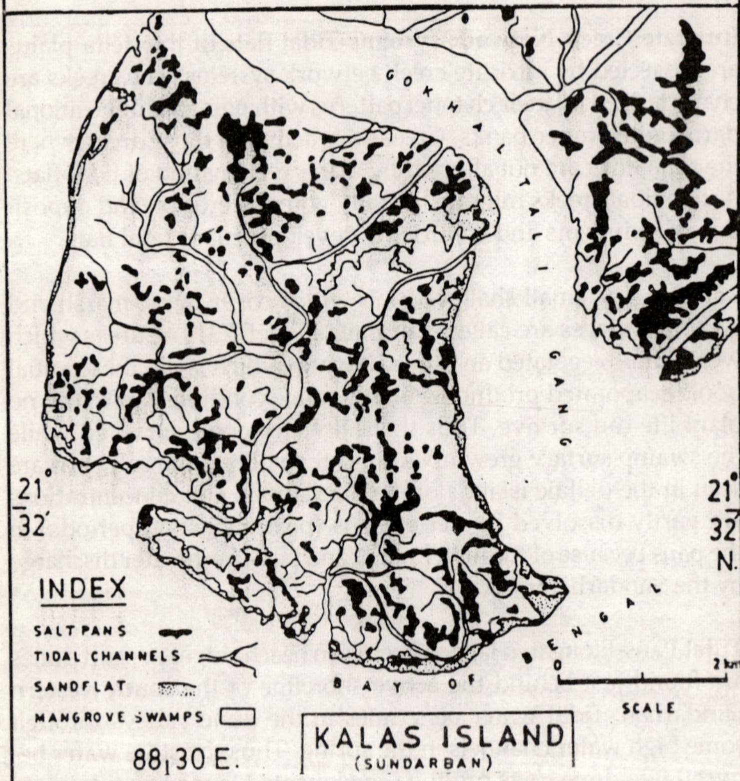

Fig. B. 73 ***Location of Primary Salt Pans in the Mangrove Swamps of Kalas Island (Sundarban)***

provided the home for many civilizations, such as those based on the Nile and Irrawaddy deltas. Most human activity within the shore zone and on continental shelves, is linked to land uses further inland. Thus recreation on tourist beaches is linked to hotel and resort developments on the coastal plain.

As with the linked beach environments, natural and managed dunes may respond very differently to sea level rise. Natural, patchly vegetated coastal dunes usually recover quickly and can migrate landwards in response **to rising sea-levels.** One of the major problems for future dune management is that a very large percentage of many dunefields has already been reclaimed and therefore the sediment is lost by building of railway, roads, industry, housing, airport and golf courses, and the dunes cannot transgress over this area.

Coastal Wetlands appear to be both important sinks of global carbon and exporters of nutrients which help sustain the productivity of estuarine and other coastal ecosystems. Coastal wetlands around Bay of Bengal in West Bengal are in fact subjected to a vast range of human activities.

The challange facing those involved in the management of coastal wetlands is to conserve the sedimentary and biological resources while tapping their economic potential in the light of an uncertain environmental future.

Integrated conservation schemes in estuary, bay and back barrier areas are clearly required to reconcile varying land uses such as wildlife conservation, coastal protection, grazing, military use and economic development. These schemes are operating against a historical background of land claim (conversion of coastal marshes to agricultural industrial and urban land), sea level changes and biological changes.

The low-lying parts of Indian coastline like the Sundarbans area which is the older deltaic plain of the Ganges is dominated by mangroves and nipa palm swamps. The Sundarbans with 401600 ha of mangroves act as a reserve for many important species of wild life. Over the past 30 years the health of the main brackish water forest trees has declined, probably as a result of salt water intrusion, linked to the decline of fresh water supply caused by the diversion of much Ganges water by the Farakka Barrages.

The most **serious problem** is the vulnerabiliy to storm surge flood events. This is the direct consequences of the natural environment, i.e. a large, active and subsiding delta in a monsoon climate and a tectonically active setting. Deforestation has produced erosion and loss of vital mangrove forests.

Many soils in this area create problems for buildings, roads and bridges. Thus subsidence is a problem faced by many embankment roads, where 1.5-3 m high embankments may subside by upto 40 cm, causing cracking and surface distortions.

The Bay of Bengal acts as a giant funnel for storm events, creating the most severe storm surge problem in the world. Storm surges, cause an elevation in sea level above the tidal height and have devastating effects on low lying coasts of West Bengal, Orissa, Andhra Pradesh and Tamil Nadu. In 1991 a cyclone surge event caused 1000 deaths in Andhra Pradesh Coast which was again attacked by cyclones in the next consecutive years.

(F) REMOTE SENSING

Remote Sensing is the science of collection of information about objects from a distance without coming into physical contact with them.

For this purpose we make use of an assembly of electro-optical devices known as Sensors as well as cameras (Fig. B.74).

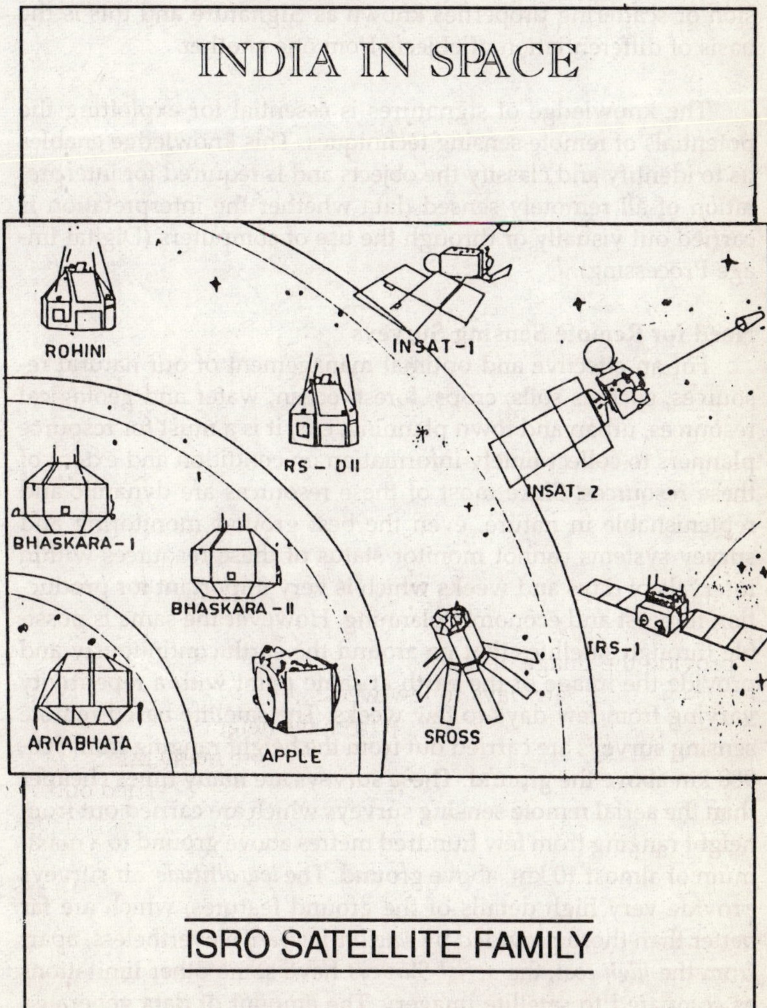

Fig. B.74 *ISRO SATELLITE FAMILY*

The most widely used remote sensing techniques today are based on the sensing of electromagnetic radiation that is reflected, emitted or scattered from the objects and hence in its current connotation the term 'Remote Sensing refers to the Sensing or detection of electro magnetic radiation which is reflected, scattered or emitted from the objects on or above the ground. The remote sensing of objects work on the principle that, each object depending on its molecular composition has the characteristic reflection, emission or scattering properties known as **Signature** and this is the basis of differentiation of objects from one another.

The knowledge of signatures is essential for exploiting the potentials of remote sensing techniques. This knowledge enables us to identify and classify the objects and is required for interpretation of all remotely sensed data whether the interpretation is carried out visually or through the use of computers (Digital Image Processing).

Need for Remote Sensing Surveys

For an effective and optimal management of our natural resources, such as soils, crops, forest, ocean, water and geological resources, urban and town planning, etc., it is a must for resource planners to collect timely information on condition and extent of these resources. Since most of these resources are dynamic and replenishable in nature, even the best ground monitoring and survey systems cannot monitor status of these resources within intervals of days and weeks which is very important for production forecast and economic planning. However the same is possible through satellites that go around the earth continuously and provide the image of the earth at same point with a repetitivity varying from few days to few weeks. The satellite based remote sensing surveys are carried out from the height ranging from 500-900 km above the ground. These surveys are many times cheaper than the aerial remote sensing surveys which are carried out from height ranging from few hundred metres above ground to a maximum of almost 10 km above ground. The *low altitude* air surveys provide very high details of the ground features, which are far better than those provided by *satellite imagery* Nevertheless, apart from the *high cost*, the *aerial Surveys* have some other limitations as compared to satellite imagery. The amount of data generated in aerial survey is comparatively much more than that of satellite surveys and hence *more time* and personnel are required for data interpretation. Besides, the aerial survey cannot be carried out in *bad weather* conditions and over difficult terrains.

Satellite Remote Sensing (How it works?)

The different stages of satellite system and how it works, is given in chart.

Advantage of Satellite Data for mapping

Some of the advantages of satellite data for mapping are given below :-

(1) Coverage-synoptic view
(2) Permanent record
(3) Mapping base
(4) Cost Saving
(5) Possibility of automation
(6) Rapid collection
(7) Monitoring
(8) Possible to conduct surveys in areas which are difficult to access.

Utility of Resource Maps

1. These maps provide a basic data on type and extent of resources at district village level for management and planning of such resources.
2. These resource maps can be used in integrated manner for making development plan.
3. The information on resources will be useful in assisting various programmes such as reclamation of degraded land, flood, ground water, mineral, afforestation programme etc.
4. The resource maps can be used for subsequent updating of details and their monitoring periodically.
5. For GIS development.

Problem in Data Collection

How do we improve the methods of collection and quality of data? The three aspects of surveys which are often discussed.

Relability
Cost and benefits
Timeliness

The above three aspects qualify using remote sensing techniques, but under conventional method these will remain unsolved.

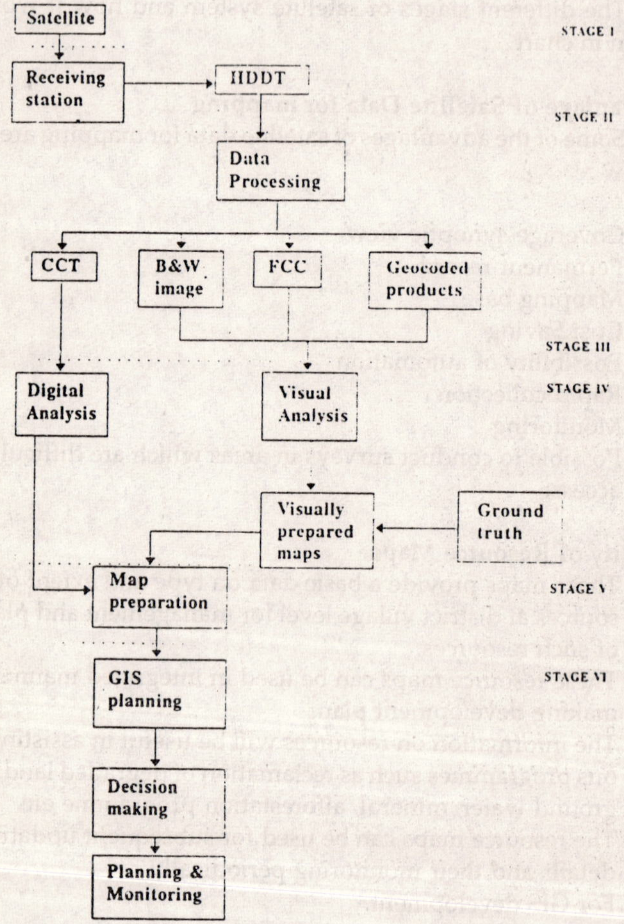

Chart 1

Image Interpretation

For extracting the meaningful information from imagery/ photographs, it is necessary to interprete them. The image interpretation depends on the purpose and the types of information required for decision making. It requires information on the sensors bands used (range of electromagnetic spectrum) and image

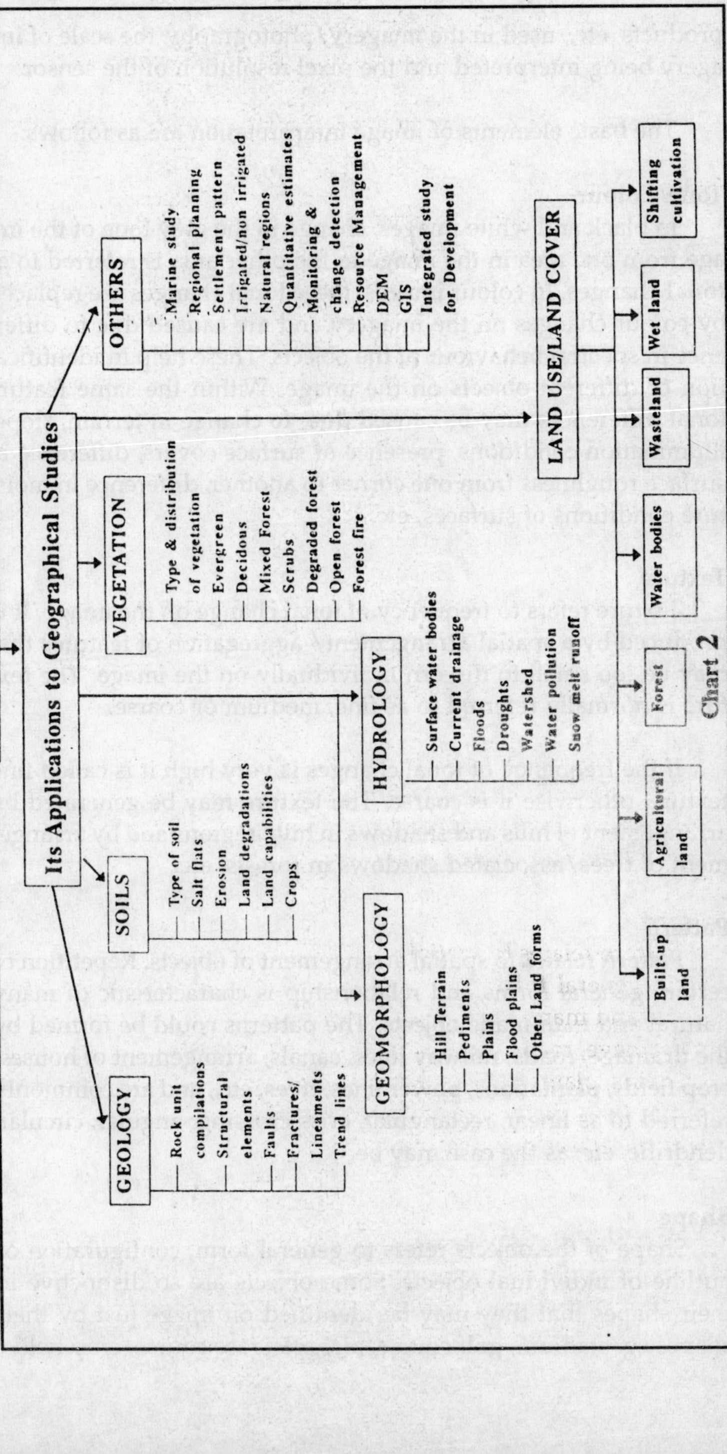
SATELLITE DATA
Its Applications to Geographical Studies
GEOLOGY
Rock unit compilations
Structural elements
Faults
Fractures/ Lineaments
Trend lines
SOILS
Type of soil
Salt flats
Erosion
Land degradations
Land capabilities
Crops
VEGETATION
Type & distribution of vegetation
Evergreen
Decidous
Mixed Forest
Scrubs
Degraded forest
Open forest
Forest fire
OTHERS
Marine study
Regional planning
Settlement pattern
Irrigated/non irrigated
Natural regions
Quantitative estimates
Monitoring & change detection
Resource Management
DEM
GIS
Integrated study for Development
GEOMORPHOLOGY
Hill Terrain
Pediments
Plains
Flood plains
Other Land forms
HYDROLOGY
Surface water bodies
Current drainage
Floods
Droughts
Watershed
Water pollution
Snow melt runoff
LAND USE/LAND COVER
Built-up land
Agricultural land
Forest
Water bodies
Wasteland
Wet land
Shifting cultivation
Chart 2

products, etc., used in the imagery/photography, the scale of imagery being interpreted and the pixel resolution of the sensor.

The basic elements of image interpretation are as follows:-

Tone/Colour

In black and white images, change in the grey tone of the image from one area in the image to the other area is referred to as **tonal** changes. In colour images, these tonal changes are replaced by colour changes on the imagery and are caused due to difference in spectral behaviour of the objects. These help in identification of different objects on the image. Within the same feature tonal differences may be caused due to change in terrain, slope, illumination conditions, presence of surface covers, difference in surface roughness from one corner to another, difference in moisture conditions of surfaces, etc.

Texture

Texture refers to frequency of tonal change on the image. It is produced by a spatial arrangement/ aggregation of features that may be too small to discern individually on the image. The texture is normally referred to as fine, medium or coarse.

If the frequency of tonal changes is very high it is called fine texture, otherwise it is coarse. The texture may be generated by arrangement of hills and shadows in hilly regions and by arrangement of trees/associated shadows in forests, etc.

Pattern

Pattern relates to spatial arrangement of objects. Repetition of certain general forms and relationship is characteristic of many natural and man-made objects. The patterns could be formed by the drainage, roads, railway lines, canals, arrangement of houses, crop fields, plantations, power lines, trees, etc., and are commonly referred to as linear, rectangular, criss-crossing, angular, circular, dendritic, etc; as the case may be.

Shape

Shape of the objects refers to general form, configuration or outline of individual objects. Some objects are so distinctive in their shapes that they may be identified on image just by their shapes eg. stadium, golf course, airports, race course, crop fields, building etc.

Size

Size of an object for interpretation should always be determined in the context of its scale. Using the concept of its relative size, a small town can be distinguished from a city, and a water tank from a reservoir, a hill from a mountain and a stream from a river, etc.

Shadow

Shadows associated with the objects facilitate interpretation in increasing cases. Mountain ridges and valleys, clouds, etc. can be interpreted on the basis of shadow effects.

Drainage

Drainage Patterns over a terrain are indicative of topography, rock types, geological structure and ground water conditions and are very useful in geological and geomorphological interpretations.

Associations

Association of objects in relation to other features is very helpful in the identification of objects on an image. Sand beaches along coast line, snow on high altitudes and higher latitudes, irrigated lands near a tank, sand dunes in desert, bridges/dams across rivers are examples of associations.

Identification of Various Features Using Different Bands

Various features/objects on the imagery can be interpreted using spectral signatures/spectral behaviour of objects in different spectral bands. Now a days use of colour imagery FCCS (False Colour Composites) are very common. In colour composites, normally information of three spectral bands are combined into a single imagery through use of different colour filters. In the standard FCCs, we always use red filter for the infra-red band information. As such information contained in infra-red band always appears to be red e.g vegetation in FCCs always appear red. In these FCCs deep, water appear in black; turbidity/shallow water in different shades of blue; red soils in yellowish white; brown soils in yellowish brown; black soils in brown to grey; snow in milky white; built-up areas in bright blue/ bluish; roads, railway lines and mountain ranges as dark linear features; and clouds as bright white features mostly associated with shadows of similar shapes. Shadows are formed by hill slopes, clouds and very rarely by vegetation and always appear as dark or black in colour.

Topograhy and drainage/stream patterns can be easily identified on imagery/photographs by their familiar patterns. General slope of the terrain porosity/permeability of sub surface materials can be interpreted by direction of stream flow and drainage density. Dry streams appear as bright irregular linear features, where as water bearing streams show water in different shades of blue or black along the river channel.

Features important for geographical study as shown in FCC are as follows :-

The information contained on imagery/photographs can be interpreted for crop types/acreage and predicting crop yields, forest types and area mapping afforestation-deforestation status studies, forest fire mapping, geological studies, identification of ground water and mineral bearing areas, mapping of soil resources and thier types, wasteland, plantations, coastal zone, land use, urban sprawls, fisheries, pollution, etc.

The **interpretation of aerial photographs** involves observation ot the marked landscapic features, their identification and declineation with the help of various conventional symbols or colours. The observer can easily visualize three dimensional view of an area from its air photos by using a mirror stereoscope. In the interpretation of aerial photographs, in addition to the equipments used the observer scientist, and the air photo, both are important. The observer should not be one eyed. He should be familiar with the subject and also his understanding of the allied subjects must be adequate, because the conventional signs/symbols are not marked on the air photos. The characteristics of the air photos depend on the following:-

(i) weather conditions during the period when the air photos are taken-often cloudless, clear sky.

(ii) the camera to be used should be as far as possible distortion free.

(iii) filter should be used to counter act the effects of ultraviolet rays during air photography.

(iv) the overlap in the stereos pairs should be a minimum of 60%.

(v) the positive copies of the air photos should be prepared in the laboratory very carefully.
(vi) for photo printing, double matt photo paper is the best. Though, when air photos printed on this paper, are viewed under the stereoscope, the grains are visible, yet the effect of weather changes as recorded in this paper are much less than in the glassy paper.
(vii) from the point of view of utility, the scale of air photo should be fixed. For general study, the scale of air photos may be small, but for any specific purpose, such as, remote sensing concerning the study of towns, forests, etc., more care must be taken.

The effect of all the above mentioned factors is felt on the tone of the air photo, and the interpreter delineates the different aspects through Black-and-White tone. Tone or at micro level grey tone indicates the reflectance capacity of the air photo objects, generally, water bodies are marked black and waterless bodies are of white tone on the air photo. Volcanic rocks, in which quartz content is less also look black on the air photo. The tones of some of the objects are noted in Table 1.

Table 1

	Object	Grey Tone
1.	Sandstone	Light brown to white.
2.	Marble	From white to deep brown, ranging according to their colour
3.	Basalt	deep brown to black.
4.	Water bodies	deep brown to black.
5.	Moist soil	deep brown to black.
6.	Dry soil	light broun to deep brown.
7.	Quartz mixed dry sandy soil	light brown to deep brown.
8.	Green leaved vegetation	deep brown to black.

In the air photo interpretation work, different coloured pencils and water colour, which may be easily washed off, are needed. Notable amongst other equipments needed are pricker, Chinese crucible plate, quill pen, weights and adjustable table lamps.

An aerial photograph (not on the original scale) is reproduced (vide Fig. B.75), potraying a Japanese landscape. On the basis of this, with the help of pocket stereoscope the general land use pattern is interpreted and mapped (vide Fig. B.76). For symbols see Table 2.

Fig. B.75

Applications of Aerial Surveys

Urban Mapping, Land use and Human settlement for urban/rural cadastral map updation, large scale maps of scales 1:2,000 and 1:4,000 scale will be required which is possible only from aerial photos. For Urban Mapping very detailed land use, utility infrastructure and contour mapping has to be carried out. Creation of a large scale topographic data base for GIS applications in various medium and big towns is a growing requirement. This is required for studies on traffic utilities, population growth etc.

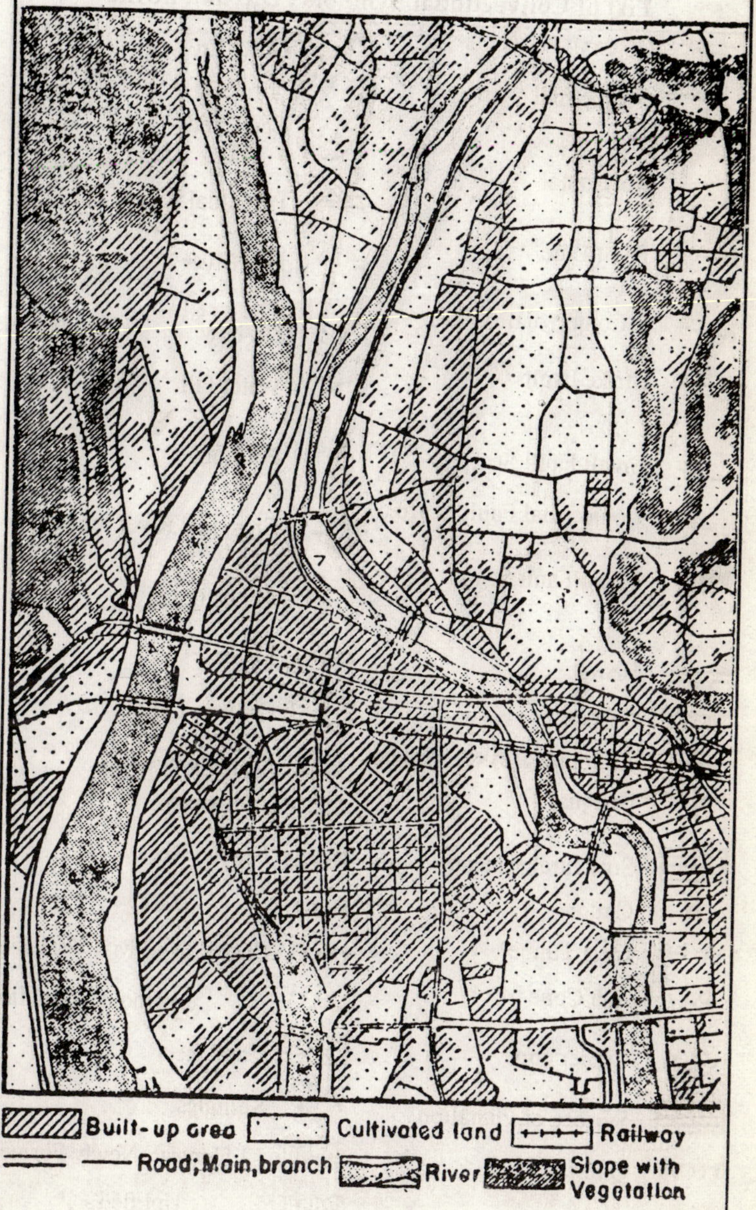
Built-up area
Cultivated land
Railway
Road; Main, branch
River
Slope with Vegetation

Fig. B.76

Table 2
List of Convectional Symbols : Dip and Strike

General	Gully Erosion
Conjectrual	Bad Lands
Horizontal	Perennial River
Fault Line	Dry River
.. Conjectrual	Ox-bow
Strike Fault	Water fall
Small Fault Scarp	Pot-hole
Conjectrual Fault Scarp	Erosional River terrace
Major Fault Scarp	Depositional
Hoarst	Levee
Graben	Ox-bow Lake
Anticlinical Axes : Equal	Permanent Lake
Unequal	Temporary ..
Structural Plateau	Beach : Rocky
Crator	.. : Sandy
Lava Tunnel	Coastal Dune with Vegetation
Ash Cone	.. .. without Vegetation
Cinder cone	Coral Reef
Surface of Planation	Shingles
Questa	Cliff coast : Newly Formed
Hogback	.. .. : Uplifted
Residual hill	Wave-cut Platform
Monad nock	Marine Terrace

- Break of slope
- Scree slope/Fan
- Land slide : small
- .. .. : Large
- Parabolic Dune
- Longitudinal Dune
- Barchan
- Horizontal Sand Dune
- Yardang
- Sandy
- Nodular
- Rocky
- Sink Hole
- Uvula
- Polje
- Karst Spring
- Swallow Hole
- Underground River
- Natural canyon with bridge
- Cirque
- Arete
- Horne
- Hanging Valley
- Drumlin
- Esker
- Kame Deposit
- Moraine : Ground
- Stable

- Mangroves
- Moraine : recessional
- Lateral moraine : Stable
- : Unstable
- : Transitional
- : Medial
- Railway Line
- Canal with sluices and culverts
- Tunnel
- Scrub
- Broad Leaves
- Coniferous
- Mixed
- Palm
- Reservoir with Embankment
- Cistern
- Coastal Bandh
- Groyne
- Mill
- Pump
- Water Logged : Permanent
- .. : Temporary
- Pipe Line
- Telephone Line
- Power Line
- Settlements
- Monuments

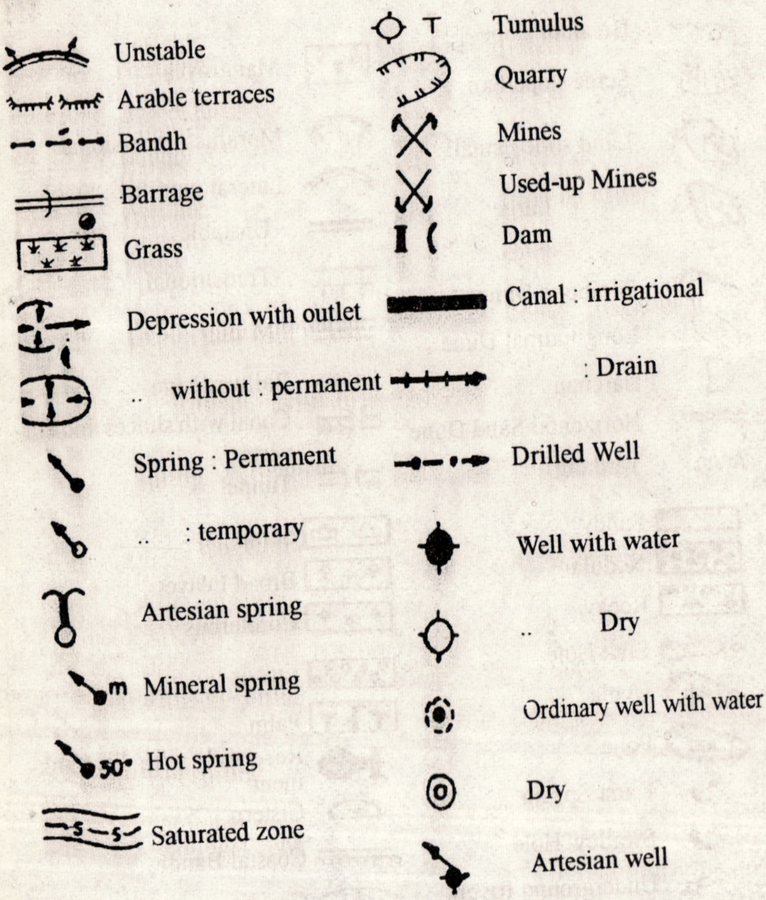
Unstable
Arable terraces
Bandh
Barrage
Grass
Depression with outlet
.. without : permanent
Spring : Permanent
.. : temporary
Artesian spring
m
Mineral spring
50°
Hot spring
s
s
Saturated zone
T
Tumulus
Quarry
Mines
Used-up Mines
Dam
Canal : irrigational
: Drain
Drilled Well
Well with water
.. Dry
Ordinary well with water
Dry
Artesian well

Forestry Application

For efficient forest management many of the Forest Departments require high resolution aerial remote sensing data using aerial photographs and scanners. (Fig. B.77).

Fig. B. 77 ***PAN image showing forest cover in parts of western U.P.***

Water Resources

Monitoring and evaluation of irrigation schemes is being increasingly attempted through Remote Sensing Techniques. While satellite can provide useful information right up to distributary level more detailed information is generally called for in the analysis of irrigation systems. During kharif season, the problems of cloud cover could be solved only by aerial remote sensing.

Aerial Remote Sensing using camera systems and synthetic Aperture Radar (SAR) significantly improve the capabilities of flood mapping and damage assesement. Only air borne SAR data Seems to be the solution for floods. For instance in 1994 flood season so far it has been possible to map only two flood events with many left unsurveyed due to cloud cover. Flood risk zone in

1:15,000 scale in sutlis basin below Bakhra reservoir can be done only with airborne scanner data. Where close contour map is not available, like in command area and flood prone areas, aerial surveys with metric camera systems are absolutely vital.

For targetting areas for **ground water exploration** the use of IRS-IA and IB data are essential. The results have been very much encouraging and the methodology has been adopted by many of the state ground water departments.

Agriculture and Soils

Aerial Remote Sensing, particularly aerial photographs had been succesfully utilised for detecting instances of plant stress due to pests and diseases, nutrient and moisture deficiencies etc. in the country and else where. It is observed that any abnormality associated and manifested on leaves could be more conveniently detected using aerial photographs. It is also reported that discriminations of vegetation is possible using aerial photographs. Aerial Multispectral Scanner data obtained in different wavelengths is used for crop identification and production estimation studies. This is more suitable in country like ours where small land holding exists.

Aerial photography are also being used for verification of crop acreage accuracies obtained from analysis of satellite data.

Geomorphology

Geomorphology deals with the study of land forms and landscapes, including their description, type and genesis. These landforms can be interpreted in excellent manner on regional scale using synoptic coverage provided by remote sensing data. The dynamic changes in physical processes and resulting landforms (eg. river migration) are documented in remote sensing data and can be studied by virtue of temporal resolution of the data. Satellite images clearly depict the different land forms like beach ridges, palaeochannels, meander scars, natural levees, structural hills, inselbergs, pediment, sand dunes, fault scarps and so on.

Finally, the analysis of landforms and drainage helps in lithological discrimination and structural mapping and understanding the geological processes operating in the region.

Mineral Exploration

The mineral deposits occur in a variety of environments which are genetically different. But the concentrated and economic deposits have particular genetic relation and mode of occurence, which form the basis for the modern concepts of exploration through remote sensing. Remote Sensing data are helpful in delineating metallogenic provinces/belts/ sites on the known models of commercial occurences of ore bodies. Here, remote sensing data are being used in two ways. First one is the delineation of features favourable for localisation of mineralisation such as folds, faults and fractures for epigenetic minerals and lithological controls for syngenetic minerals, which the second one is to identify the features directly related to mineralisation.

Secondly, the data are of proven utility for identification of limonite and hydroxy/minerals which form significant guides for hydro thermal mineral deposits.

Urban Sprawl/Urban Spatial Growth Trend Analysis

Urban Sprawl and Urban Growth indicate the overall development pattern of a town or city over a period of time and the information is essential to carry trend analysis for planning its future synoptic view and repetitive coverage is ideally suited for monitoring the urban growth pattern, rate of growth of urban development on to agricultural lands and water bodies. For example, the urban sprawl study of Srinagar indicated encroachment along the margins of Dal Lake. Urban growth of Madras city increased from 188 sq. km in 1971 to 491 sq. km in 1989 with 9.16% annual growth rate with a population of 54.97 million at 2.45% annual growth rate (1981-91). During the same period, agricultural land decreased from 791 sq. km (1974) to 488 sq. km (1988). Showing a loss of 38.3% and the surface water tank area decreased from 47 sq. km to 42 sq. km. showing a loss of 5 sq. km. or 9.7%. (Fig. B.78).

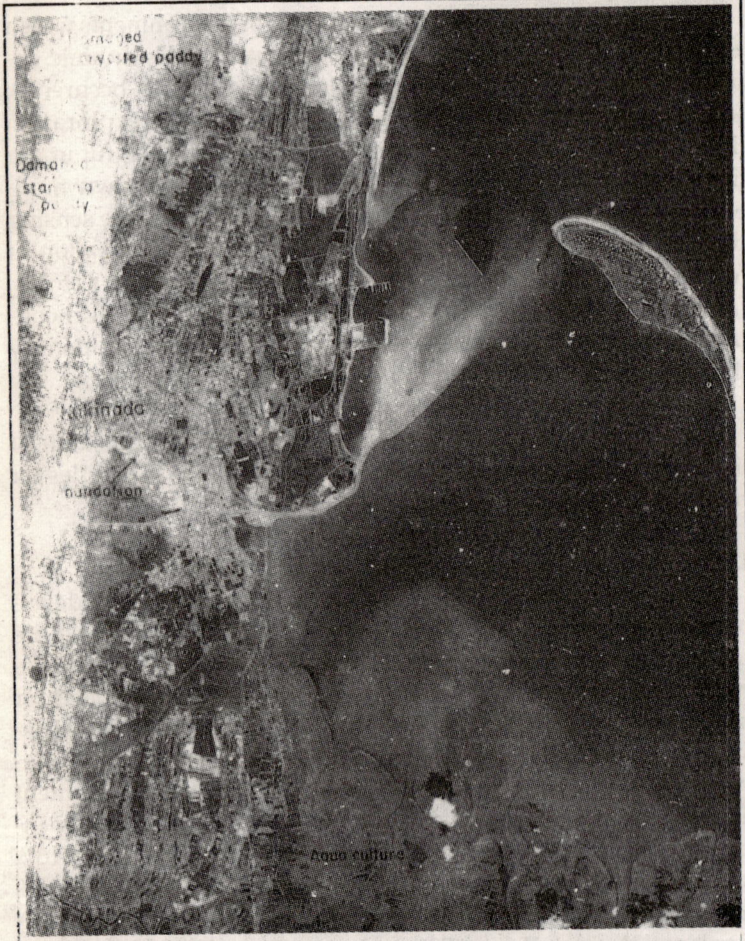

Fig. B. 78 ***IRS-1C PAN image (cyclone impact) of Kakinada and its surroundings, A.P. India***

3

Weather And Climate

The behaviour of the atmosphere has fundamental and far-reaching influence on the existence, growth and well being of all life. Distribution of land and water, alignment of mountain barriers and ocean currents, are all factors which influence weather. **Weather** is the day to day change in climatic elements i.e temperature, pressure, wind, humidity, cloud and precipitation.

Climate is the long term regime of the atmospheric elements for a given place or area for a given period of 35 years.

A weather map is the representation of the weather of a portion of the earth or part of it on a flat surface. The necessity of starting a Meteorological Service in India was first brought to the notice of the Government by the Asiatic Society of Bengal. The Service was started by the government in 1864 andt its headquariers at Simla. After the world war of 1914-18 the Department was expanded and the central office shifted to Poona.

At fixed hours in observatories the trained observer reads the barometer on barograph, notes the temperature and the directions and strength of the wind; also the amount and type of cloud; amount of precipitation if any and the visiblity.

(a) The observations

Pressure

Of all the weather elements which enter into the preparation of the weather chart atmospheric pressure is the most important. Air has weight and thus it exerts a pressure on the earth's surface.

Pressure is **measured** with tha help of a **barometer**.

Mercury Barometer- The ordinary mercury barometer consists of a long glass tube sealed at the upper and opened at the lower end. The lower end is inverted in a bowl of mercury whose surface is exposed to the air (Fig C.1)

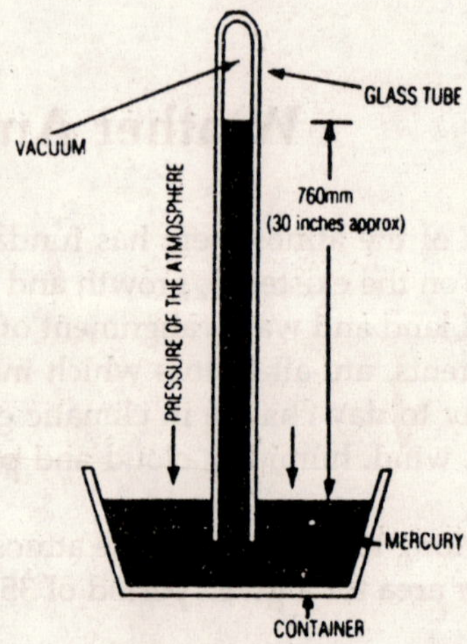

Fig. C.1 ***Mercury barometer***

Variations in the atmospheric pressure on the mercury surface is balanced by the column of mercury in the glass tube. Any liquid could be used for this purpose but mercury has been chosen as it is the heaviest liquid known. If the pressure increases then the air pressing on the surface will force up the mercury column to about 760 km where as at sea level mercury column is 1013 mb.

As pressure is a force it is approximately measured in terms of unit of force called millibar (mb) A new unit for pressure has been introduced which is called hectapasta (hpa).

Aneroid Barometer- Since mercury barometer dips in liquid mercury it is inconvenient for outdoor measurement. The aneroid barometer is a sort of a metallic chamber with a thin lid of elastic metal. Almost all air has been extracted from the box and it is hermetically sealed. There is a spring inside the box pressing the lid outwards against the pressure of the atmosphere. When the pressure of the atmosphere increases the lid is pressed inwards;

and when the pressure decreases this spring inside the box forces the lid outside. These relative movements are made to rotate a needle over a dial which, thus indicates the atmospheric pressure (Fig. C.2).

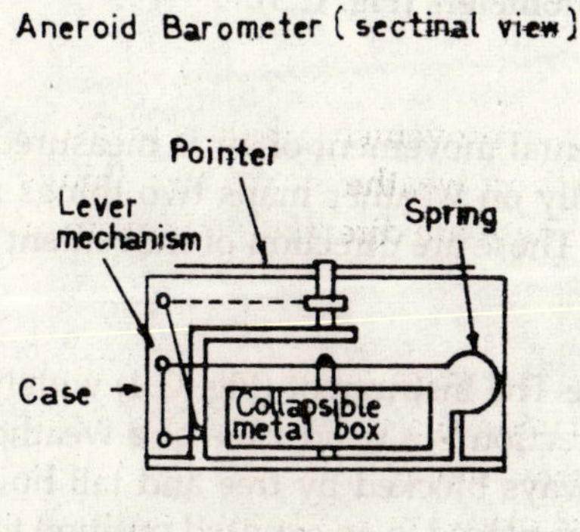

Fig. C.2

Temperature

In meteorology the real air temperature is generally obtained by means of a sheltered thermometer. The shelter is used to screen

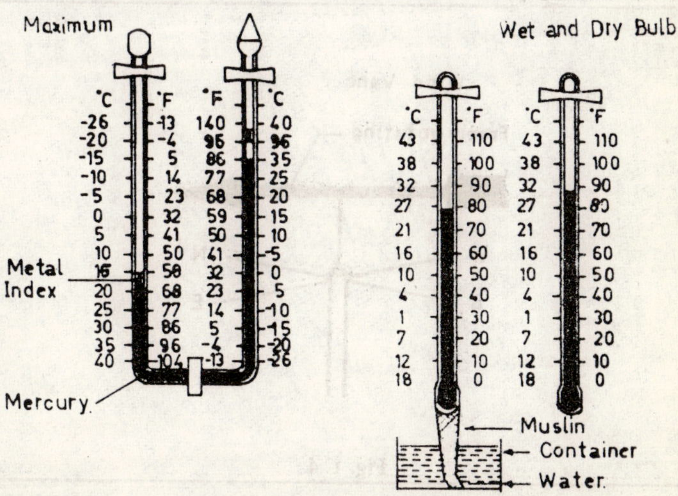

Fig. C.3

the thermometer from direct sunshine or reflected radiant heat. The Stevenson's screen is generally used for this purpose. It is a double walled wooden box which admits a free movement of air. The is painted white on the surface to reflect direct heat.

Inside the Stevenson's screen lies the Maximum and Wet and Dry bulb thermometers (Fig. C.3).

Wind

The horizontal movement of air is measured under the term "wind. Generally on weather maps two things are indicated regarding wind. These are direction of movement and the velocity of movement.

Wind Vane-The instrument (Fig. C.4) widely used for measuring wind direction is a wind vane or a weather cock. As wind direction is always blocked by tree and tall building thus wind vanes need to be placed in an exposed position to get a true direction. It is made up of two parts : One part is an arrow or the vane on top of a mast which is free to move with the prevailing wind. The other part with four compass points is stationary and shows in which direction the wind is moving. Winds are always named from the direction they blow i.e the east wind is that which blows form east to west direction.

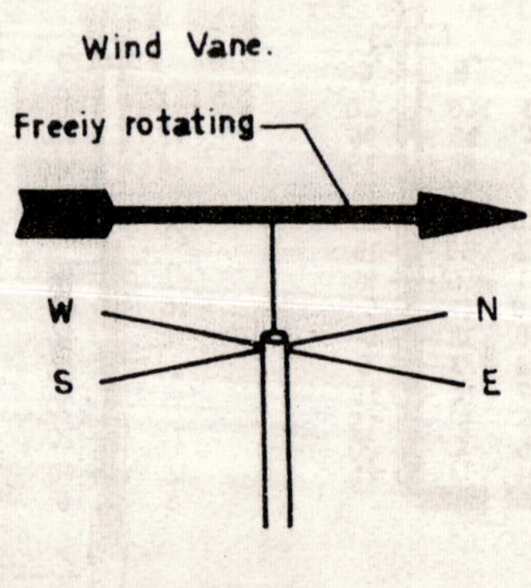

Fig. C.4

Anemometer- The Speed of wind is measured by anemometer. It consists of three or four semi-circular cups attached to the ends of horizontal spikes mounted on high vertical spindle. The concave side of the cup is of greater resistence to the winds (Fig.C. 5).

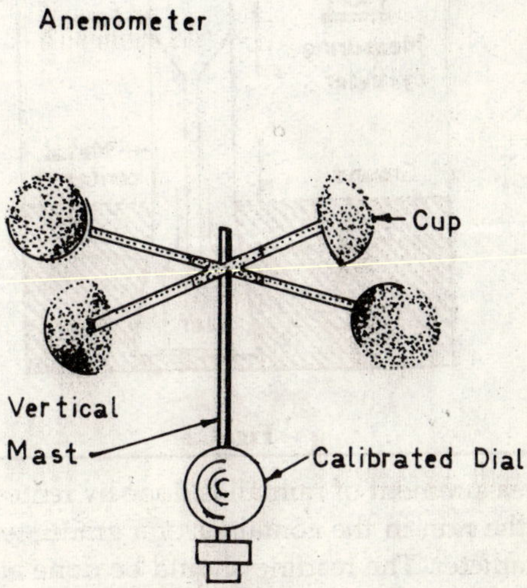

Fig. C.5

The horizontal wheel rotate moving along a central rod which transmit the velocity of wind in km per hour to an electrically operated dial. But the speed recorded is not absolutely recorded because even after the wind has abated the rotation continues due to its own momentum. With some modifications, the anemometer can even record wind direction.

Rainfall

The amount of rain is recorded with the help of a rain-gauge (Fig. C.6) It consists of a copper cylinder with a metal funnel about 12.5 cm in diameter which leads into a smaller copper or glass container. The hole in the funnel that leads down to the container is very small, so that evaporation of the collected rain is minimised. The mouth of the gauge should be at least 30 metre above the ground, away from high trees and other objects which would shelter it. The rain gauge must be kept away from tall building as well.

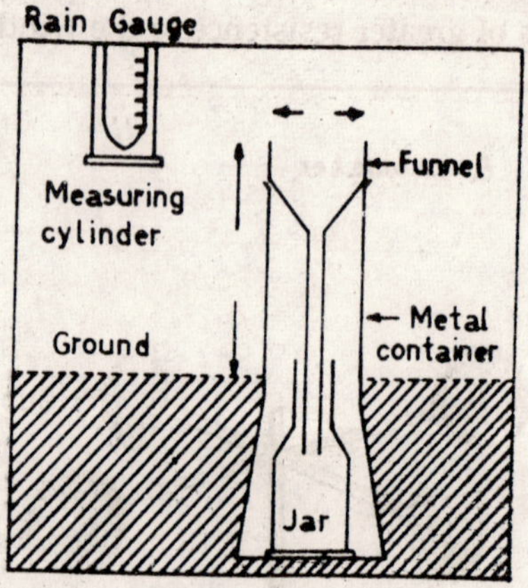

Fig. C.6

The measurement of rainfall is done by removing the funnel, emptying the rain in the container of a graduated cylinder with 1½ inch diameter. The reading should be done at eye label to an accuracy of .025 cm. For greater accuracy of about .073 cm readings are to be taken on the caliberated measure. Few cms of rainfall means the amount of water that would cover the ground to a depth of 2.54 cms provided none of water had evaporated, percolated away or drained away.

The daily records of rainfall are added at the end of the month to find total for that month. The total for each month is again added at the end of the year to find the annual rainfall of the year. The mean annual rainfall rainfall is obtained from the average of annual rainfall taken over a long period of about 35 years. Fig. C.14 shows the wind character after A. Beaufort, 1806.

Cloudiness

The amount of sky covered by cloud is usually estimated in tenths of the sky covered with clouds. On this scale O represents an entirely cloudless sky, and 10 represents a sky totally covered by clouds; and if the cloudiness is 7, it means that 7/10 of the sky is covered with clouds. The observers usually sub-divide the sky mentally into form quadrants and then combine the estimates of each quadrant. For symbols of cloud cover see Fig. C.14.

(b) Different types of rainfall

(i) **Convectional rainfall-** As a result of the heating of surface air it expands and is forced to rise by the cooler, heavier air above and around it. At that point where the rising air reaches air strata of its own temperature and density, further ascent ceases. Thus on a hot, humid summer afternoon, when surface heating is intense and condensation abundant, the towering cumulonimbus clouds resulting from convectional ascent may be several metres in vertical depth, and precipitation from them may be copious (Fig. C.7).

Connectional rainfall.

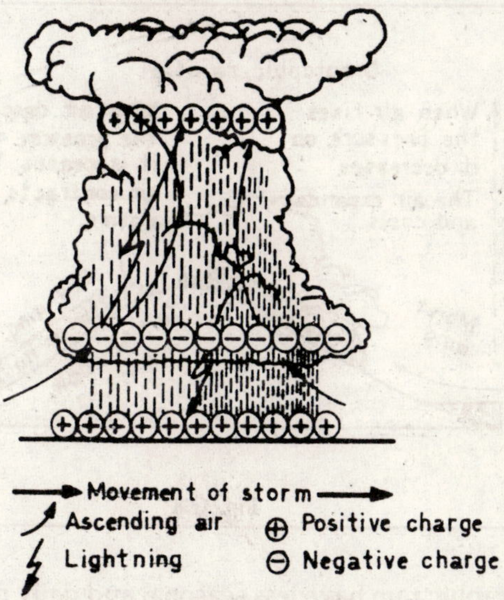

Fig. C.7

Convectional rain, because it covers frequently in the form of heavy showers, is less effective for crop growth, since much of it, instead of entering the soil, goes off in the form of surface drainage. On the other hand, for the middle and higher latitudes, convectional rain, since it occurs in the warm season of the year when vegetation is active and crops are growing, comes at the most strategic time and provides maximum rainfall with minimum amount of cloudiness.

(ii) **Relief or Orographic Rainfall-** Air may be forced to rise when landform barriers, such as mountain ranges, plateau escarpments, or even high hills, lie on the paths of deep and extensive air masses. Since water vapour is largely confined to the lower layers of atmosphere and rapidly decreases in amount upward, heavy orographic rainfall is the result of such forced ascent of air, associated with the blocking effect of landform obstacles.

The abrupt west coast of India which the westerly currents of the summer monsoon meet practically at right angles experiences relief rainfall. The **leeward** sides of such mountain barriers, where the air is descending and warming, are characteristically drier. This is called the **rain shadow** (Fig. C.8).

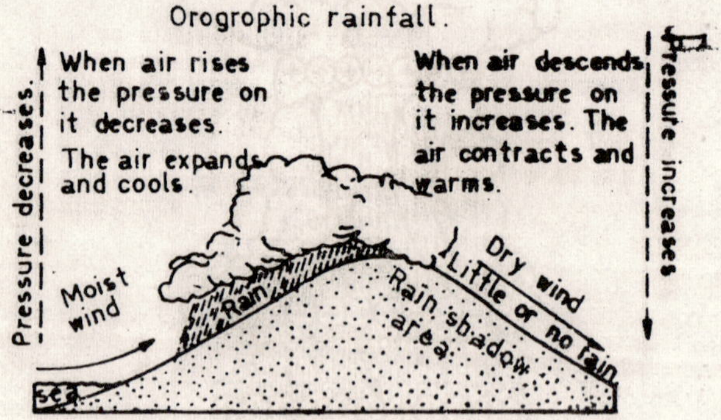

Fig. C.8

Orographic rain have less seasonal and daily periodicity than do those of convectional origin. In monsoon region like India, the maximum is at the time when air is moving from sea to land, usually high sun, or summer.

(iii) **Cyclonic Rainfall-** Where convergence exists in the horizontal flow of thick and extensive masses of the atmosphere, a slow upward movement of air must result. In many convergent areas, especially those of the middle latitudes, the converging air masses are likely to be characterized by contrasting temperatures and densities, so that true density fronts may be formed in the zone of air-mass conflict.

Where two horizontally converging air masses of contrasting temperatures and densities meet, the warmer and less dense air mass is forced to ascend over the colder, denser air along a mildly inclined surface of discontinuity or **Front**. (Fig. C.9).

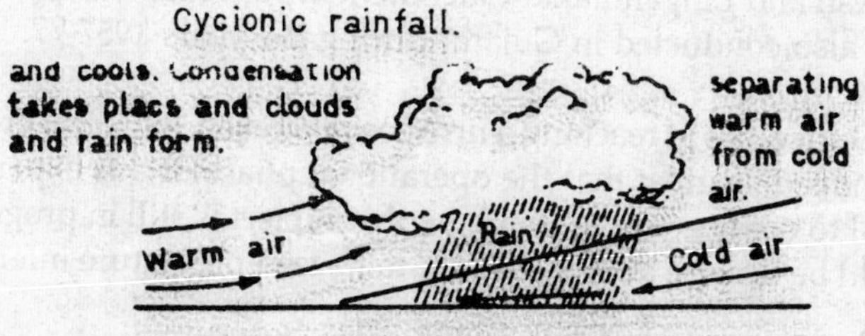

Fig. C.9

Cyclonic storms and their associated fronts are most numerous and best developed during the cool season. In the tropics, as well as in the middle latitudes, cyclones are important generators of precipitation.

(iv) **Artificial Rainfall**- The atmosphere does not convert gaseous vapour into liquid water in a very efficient manner. Substantial material benefits could be derived if the efficiency could be enhanced.

With this objective in mind, a number of experiments have been designed in the last two decades to induce clouds to release precipitation. More than twenty years ago, **Vincent Schaefer**, an American Scientist, discovered that a tiny piece of dry ice, when dropped into a cold chamber filled with super cooled cloud, resulted in the formation of a very large number of ice crystals. Schaefer was closely associated in this work with Irving Langmuiro, who had earlier won a Nobel Prize for his research in physical chemistry, and they estimated that a pellet of dry ice, about the size of a pea, could produce about 10^{16} ice crystals in its passage through a super cooled cloud. The first field trials on cloud seeding appear to have been conducted by schaefer and Langmu towards the end of 1946.

In India, field experiments along these lines were initiated by Professor S.K. Banerji nearly thirty years ago. A series of 35 experiments were made by Prof. Banerji in which he reported rainfall varying from drizzle to heavy rain on 28 occasions. Many experiments were conducted over the Rihand catchment in Uttar Pradesh and Linganmakki Catchment in Karnataka. Experiments were also conducted in Gujarat-during the years 1957-77.

Difficulties in reaching a firm conclusion on statistical grounds are indeed so great that the operational phase of this experiment is still to commence. Research on this subject is still in progress. It would be unwise at this juncture to hazard premature inferences.

(c) Indian Weather

It is a customary to divide the Indian year into three distinct seasons.

(i) The cool dry season, from November to the end of February.
(ii) The Hot dry season, from early March to early or mid-June.
(iii) The Monsoon, from early or middle June to the end of October.

The winter weather does not quite set in from October. The weather of this month is rather variable and with the decrease in the amount of rainfall there is a slight rise in the temperature and it is not before November that one feels the cool breeze of the winter monsoon.

(i) **The Cool-dry season-** The months of January and February represent the cold-weather season in India. During these months the weather is one of the most charming, and this is specially the case for the plains of Northern India. The days are warm and sunny and the nights are cold. Sometimes due to the passage of western disturbances through Northern India the serenity of the weather is disturbed and we get some rainfall in Northern India.

Fig. C.10 shows the average pressure, temperature, rainfall, wind direction and velocity for the month of January. Isobars trend east to west almost running parallel with the latitude. The pressure value increases from 1012 mb in the south to 1016 mb in the north. The temperature decreases from 26°C in the extreme south to 10°C in the north. The rainfall shows a decrease from the Punjab to the plains of Bengal and then it increases again to the south

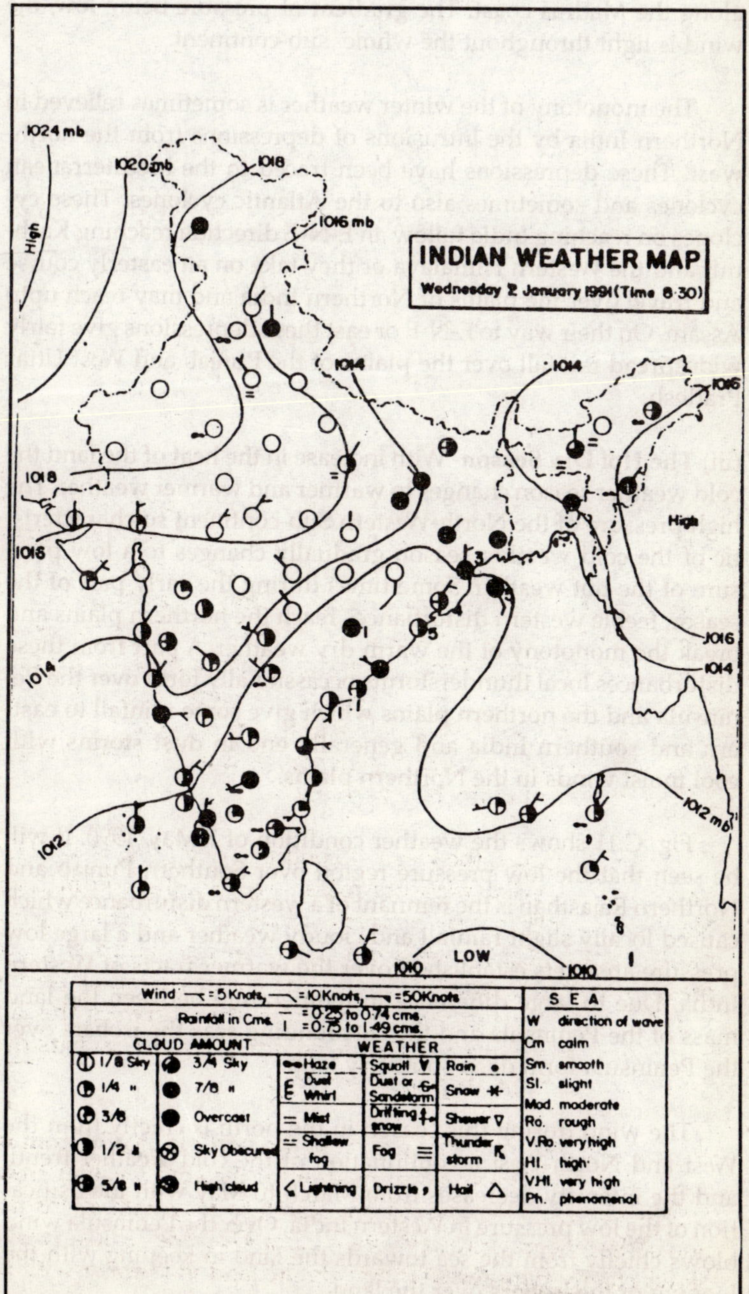

Fig. C.10 *Indian Weather Map - January*

along the Madras coast. The gradient of pressure being low, the wind is light throughout the whole sub-continent.

The monotony of the winter weather is sometimes relieved in Northern India by the intrusions of depressions from the north-west. These depressions have been traced to the Mediterranean cyclones and sometimes also to the Atlantic cyclones. These cyclones on reaching India follow an E-N-E direction reaching Kashmir and the Western Himalaya or they take on an easterly course and travel over the plains of Northern India and may reach upto Assam. On their way to E-N-E or east these depressions give fairly widespread rainfall over the plains of the Punjab and West Uttar Pradesh.

(iii) **The Hot Dry Season-** With increase in the heat of the land the cold weather season changes to warmer and warmer weather. The high pressure of the North-Western Sub-continent so characteristic of the cold weather season gradually changes to a low pressure of the hot weather. Some times during the early part of the season feeble western disturbances reach the northern plains and break the monotony ot the warm dry weather. A part from these disturbances local thunderstorms occassionally form over the Peninsula and the northern plains which give some rainfall to eastern and southern India and generally end in dust storms with cool moist winds in the Northern plains.

Fig. C.11 shows the weather condition of 7 May, 1990. It will be seen that the low pressure region over Southern Punjab and Northern Rajasthan is the remnant of a western disturbance which caused locally slight rainfall and cloudy weather and a large low pressure area gets established over the warmer tracts of Western India. Due to large difference in temperature between the land mass of the Peninsula and the surrounding seas the isobars over the Peninsula form deep southerly loop.

The wind during this season in the north is chiefly from the West and North-West a continuation of the cold weather trend, and the intensity decreases from March to May with intensification of the low pressure in Western India. Over the Peninsula wind blows chiefly from the sea towards the land in keeping with the looping of the isobars over the land.

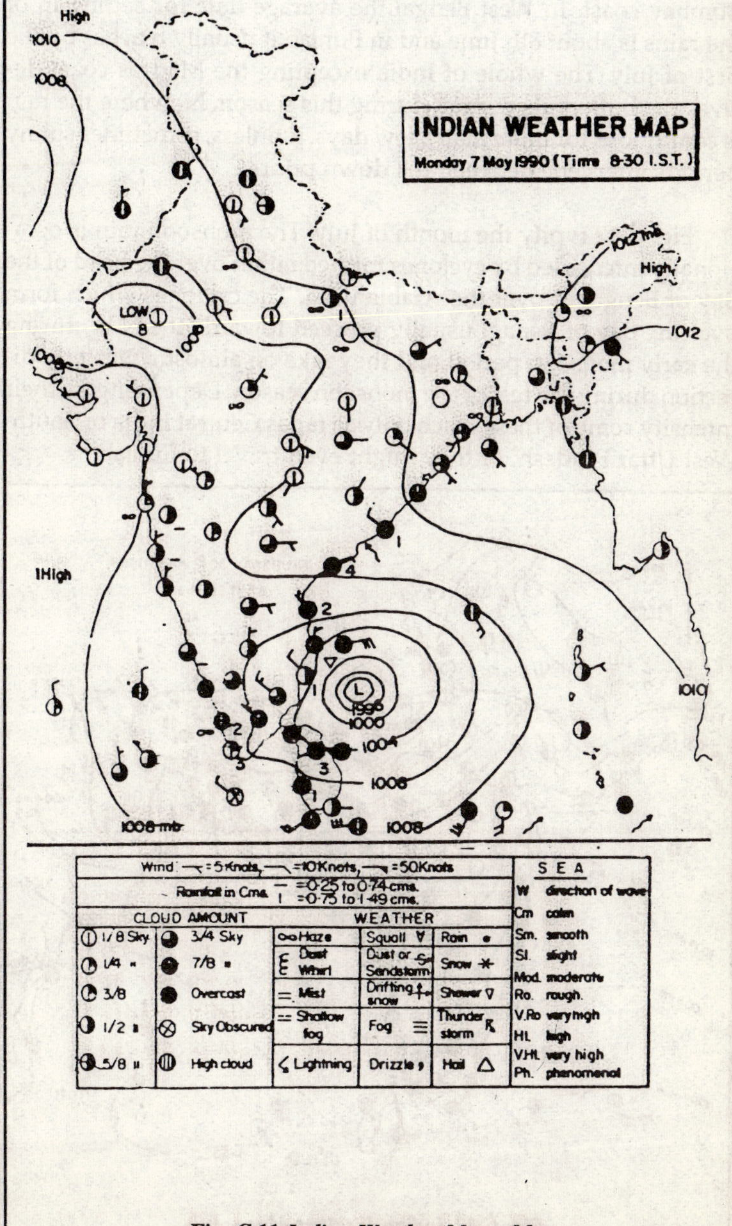

Fig. C.11 *Indian Weather Map - May*

(iii) **Monsoon Season**-The sudden change of weather brought in by the bursting of the Summer Monsoon is well marked almost all over India. The rainy season sets in by the first week of June in Bombay coast. In West Bengal the average date for setting in of the rains is about 8th June and in Punjab it usually reaches by the first of July. The whole of India excepting the Madras coast derives the bulk of its rainfall during this season. Nowhere the rain is continuous for more than a few days. Rainless, sometimes sunny periods intervene between the down pours.

Fig. C.12 typify the month of July. The monsoon rain is occasionally intensified by cyclones formed either over the head of the Bay of Bengal or over the Arabian Sea. The cyclones which form over the Bay of Benagl usually proceed towards the N.W during the early monsoon period and they take on almost a westerly direction during the rest of the monsoon season. Depending on their intensity some of these reach only as far as Central India or South-West Uttar Pradesh, or they might even travel to Punjab.

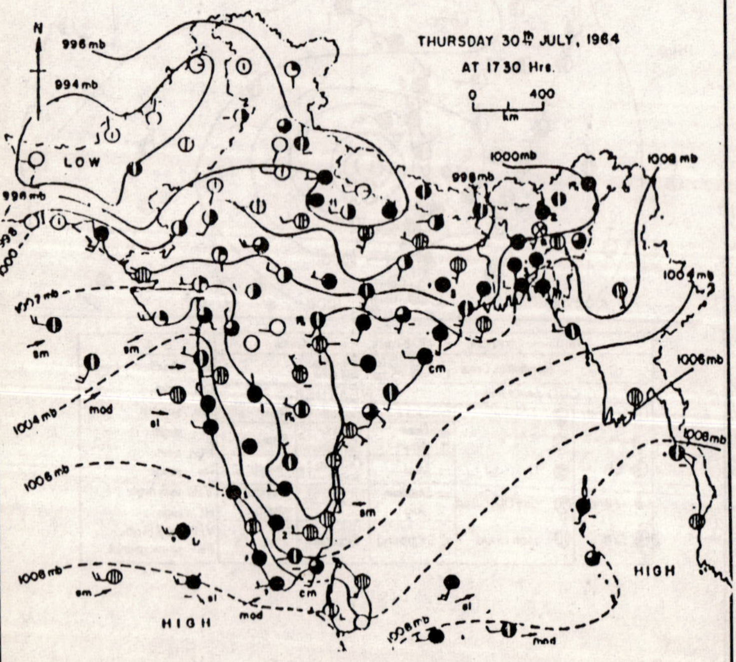

Fig. C.12 *Indian Weather Map - July*

The Arabian Sea cyclones are usually of a comparison with the weather map for the Hot season (May) indicates a slight fall in the average pressure in the north and a slight rise of pressure on the Travancore (Malabar) coast in the south. The isobars run obliquely across the Peninsula from west to east. The normal trend of the axis of the trough of low pressure over the Ganga plain is from Ganga to Allahabad. The shifting of this axis either to the north towards the hill or to the south much influences the distribution of rainfall.

The monsoon rain is occasionally intensified by cyclones formed either over the head of the Bay of Bengal or over the Arabian Sea. The cyclones which form over the Bay of Bengal usually proceed towards the N.W during the early monsoon period and they take on almost a westerly direction during the rest of the monsoon season. Depending on their intensity some of these reach only as far as Central India or South-West Uttar Pradesh or they might even travel to Punjab.

The Arabian Sea cyclones are usually of lesser frequency. From the Arabian Sea they generally move to the east or north east and after causing cyclonic weather over the western coast they recurve and proceed over Kathiawar and Sind towards the low pressure centre in Baluchistan.

(iv) **Season of the Retreating Monsoon-** In Northern India the summer monsoon almost ceases by the middle of September. The serenity of the weather is occasionally disturbed by the appearance of sporadic cyclones. In Bengal and Assam the rains last well into October and cyclonic storms sometimes reach Southern Bengal. By October the monsoon completely retreats from Northern India and the influence of the Bay of Bengal monsoon is felt only along the eastern coast. Low pressure of North-Western India still persists but the intensity is much reduced. The retreat of the Bay monsoon is felt along the east coast by light north-easterly winds and these bring some amount of rainfall. By the middle of October or little later the Madras coast receives heavy rainfall due to predominance of moist north-east wind. Fig. C.13 Shows the weather conditions in the month of October.

Reading a Weather Map

Before proceeding to read the Indian Daily Weather Map one

should get familiar with the various symbols used on such maps which is given below.

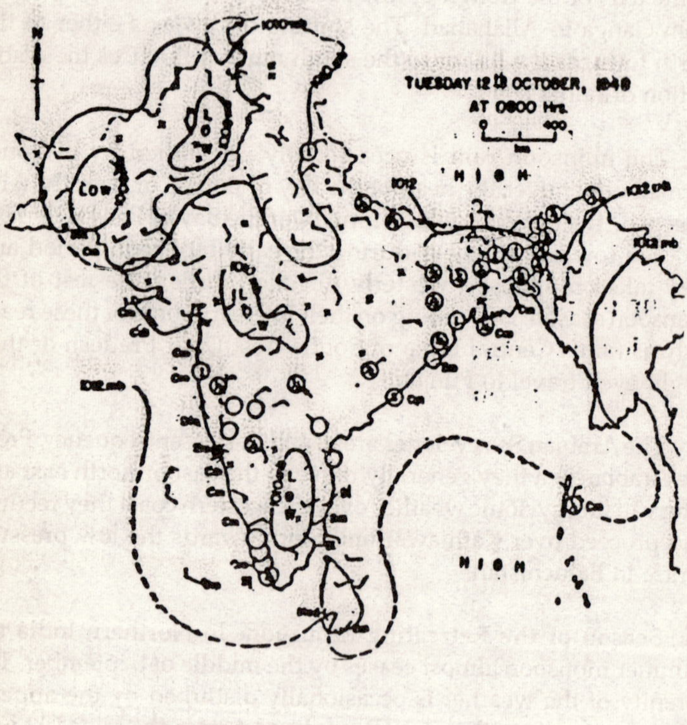

Fig. C.13 *Indian Weather Map - October*

The following points are to be described while reading the Weather map:

1. **Pressure**
(a) location of bar high
(b) location of bar low
(c) trend of isobars
(d) gradient of pressure

2. **Wind**
(a) direction, (b) velocity
In relation to pressure variation.

3. **Sky Condition**
(a) cloud cover
(b) nature of the cloud
(c) other atmospheric phenomena.

4. **Precipitation**
(a) general distribution
(b) Special area of heavy precipitation.

5. **Pressure Departure From Normal**

6. **Temperature Departure From Normal**

7. **Sea-condition**

Some Notes on the Weather Maps of India

With a view to making improvements in the representation of weather conditions several changes have been introduced in the 'Weather Reports of India' in recent years. Up to the end of the year 1948 the weather maps in the 'Reports' used to show (a) pressure in the millibars, (b) wind direction and speed in miles, (c) rainfall in inches and sea-condition. There was, thus, no indication of cloud cover on the weather-maps. The symbols used were also different from those of later weather maps.

On Ist January, 1949 various new informations regarding cloud cover and other atmospheric phenomena were introduced. The new maps, thus, gave a better picture of the weather conditions than the old maps.

Further modifications, though only minor, have been made since January 1, 1957 so as to represent more clearly the wind condition on the weather-maps.

Fig. C.14 shows the changes introduced during the past one decade in the Daily Weather Maps of India.

Metric Units for Weather Reports

From Ist January, 1957 weather reports in India are giving rainfall in millimetres, temperatures in degrees centigrade and cloud heights and distances of visibility in metres and so on. Wind speed generally meant for navigational purposes will continue to be

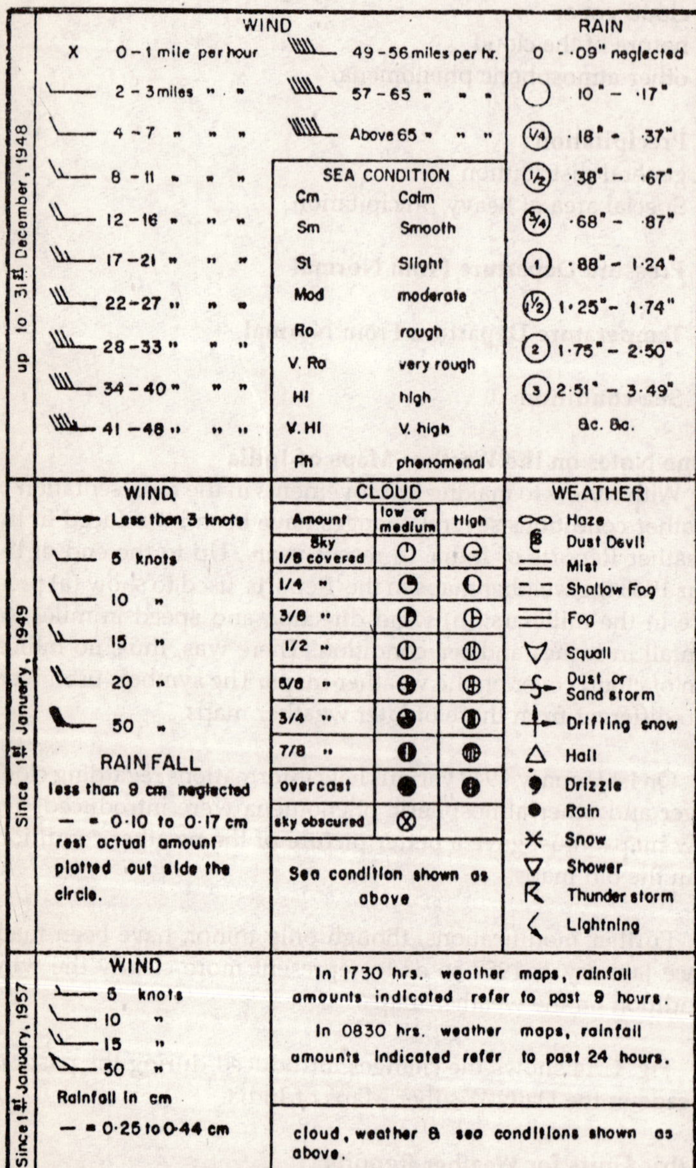
up to 31st December, 1948
WIND
X 0 - 1 mile per hour
2 - 3 miles " "
4 - 7 " " "
8 - 11 " " "
12 - 16 " " "
17 - 21 " " "
22 - 27 " " "
28 - 33 " " "
34 - 40 " " "
41 - 48 " " "
49 - 56 miles per hr.
57 - 65 " " "
Above 65 " " "
SEA CONDITION
Cm Calm
Sm Smooth
Sl Slight
Mod moderate
Ro rough
V. Ro very rough
Hi high
V. Hi V. high
Ph phenomenal
RAIN
0 - ·09" neglected
·10" - ·17"
·18" - ·37"
·38" - ·67"
·68" - ·87"
·88" - 1·24"
1·25" - 1·74"
1·75" - 2·50"
2·51" - 3·49"
&c. &c.
Since 1st January, 1949
WIND
Less than 3 knots
5 knots
10 "
15 "
20 "
50 "
RAIN FALL
less than 9 cm neglected
— = 0·10 to 0·17 cm
rest actual amount plotted out side the circle.
CLOUD
Amount
low or medium
High
Sky 1/8 covered
1/4 "
3/8 "
1/2 "
5/8 "
3/4 "
7/8 "
overcast
sky obscured
Sea condition shown as above
WEATHER
Haze
Dust Devil
Mist
Shallow Fog
Fog
Squall
Dust or Sand storm
Drifting snow
Hail
Drizzle
Rain
Snow
Shower
Thunder storm
Lightning
Since 1st January, 1957
WIND
5 knots
10 "
15 "
50 "
Rainfall in cm
— = 0·25 to 0·44 cm
In 1730 hrs. weather maps, rainfall amounts indicated refer to past 9 hours.
In 0830 hrs. weather maps, rainfall amounts indicated refer to past 24 hours.
cloud, weather & sea conditions shown as above.

Fig. C.14

printed in knots as hitherto, while those for other purposes will be expressed in kilometres per hour, consequently an inch of rainfall at any station will be reported as 25.4 millimetres of rainfall; 2 inches as 51 millimetres and so on. The conversion is very simple being proportional at a rate one inch = 25.4 millimetres.

In the case of temperature, the conversion is not so simple. To convert degrees Fahrenheit to degrees Centigrade, equations are used.

The Table 3 gives some equivalents:

Table 3

Fahrenheit, x^0	Centigrade, y^0
100	37.48
80	26.47
60	15.56
50	10.00
40	4.44
30	-1.11
20	-6.67
10	-12.00
0	-32.00
-10	23.00
-20	28.50
-30	34.00
-40	40.00

In the case of distances the conversion factors are

1 inch = 2.54 centimetres.

1 yard = 91.44 centimetres.

1 mile = 1.61 kilometres.

The above changes have been affected as a result of the decision of the Government of India to change over to metric system in all phases of the activities of the country. Therefore, the data included in the publications of the Indian Meteorological Department, like the Indian Daily Weather Reports, Weekly Weather Reports, Regional Daily Weather Reports and also all data which are being supplied to daily newspapers for publication are being expressed in the metric units with effect from Ist January 1957. All data included in weather warnings and messages are also given in the new metric units.

Cyclonic Storms-Depressions-Thunder Storms

(i) A cyclonic storm appears on the weather map as a system of closed isobars enclosing a region of low pressure. The winds blow around these isobars in an anticlockwise direction and with a speed of 34 m.p.h or more in at least some part of the storm area. When the winds, however, do not reach 34 m.p.h. the system is called a depression. In the area where a cyclonic storm or a depression is situated the pressures will also be much lower than they would normally be in that area on that particular from normal over that region will be considerably negative.

(ii) The cyclonic storms and depressions travel as definite entities from one part of the country to another and their movements can be easily scen by marking the positions of the centres of these systems on a succession of weather charts. For an instance a cyclonic storm which formed in the Bay of Bengal and weakened into a depression after moving inland and lay over Uttar Pradesh see the maps in the Indian Daily Weather Reports for the period 12th to 18th August, 1948. It will be seen from these maps that cyclonic storm was centred about 240 km south-west of Calcutta at 08 hrs., on the 14th August, 1948. It lay as a depression centred near Pendra in Madhya Pradesh on the 16th August, 1948, and over the southern districts of Uttar Pradesh on the 18th August, 1948. It will also be seen that the departures of pressure from normal (see the smaller map in the Report which gives the 17 hours pressure departures) was considerably negative in the region of the cyclonic storm as well as the depression.

(iii) A thunderstorm is a very much more localised phenomenon. It may occur, for instance, in Varanasi but not at a place even 24 km away. It is also a shortlived phenomenon; it hardly lasts for more than 2 or 3 hours at any particular station. As its name implies it is accompanied by peals of thunder. Thunderstorms also move from place to place but they travel very much less distance than cyclonic storms and depression. Thunderstorms may or may not occur in association with low pressure systems. For occasions when thunderstorms were not connected with any low pressure system see the map of the I.D.W. Reports for the 13th and 16th May, 1949 recorded at 08.30 hrs.

In view of the above it will not be correct to say that a thunderstorm occurs only around a low pressure area.

The area of thunderstorms may not always be evident on maps in the I.D.W.R. In order to find out the area where the thunderstorms are occurring or have occurred, one has to refer to the columns WW and W against the various stations in the tables published in the Daily Weather Reports. If, however a thunderstorm was occurring at the time of observation (represented by the weather map) at a Station printed on the Daily Weather Map, it will be shown by the appropriate symbol (for thunderstorm) to the left of the circle for the station. For instance, it will be seen from the map of the I.D.W.R. for 16-5-1949 that a thunderstorm occurred at Dibrugarh at 08.30 hrs. I.S.T. on that day.

Example I

Date

The Fig. C.15 shows the weather condition observed on Tuesday, 18th January, 1949, at 8 hrs. I.S.T.

1. **Pressure**

In general the pressure increased from south to north with local variations.

(a) **Location of Bar High**: Two areas of high pressure were well marked. One was in the north-western part of the subcontinent where the isobar of 1018 mb enclosed a small area round Quetta in Baluchistan and the northern portion of N.W.F. Province and Kashmir. The other areas of high pressure occupied almost the central part of the subcontinent. The boundary was demarcated by 1,018 mb isobar which enclosed south-eastern Rajasthan, West-Central India, almost the whole of Madhya Pradesh, Eastern Hyderabad and Eastern Bombay Province (Maharashtra).

(b) **Location of Bar Low** : The areas of low pressure existed over the sub-continent and another over Southern Bay of Bengal. Of the two subcontinental L.P. areas, one was in the form of an oval patch covering Central and North-Eastern Sind and Southern, West Punjab. The area was encircled by 1,016 mb. It was the remnant of a shallow temperate depression which travelled in from the west. The other sub-continental low pressure extended as an elongated trough along the foot of the Himalaya from the West Uttar Pradesh

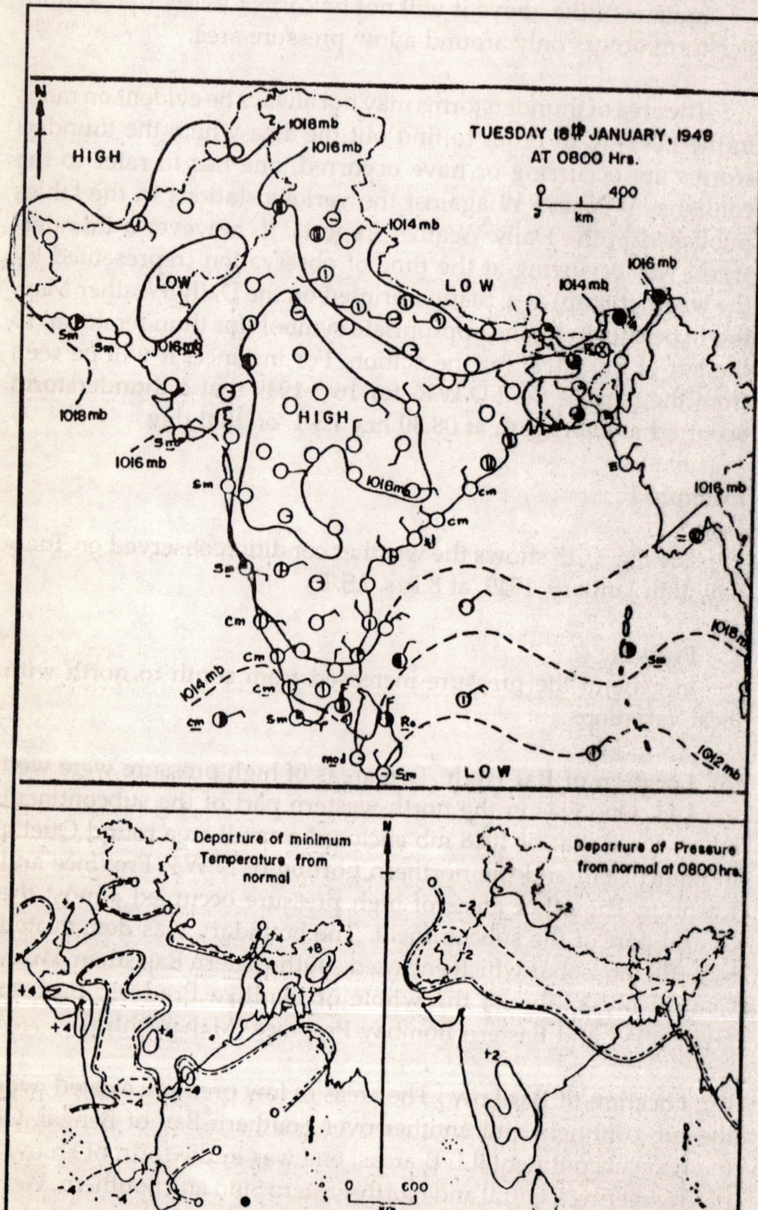
TUESDAY 18th JANUARY, 1949
AT 0800 Hrs.
N
HIGH
LOW
HIGH
LOW
LOW
1018 mb
1016 mb
1014 mb
1012 mb
400
km
Departure of minimum Temperature from normal
Departure of Pressure from normal at 0800 hrs.
600
km

Fig. C.15

of North-Western Assam. It was a bit more deeper than the former and had an isobaric value of 1,014 mb. The temperature in this region had been uniformly high for the last few days and the low pressure might have been created due to local convection.

In the southern part of the Bay of Bengal off South-Eastern Ceylon there was a large area of relative low pressure enclosed by the isobar of 1,012 mb.

(c) **Trend of the Isobars**: The seasonal trend of isobars indicate that a gentle gradient of pressure existed throughout the whole of sub-continent excepting at a few localities like the region near Bombay coast, Northern Bengal and the extreme southern portion of the Peninsula where the isobars were relatively closer and the gradient moderate.

2. **Wind**

(a) **Direction**: In keeping with the general law wind motions from high pressure centres to low pressure areas, land wind prevailed over the sub-continent blowing out from the relative high pressure over the land towards the seasonal lows on the seas. The direction of wind motion in the north-west was chiefly controlled by the seasonal high and the cyclonic low. Local variations were observed at Quetta and Peshawar where apparently the wind blew from regions of low pressure to areas of high pressure. In Northern and Eastern India the wind blew from almost west to east and was controlled by the low pressure trough at the foot of the Himalaya. The direction of wind over the Peninsula was determined by the tongue which projected to the south from the centre of high pressure over the Peninsula was determined by the tongue which projected to the south from the centre of high pressure over the middle of the sub-continent. Over the eastern half, the wind had an almost north-west to south-east direction, excepting in the open sea where it blew from north-east to south-west. Over the western half, the direction was from some quarter in the east to that of the west. It varied from north-east to south-west direction as was at Cochin, Calicut, Gadag and Veraval to almost south-east to north-west direction as was at Marmogoa and Trivandrum.

(b) **Velocity**: The velocity primarily depends on the gradient of pressure; and since the gradient was gentle the wind velocity almost throughout the whole sub-continent was low. Calm to light conditions prevailed over West and North-West India, Uttar Pradesh, Bihar, Bengal and Assam. Light air was recorded at Dehradun and Calcutta; light breeze at places like Mainpuri, Gorakhpur, Darbhanga, Purnea, Naya Dumka, Jalpaiguri, Burdwan, Asansol, Decca, Dibrugarh, Gauhati, Sibsagar, etc.; and moderate breeze at Delhi, Lucknow, Gaya and Daltonganj. In Madhya Pradesh, Orissa, Hyderabad and Bombay the wind was mostly calm or light. Over the East Coast light air to light breeze had away excepting at Madras where wind with a higher velocity than 10 knots was recorded. The Konkan and Malabar coast had also light air or light breeze.

3. Sky Condition

(a) **Cloud Cover** : In Northern India the sky was almost clear of cloud excepting locally at a few places where the cloud cover varied from 1/8 to 1/2. One notable exception was eastern India where at Dibrugarh and Tezpur the sky was overcast. In the south at many stations 1/8 cloud cover was recorded, and at Cuddalore and Trivandrum the sky was more than 3/8 clouded.

(b) **Nature of the Cloud** : Low clouds prevailed over Assam and Bengal. High or medium clouds were recorded from Uttar Pradesh, Punjab, Rajasthan and Sind. The Peninsula had chiefly high or medium clouds excepting at few places in the south like Vellore, Nellore, and Cuddalore where there had been low clouds.

(c) **Other Atmospheric Phenomena:** The sky was obscured at Cherrapunji and Akyab. Thunderstorms were reported from Dibrugarh, Tezpur and Cherrapunji, Fog and mist were noted at Akyab and Rangoon respectively.

4. Precipitation

Highest amount of rainfall was recorded from North-East Assam where Dibrugarh had 1" and Tezpur 1/4". Rest of the sub-continent was almost dry except a few scattered showers ranging from 0.10" to 0.17" at places like Ormara and Sandeman in Baluchistan; Jodhpur and Jaipur in Rajasthan; Dehra Dun, Bahraich, Lucknow, Allahabad in U.P.; Ahmedabad, Sholapur and Gadag in Bombay; Gujarat; Anantpur and Masulipatam in Andhra Pradesh and Balasore in Orissa.

5. **Pressure Departure from Normal**

The pressure was uniformly below normal throughout the whole of Northern India and the departure varied from 0 to-2 mb, excepting locally in Western Rajasthan, Sind, North-Eastern Punjab and Kashmir where the pressure was less than-2 mb from normal. In the South, Western Hyderabad, South-East Bombay, South Central Madras and Mysore had +2mb pressure above normal.

6. **Temperature Departure from Normal**

The minimum temperature was below normal in Travancore, Central and Southern Madras (Tamil Nadu), Eastern and Southern Mysore (Karnataka), Eastern Bombay (Maharashtra), Western Madhya Pradesh, Eastern Rajasthan, South-Eastern Punjab and North-West Uttar Pradesh. It was below-20^{0}C. from normal in the extreme Southern Travancore, Southern Madras, Western Andhra and round Vishakhapatnam. It was +4^{0}F. in Northern Bombay, Western Rajasthan, Northern Sind and South-West Punjab in the west, and North-West Orissa, Western and Northern Bengal and almost the whole of Assam in the east. It was +8^{0}F. in the N.E. region-Dibrugarh, Tezpur Sibsagar and Silchar in Assam. The foothills of the Punjab had minimum temperatures just below normal.

7. **Sea-Condition**

In accordance with light winds over the northeast coast the sea was mostly calm. Further south the winds were stronger and the sea was slightly wavy near Coconada, Madras and Pamban, The sea on the west was calm along Malabar coast and smooth in Konkan, Kathiawar Sind coast.

(d) **Climatic Types**

It is necessary to divide the world into several **climatic zones** each with its own climatic characteristics, natural vegetation (forests, grasslands or deserts) crops, animals and human activities. Though the geographical characteristics may not be absolutely uniform in each climatic type, they have many things in common.

(i) **The Hot, Wet Equatorial Climate**

Distribution: The equatorial, hot, wet climate is found between 5^0 and 10^0 north and south of the equator. Its greatest extent is found in the lowlands of the Amazon, the Congo, Malaysia and the East Indies. Within the tropics, the equatorial high lands have a distinctively cooler climate, modified by altitude, such as the Cameron Highlands in Malaysia, the Northern Andes, and the Kenyan Highlands in East Africa. Fig. C.16 shows the regions of the world which experience the hot, wet equatorial climate.

Climate

Temperature: The most outstanding feature of the equatorial climate is its *great uniformity* of temperature through out the year. The mean monthly temperatures are always around 26.47ºC with very little variation. There is no winter. Cloudiness and heavy precipitation help to moderate the daily temperature, so that even at the equator itself, the climate is not unbearable. In addition, regular land and sea breezes assist in maintaining truly equable climate. The *diurnal range* of temperature is *small*, and so is the annual range.

Precipitation-Precipitation is *heavy*, between 152.4 cms to 250 cms, and well distributed through out the year. There is no month without rain, and a distinct dry season like those of the Savanna or the Tropical Monsoon Climate is absent. Instead, there are two periods of maximum rainfall, in April and October which occur shortly after the equinoxes. Least rainfalls at the June and December solstices. The double rainfall peaks coinciding with the equinoxes are a characteristic feature of equatorial climates not found in any other type of climate. As one goes further north and south of the equator, particularly in coastal districts open to the influences of the trades, the tendency is towards a monsoonal pattern with the *heaviest rainfall* coming in the *Summer* months, i.e June, July and August in the northern hemisphere and December, January and February in the southern hemisphere. Due to great heat in the equatorial belt, mornings are bright and sunny. There is much evaporation and convectional air currents are set up, followed by heavy downpours of convectional rain in the afternoon from the towering cumulonimbus clouds. Thunder and lightning often accompany the torrential showers and the amount of rainfall recorded in one single afternoon may be as much as the deserts receive for the entire year.

The relative humidity is constantly high (over 80%) making one feel 'sticky' and uncomfortable. The monotonous climate, oppressive and enervating, taxes one's mental alertness and physi-

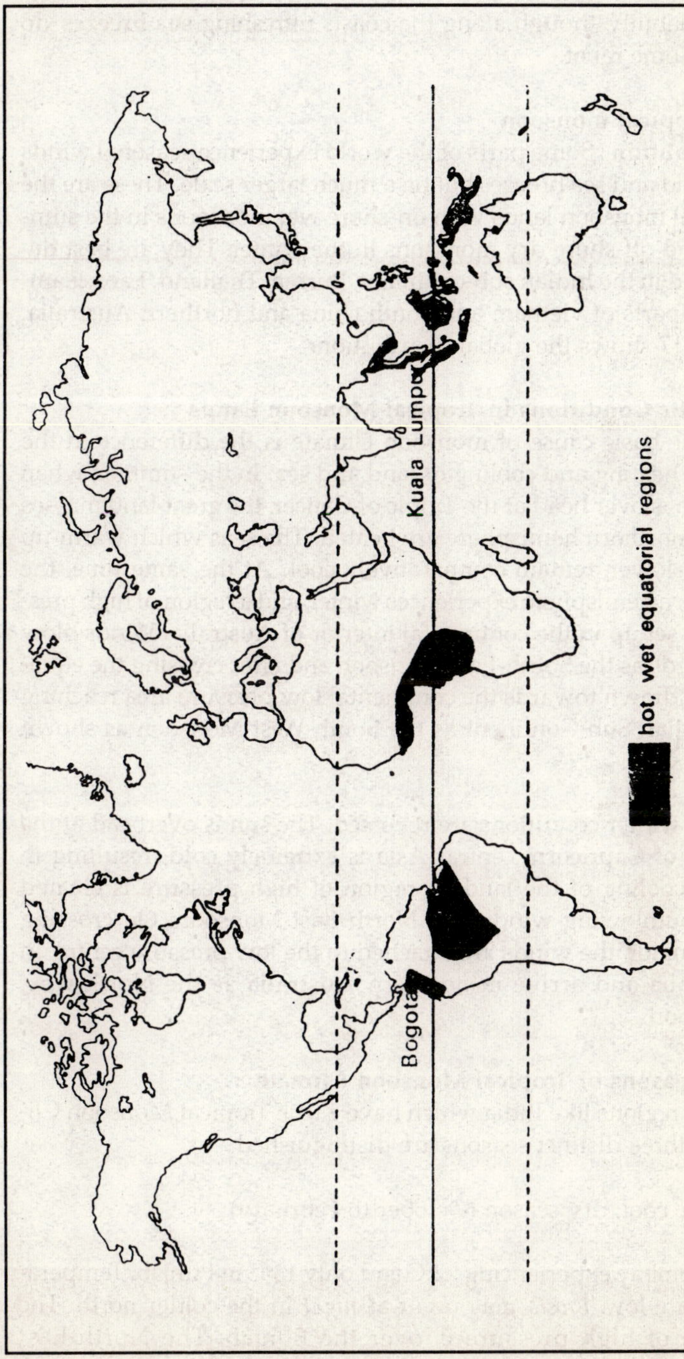

Fig. C.16 ***The hot, wet equatorial regions***

cal capability, though along the coasts refreshing **sea breezes** do bring some relief.

(ii) **Tropical monsoon**

Distribution : Some parts of the world experience seasonal winds like land and sea breezes but on a much larger scale. These are the tropical monsoon lands with on-shore wet monsoons in the summer and off-shore dry monssons in the winter. They are best developed in the Indian sub-continent, Burma, Thailand, Laos, Cambodia, parts of vietnam and south china and northern Australia. Fig. C.17 shows the global distribution.

Climatic Conditions in Tropical Monsoon Lands :

The basic cause of monsoon climate is the difference in the rate of heating and cooling of land and sea. In the summer, when the sun is over head at the Tropic of Cancer, the great land masses of the northern hemisphere are heated. The seas which warm up much slower, remain comparatively cool. At the same time, the southern hemisphere experiences winter, and a region of high pressure is set up in the continental interior of Australia. Winds blow outwards as the South-East Monsoon and after crossing the equator are drawn towards the continental low pressure area reaching the Indian Sub-Continent as the South-West Monsoon as shown in Fig. C.17.

In winter conditions are reversed. The sun is overhead at the Tropic of Capricorn, central Asia is extremely cold, resulting in rapid cooling of the land. A region of high pressure is created with outblowing winds- the North East Monsoon. On crossing the equator, the winds are attached to the low pressure centre, in Australia and arrive in northern Australia as the North-west Monsoon.

The Seasons of Tropical Monsoon Climate

In regions like India which have a true Tropical Monsoon Climate, three distinct seasons are distinguished.

(a) The cool, dry season (October to February)

Bombay experiencing 22^{0}C and only 13^{0}C in Punjab. Temperatures are low. *Frosts* may occur at *night* in the colder north. The centre of high pressure is over the Punjab. The North-East

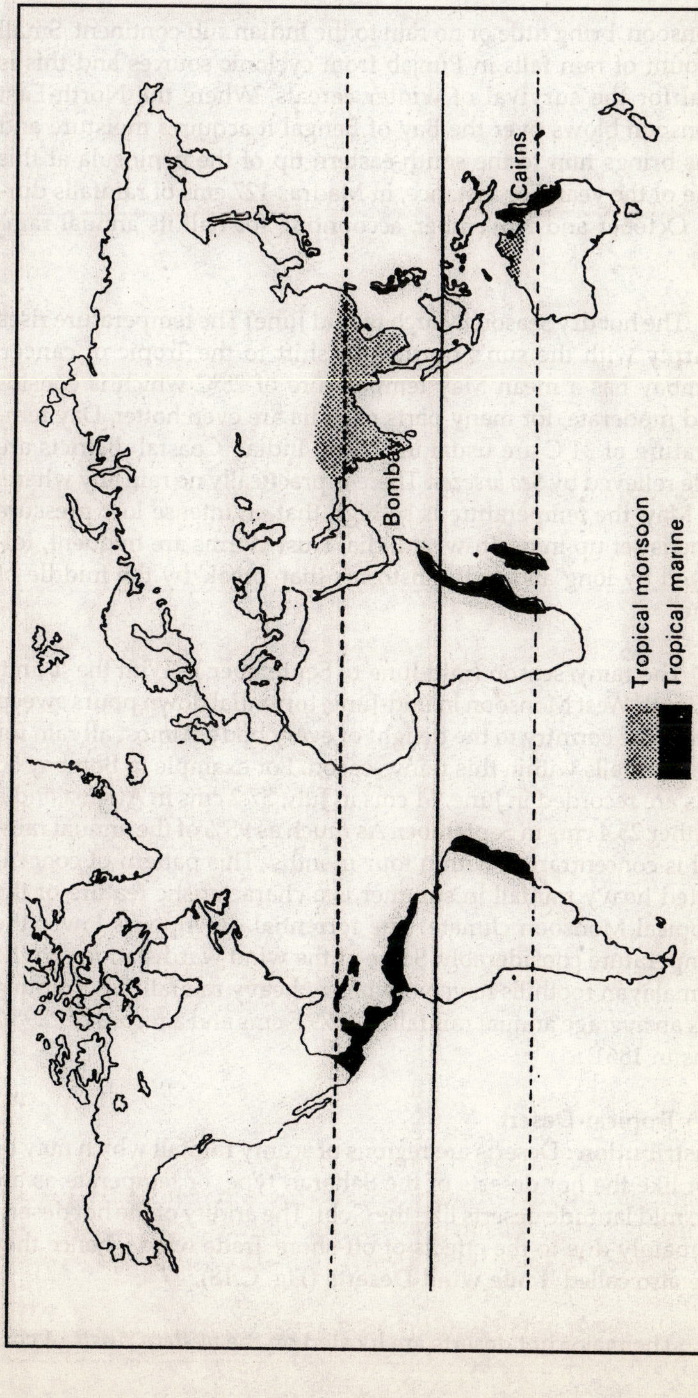

Fig. C,17 ***The tropical monsoon and marine regions***

Monsoon, bring little or no rain to the Indian sub-continent. Small amount of rain falls in Punjab from cyclonic sources and this is vital for the survival of winter cereals. Where the North-East Monsoon blows over the Bay of Bengal it acquires moisture and thus brings rain to the south-eastern tip of the peninsula at this time of the year. For instance, in Madras 127 cms of rainfalls during October and November, accounting for half its annual rainfall.

(b) The hot dry season (March to mid June) The temperature rises sharply with the sun's northward shift to the Tropic of cancer. Bombay has a mean May temperature of 28°C which is considered moderate, for many parts of India are even hotter. Day temperature of 31°C are usual in central India. Coastal districts are little relieved by *Sea breezes*. There is practically no rain any where. By May, the temperature is so high that an intense low pressure zone is set up in north-west India. Dust storms are frequent, followed by long awaited rainstorms that 'break' by the middle of June.

(c) The rainy, season (mid June to September):- With the **'burst'** of South West Monsoon in mid-June, torrential down pours sweep across the cormtry to the delight of every body. Almost all rain for the year falls within this rainy season. For example in Bombay 50 cms are recorded in June, 61 cms in July, 37.2 cms in August and a further 25.4 cms in September. As much as 95% of the annual rainfall is concentrarted within four months. This pattern of concentrated heavy rainfall in summer is a characteristic feature of the Tropical Monsoon climate. The torrential downpours lower the temperature considerably. Some of the wind ward stations on the Himalayan foothills have very heavy heavy rainfall. Cherrapunji has an average annual rainfall of 1079.5 cms and a record of 2298.7 cms in 1861.

(iii) **Tropical Desert**

Distribution : Deserts are regions of scanty rainfall which may be hot like the hot deserts of the Saharan type, or temperate as are the mid latitude deserts like the Gobi. The aridity of the hot deserts is mainly due to the effects of off-shore Trade winds, hence they are also called **Trade wind Deserts** (Fig. C.18).

The major hot deserts are located on the *western coasts* of con-

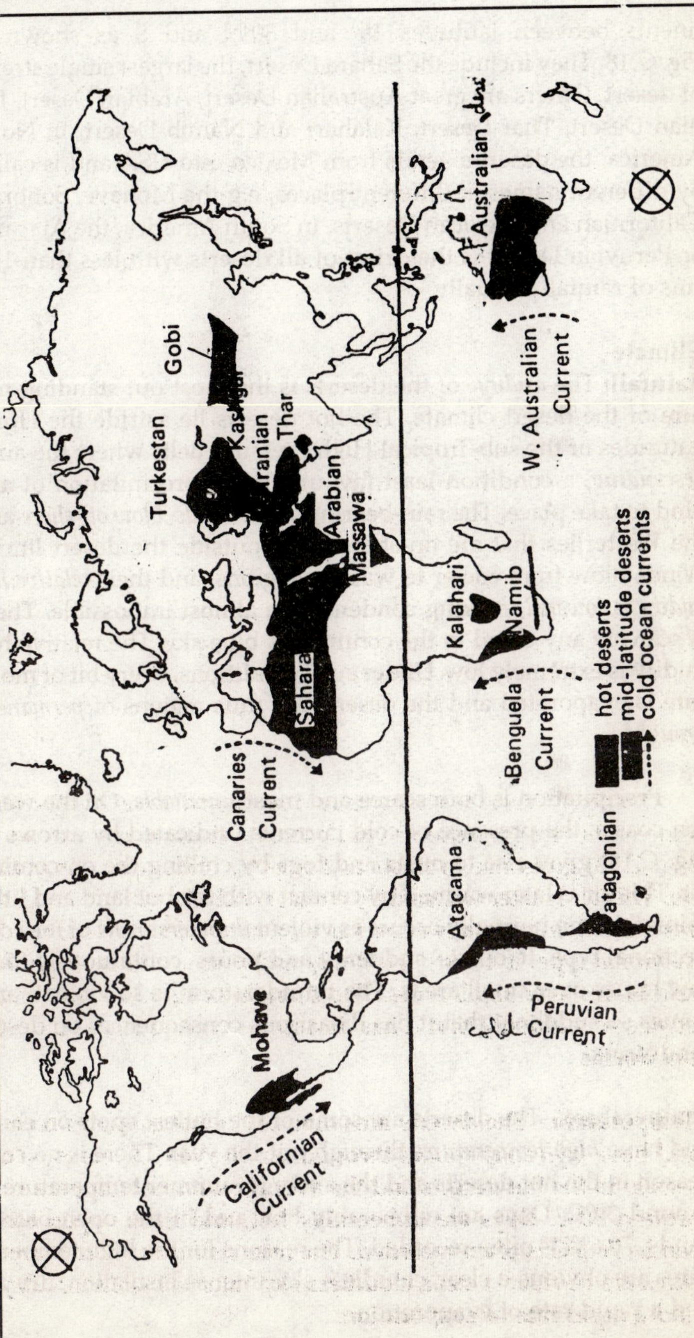

Fig. C.18 *The hot deserts and mid-latitude deserts of the world*

tinents between latitudes 15^0 and 30^{0}N and S as shown in Fig. C.18. They include the Sahara Desert, the largest single stretch of desert. Others are great Australian Desert, Arabian Desert, Iranian Desert, Thar Desert, Kalahari and Namib Desert. In North America, the desert extends from Mexico into USA and is called by different names at different places, e.g the Mohave, Sonoran, Californian and Mexican Deserts. In South America, the Atacama or Peruvian Desert is the driest of all deserts with less than 1.24 cms of rainfall annually.

Climate

Rainfall: The *aridity* of the deserts is the most out standing feature of the desert climate. The hot deserts lie astride the Horse Latitudes or the sub-Tropical High Pressure Belts where the air is *descending*, a condition least favourable for precipitation of any kind to take place. The rain-bearing *Trade winds blow off-shore* and the Westerlies that are on-shore blow outside the desert limits. Winds blow from cooler to warmer regions, and their *relative humidity* is *lowered*; making condensation almost impossible. There is scarcely any cloud in the continuous blue sky. The relative humidity is extremely low. Under such conditions, every bit of moisture is evaporated and the deserts are thus regions of *permanent drought*.

Precipitation is both scarce and most *unreliable*. On the western coasts, the presence of cold currents (indicated by arrows in Fig. C.18) gives rise to mists and fogs by chilling the on-coming air. This air is later warmed by contact with the hot land and little rainfalls. Rain normally occurs as violent *thunderstorms* of the convectional type. It 'bursts' suddenly and pours continuously for a few hours over small areas. The thunderstorm is so violent, and comes so suddenly that it has disastrous consequences on desert landforms.

Temperature:- The deserts are some of the hottest spots on earth and have *high temperatures* through out the year. There is no cold season in the hot deserts and the average summer temperature is around 30^{0}C. Days are unbearably hot, and in the open barren sands, 76.6^{0}C is often recorded. The reasons for the high temperatures are obvious-a clear, cloudless sky, intense insolation, dry air and a rapid rate of evaporation.

Coastal deserts by virtue of their maritime influence and the cooling effect of the cold currents have much *lower temperatures.*

The *desert interiors* however experience much higher summer temperatures and the winter months are rather cold.

The *diurnal range* of temperature in the deserts is *very great.* In tense insolation by day in a region of dry air and no clouds causes the temperature to rise with the sun. The barren ground is so intensely heated that, by noon, particularly in summer, a reading of 48°C is common. But as soon as the sun sets, the land loses heat very quickly by *radiation,* and the mercury column in the thermometer drops to well below the mean temperature. *Frosts* may occur at night in winter. These extremes of temperature make desert living most trying.

Mediterranean Climate

Distribution: The mediterranean climate is found entirely on the western portion of continental masses, between 30° and 45° north and south of the equator (Fig. C.19). The basic cause of this type of climate is the **shifting of the wind belts.** Though the area around the mediterranean Sea has the greatest extent of this type of 'winter rain climate' and gives rise to the more popular name mediterranean Climate, the best developed form of this peculiar climatic type is found in central chile-Other regions are California, the south-western tip of Africa, southern Australia and south-west Australia.

Climate

This climate is characterised by very distinctive climatic features.

(a) **A dry, warm Summer with off-shore trades** : The summer months have a relatively high temperature (24°C in July in Rome and 21°C in January in Cape Town). In summer when the sun is over head at the Tropic of Cancer, the belt of influence of the westerlies is shifted a little polewards. Rain bearing winds are not likely to reach the Mediterranean lands. The prevailing *Trade winds are off-shore* and there is practically **no rain.** The air is dry, the heat is intense and the relative humidity is low. Days are excessively warm and in the interiors, *prolonged droughts* are common.

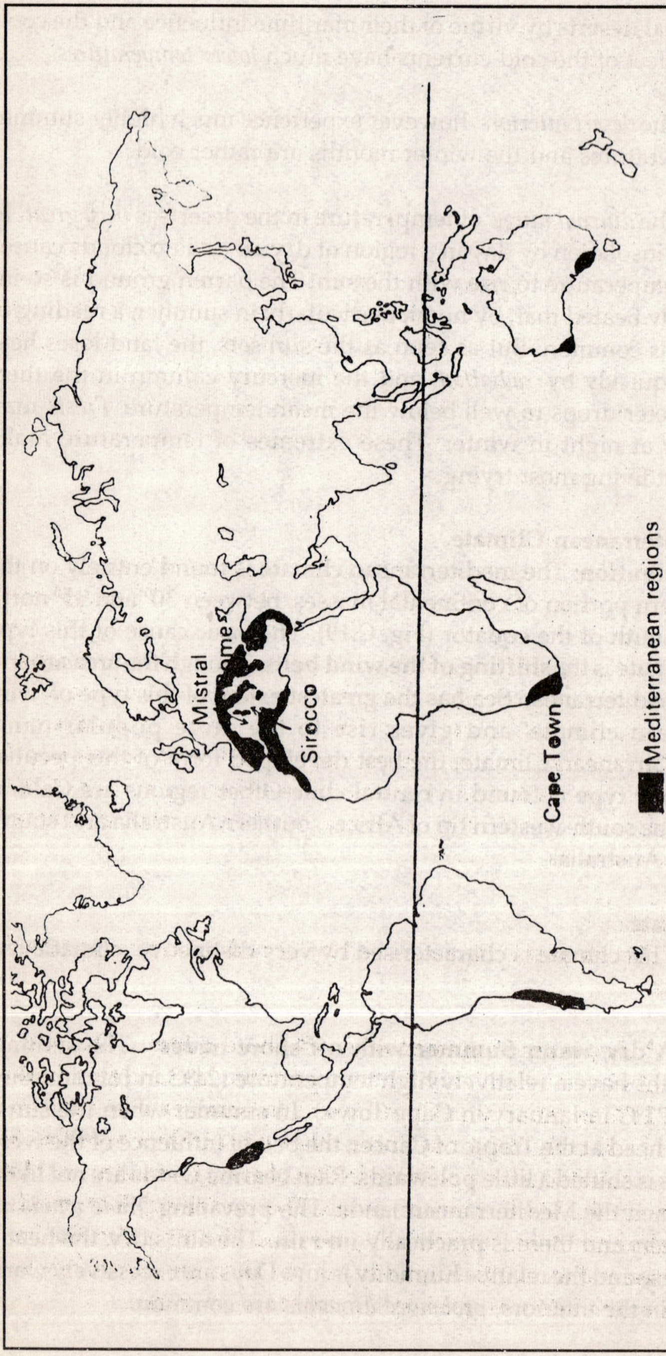

Fig. C.19 ***Regions with a Mediterranean Climate***

(b) **A concentration of rainfall in winter with on-shore westerlies**:- The Mediterranean lands receive most of their precipitation in *winter* when the Westerlies shift equator wards. In the northern hemisphere, the prevailing *on-shore westerlies* bring much cyclonic rain from the atlantic to the countries bordering the Mediterranean Sea. The rain comes in *heavy showers* and only on a few days with *bright sunny periods* between them. The Mediterranean regions are often backed by **mountains** of some kind. Much heavier precipitation has been recorded in the highlands on windward slopes facing the westerlies. The downpours are infrequent but are torrential with *floods*. **Snow** rarely occurs on lowlands and coastal districts and even if it does fall on highlands, it is moderate and is a source of water supply for hydroelectric power generation and for irrigation.

(c) **Bright, sunny weather with hot dry summers and wet, wild winters** : Considering its mid-latitude position, the mediterranean regions have a very favourable climate, unrivalled by any other climatic regions.

The sky is almost cloudless and *sunshine* **is always *abundant***. But even in mid-summer, the intense heat is never sultry. The combined effects of on-shore winds and the maritime breezes keep the temperature down to about 10ºC, in winter and not often exceeding 24ºC in summer.

(d) **The prominance of local winds around the Mediterranean Sea** : Many **local winds** some hot, others cold are common around the Mediterranean Sea. The *topography* of the region with the high Alps in north, the Sahara desert in south, continental interiors in the east and the open Atlantic on the west give rise to great differences in temperature, pressure and precipitation. The passing cyclones from the Atlantic, the anticyclones from the north and the cold masses from the continental interiors are often *interrupted or channelled* by relief features resulting in the birth of local winds around the Mediterranean. Fig. indicates the location and direction of some of these local winds and the more important ones are described below.

(i) **Sirocco**-This is a hot, dry dusty wind which originates in the Sahara Desert. It is most frequent in *spring* and normally lasts for only a few days. The Sirocco blows outwards in a southerly direction from the desert interiors into the cooler Mediterranean Sea. It is usually associated with depressions from the Atlantic passing from the coast eastwards inland. It is hot and dry with a temperature of 41°C. Its scorching breath withers vegetation and crops. The damage is particularly serious when it comes at the times during which vines and olives are in blossom. The Sirocco is so prominent that it is called by many other local names, such as *Chili* in Tunisia, *Ghibli* in Libya, *Khamsin* in Egypt and Malta.

(ii) **Mistral** -In contrast, the Mistral is a cold wind from the north, rushing down the Rhone valley in violent gusts. The velocity is intensified by the funnelling effect in the valley between the Alps and the Central Massif. In *Winter* when the Mistral is most frequent the temperature of the wind may be below freezing point, though the sky may be clear and cloudless. As a protective measure, many of the houses and orchards of the Rhone valley and the Riviera have thick rows of trees and hedges planted to shield them from the Mistral.

A similar type of cold north-easterly wind experienced along the Adriatic coast is called the **Bora**. It is caused by a difference in pressure between continental Europe and Mediterranean. This usually occur in *winter* when the atmospheric pressure over continental Europe is higher tham that of the Mediterranean Sea. This dry, icy wind is even more violent than Mistral.

Cool Temperate Climate
Distribution

Bordering the deserts, away from the Mediterranean regions and in the interiors of continents are the temperate lands. Though they lie in the westerly wind belt, they are remote from maritime influence. (Fig. C.20).

Climate

Temperature: Their location in the heart of the continents mean that they have little maritime influence.

Their climate is thus *continental* with *extremes of temperature*. Summers are warm, over 19°C. Winters are very cold in the continental Eurasia because of the enormous distances from the nearest sea. The winter months are well below freezing point. In contrast the climate in the *Southern hemisphere* is never severe. The

Fig. C.20 ***The Temperature Grasslands***

winters are so wild that the mean temperature for any of the winter months is usually between 2.5 and 12.8^{0}C. Temperatures below freezing point even in mid-winter (July in the southern hemisphere) are exceptional.

The *Annual range* of temperature is *great,* a direct result of continentality. Winters are so cold that parts of Eurasia are *snow-covered* for several months. The snow melts with the return of spring and by mid-summer temperatures soar to over 18.3^{0}C. It is really hot for its latitude.

Precipitation : In its continental position, the annual precipitation of this climate can be expected to be *light.* The average rainfall may be taken as about 50.8 cms, but this again varies according to location from 25.4 cms to 76.2 cms. The heaviest rain comes in the middle of the year with 78.7 cms each in June and July. Most of the winter months have about few cms of rainfall, brought by the occasional *depressions* of the westerlies and coming in the form of snow. In many other continental stations, the annual precipitation is even less, though the general pattern remains the same with most of the rain falling in the summer.

The southern hemisphere is even better brought out by the *rainfall regime,* Its annual precipitation is always more than the average 50.8 cms because of the *warm Ocean currents* that wash the shores. The westtest months are November, December, January and February, the summer season of southern hemisphere. There are three months (June, July and August) without any rain. This is the period of *drought.*

On the eastern slopes of the Rockies in Canada and USA, a local wind, similar to the Fohn in Switzerland, called the *Chinook,* comes in a south westerly direction to the Prairies and has a considerable effect on the local pastures. It actually comes with the depressions in *winter or early spring* from the Pacific coast as cending the Rockies and then descending to Prairies. It is a hot wind and may raise the temperature by 4.5^{0}C within a matter of 20 minutes. It melts the snow-covered pastures and animals can be driven out of doors to graze in the open fields. The agricultural year is thus accelerated. Local farmers welcome the Chinook for frequent chinooks mean mild winters.

Cool Temperate Western Margin (British Type) Climate

Distribution :- The cool temperate western margins are under the permanent influence of the westerlies all round the year. They are also regions of much *cyclonic activity*, typical of Britain and are thus said to experience the British type of climate. From Britain, the climatic belt stretches far inland into the lowlands of North-West Europe, including such regions as northern and western France, Belgium, Netherlands, Denmark, western Norway and also north western Iberia. There is so much oceanic influence on both the temperature and the precipitation that the climate is also referred to as the **North-West European Maritime Climate**.

In the *Southern hemisphere*, the climate is experienced in southern Chile, Tasmania and most parts of New Zealand, particularly in South Island. (Fig. C.21).

Climate

Temperature: The mean annual temperatures are usually between 4.5⁰C and 15.6⁰C. *Summers* are, in fact, never very warm. Monthly temperatures of over 18.3⁰C even in mid-summer are rare. 'Heat waves', as they are popularly called (that is a short spell of warm summer days) are a welcome feature in such cool temperate latitudes, where people do not often see enough of the sun. *Winters* are abnormally mild, and no stations actually record mean January temperatures below freezing-point in north-western Europe. This is attributable to the warming effect of the warm North Atlantic Drift and the prevalence of the South-Westerlies. Night frosts do occur and snow falls in winter too. Sometimes, unusual *cold spells*, caused by the invasions of cold polar continental air from the interiors, may hit the western margins for a number of weeks. The climate of the maritime regions as a whole may be described as *equable* with moderately warm summers and fairly mild winters.

The oceanic influences not only keep the *winters very mild* but also keep the *summers cool*.

Precipitation: The British type of climate has adequate rainfall through out the year with a tendency towards a slight *winter or autumn maximum* from cyclonic sources. Since the rain-bearing winds come from the west, the western margins have the heaviest rainfall. The amount decreases eastwards with increasing dis-

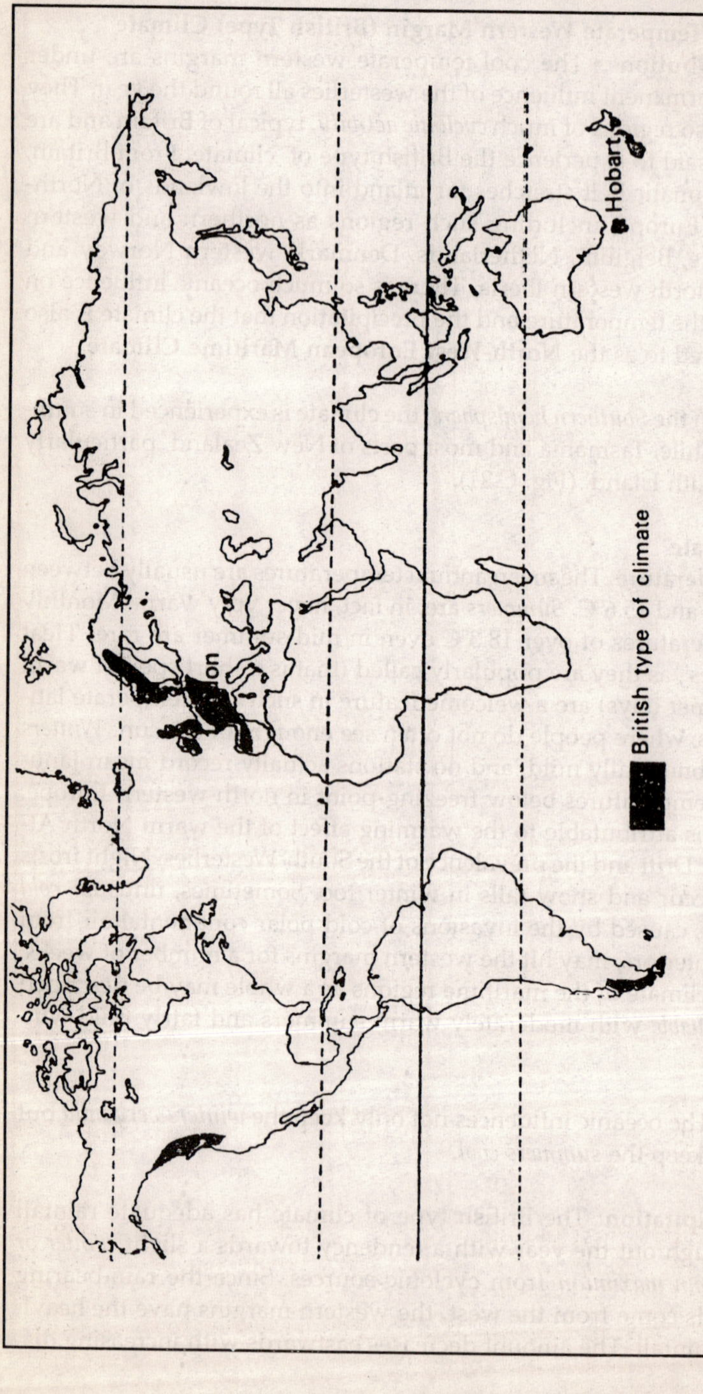

Fig. C.21 ***Regions with Cool Temperate Western margin Climate (British type)***

tance from the sea. **Relief** can make great differences in the annual amount. For example the western slopes of the southern Alps of South Island, New Zealand have as much as 500 cms of rainfall (Mainly orographic rain) whih the Canterbury Plain, in the *rain-shadow* area has as little as 63.5 cms.

As in other temperate regions there are four distinct *seasons* in the British climate type-Light snowfalls can be expected in the winter months normally only of short duration because of the comparatively mild weather. But over the highlands such as the Scandinavian Mountains and the American Rockies, snowfall is heavy and feeds the mountain glaciers that move down the valleys. Winter is the season of cloudy skies, foggy and misty mornings, and many rainy days from the passing depressions. Out on sea, gales are frequent and can be dangerous to shipping. Spring is the driest and the most refreshing season when people emerge from the depressing winter to see everything becoming green again. This is followed by the long, sunny **summer**. With the roar of gusty winds and the fall of 'golden' leaves, autumn is ushered in, and the cycle repeats itself.

Taiga

Distribution: The broad east-west spread of cool temperate continental (Siberian) climate is only experienced in the northern hemisphere. (Fig. C.22) On its poleward side, it merges into the Arctic **tundra** of canada and Eurasia at around the Arctic Circle. Southwards the climate becomes less severe and fades into the temperate *Steppe Climate*.

The predominant vegetation of this Siberian or 'sub-Arctic' type of climate is evergreen coniferous forests called '**taiga**'. In Europe the countries that have a similar type of climate are mainly in northern Europe, sweden and Finland. In North America, this climate stretches from Alaska across Canada into Labrador, and is found on the high Rocky Mountains farther south.

This type of climate is absent in southern hemisphere because of the *narrowness* of the southern continents in the high latitudes.

Climate

Temperature: The climate is characterized by a bitterly *cold winter* of long duration, and a *cool brief summer*. Spring and autumn are

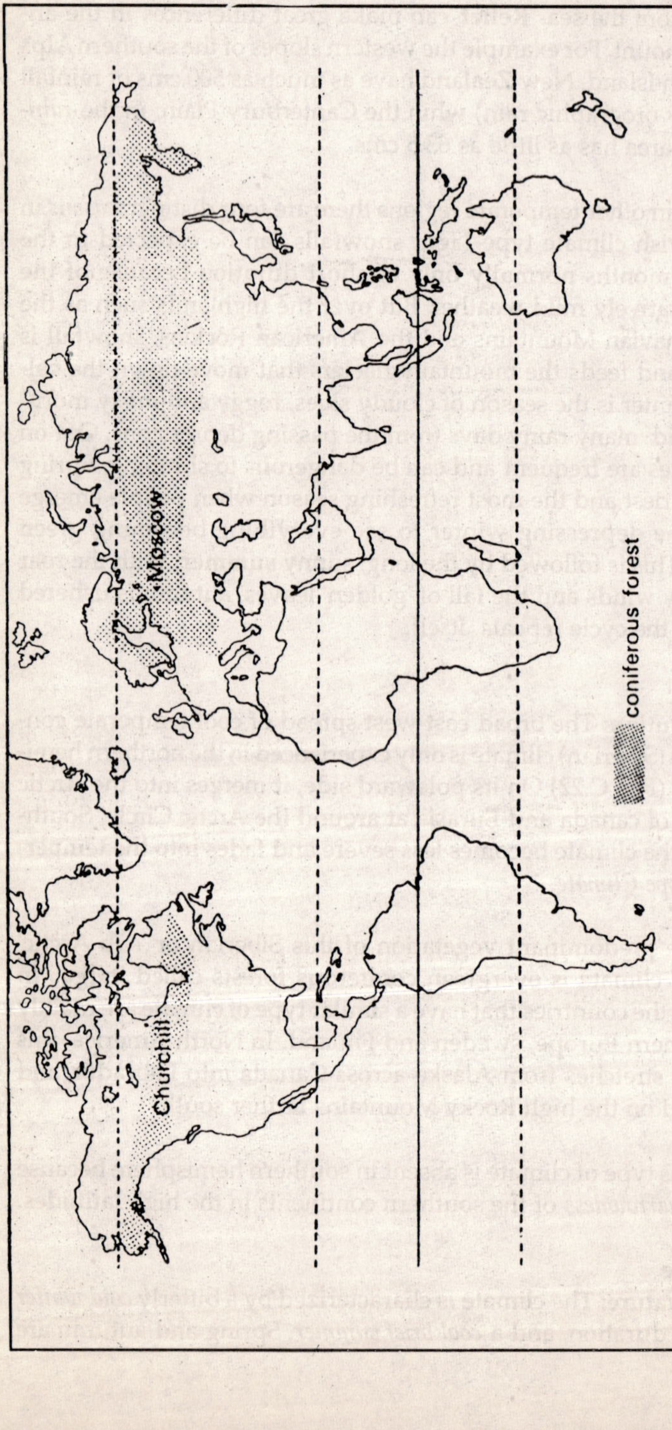

Fig. C.22 The cool temperate coniferous forest

merely brief transitional periods. The isotherm of 10°C for the warmest month forms the poleward boundary of the Siberian climate and the winter months are always below freezing. The coldest month in Moscow is January with-11°C. The warmest month (July) is as high as 19°C. With such low temperatures in the cold-season, *heavy snowfall* can be expected, Frosts occur as early as August and by September lakes and ponds are already ice-bound. All over Russia, nearly all the *rivers are frozen*.

Occasionally cold northerly polar winds such as the *blizzards* of Canada and *buran* of Eurasia blow violently at 50 m.p.h or more at a temperature of 10°C. The powdery snow-flakes are blown around in the lower atmosphere and stability is greatly reduced.

Precipitation: The interiors of the Eurasian continent are so remote from maritime influence that annual precipitaion cannot be high. Generally speaking, a total of 38 cms to 64 cms is typical of the annual precipitation of this sub-Arctic type of climate. It is quite well distributed through out the year with a *Summer maximum* from convectional rain when the continental interiors are greatly heated. In winter, the precipitation is in the form of snow, as mean temperatures are well below freezing all the times.

In a region where overall temperature is low, evaporation is not rapid and the relative humidity is high, this small amount of precipitation is adequate for tree-growth.

The total precipitation of the Siberian climate is determined by such factors as altitude, latitude, proximity to the poles, amount of exposure to influences by westerlies (on western parts of continents), temperate monsoons (on the eastern parts of continents) and the penetration of the *cyclones*.

European Russia usually has more than 50 cms of annual precipitation because of some on-coming westerlies and the periodic penetration of cyclones. Eastern Siberia also has over 50 cms. being moistered by the SE Monsoon from the Pacific Ocean. Central Siberia and Canada have about 35 cms due to their continentality and lack of sea influence. Polewards and southwards, the amount again decreases to only 25 cms or less.

Snow falls nearly every where in Russia in the long, cold winter. The amount varies from place to place. Permanent snowfields like those of the Alps or the Himalayas, are absent, because any accumulation of snow is melted with the return of spring and the warm summer. Frozen rivers are thawed, causing a rise in the water level and extensive floods occur. Snow is a poor conductor of heat and protects the ground from the severe cold above, which may be as much as-1.11^0 to 10^{0}C colder.

Tundra Climate

Distribution: The polar type of climate and vegetation is found mainly north of the Arctic Circle in the northern hemisphere. The ice-caps are confined to Greenland and to the highlands of these high latitude regions, where the ground is permanently snow-covered. The lowlands, with a few months ice-free, have tundra vegetation. They include the coastal strip of Greenland, the barren grounds of northern Canada and Alaska and the Arctic seaboard of Eurasia (Fig. C.23). In the southern hemisphere, the virtually uninhabited continent of Antarctica is the greatest single stretch of ice-cap where the layers of permanent ice are as thick as 3048 metres.

Climate

Temperature : The polar climate is characterized by a *very low mean annual temperature* and its warmest month in June seldom rises to more than 10^{0}C . In mid-winter (January) temperatures are as low as-37^{0}C and much colder in the interior. Normally not more than four months have temperatures above freezing point. *Winters* are long and very severe; Summers are cool and brief.

Within the Arctic and Antarctic Circles, there are weeks of continuous darkness. At the North Pole, there are six months without light in winter. Despite the long duration of sunshine in summer, when the sun does not set, temperatures remain low because the sun is low in the sky and much of the warmth of its faint rays is either reflected by the ground snow, or used up in melting, the ice. It has little power left to raise the air temperature. Water in the soil is frozen to great depths and the summer heat can only than the upper 15 cms of the soil. The ground remains solidly frozen for all but four months, in accessible to plants. *Frost* occurs at any time and *blizzards*, reaching a velocity of 200 km/hr are not frequent. They can be very hazardous for the polar inhabitants. In coastal districts, where warmer water meets cold land thick fogs

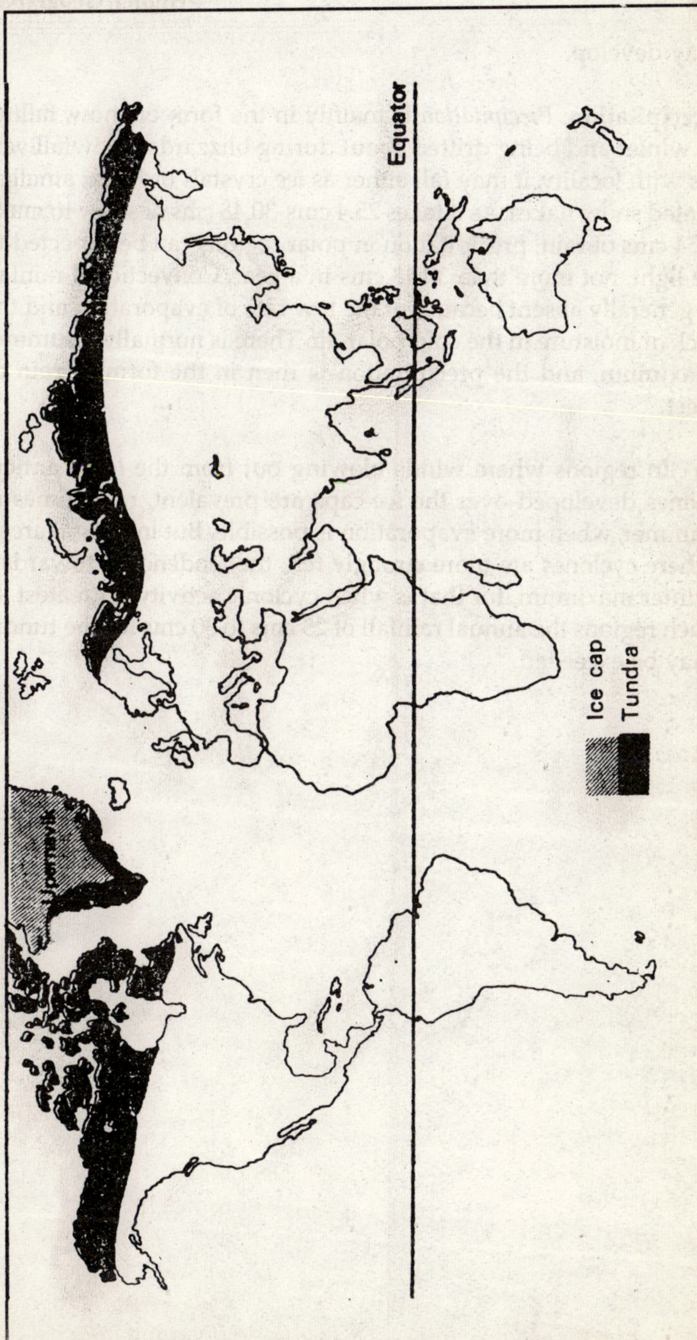

Fig. C.23 *Ice Cap and Tundra*

may develop.

Precipitation: *Precipitation* is mainly in the form of snow, falling in winter and being drifted about during blizzards. Snowfall varies with locality, it may fall either as ice crystals or large, amalgamated snow flakes. As it takes 25.4 cms-30.48 cms of snow to make 2.54 cms of rain, precipitation in polar regions can be expected to be light, not more than 30.48 cms in a year. Convectional rainfall is generally absent because of the low rate of evaporation and the lack of moisture in the cold polar air. There is normally a summer maximum, and the precipitation is then in the form of rain or sleet.

In regions where winds blowing out from the large anticyclones developed over the ice-caps are prevalent, rain comes in summer, when more evaporation is possible. But in coastal areas, where cyclones are more strongly felt, the tendency is towards a winter maximum, for that is when cyclonic activity is greatest. In such regions the annual rainfall of 25 cms to 30 cms for the tundra may be exceeded.

4

Vegetation and Soils

The soil is a very important element of the environment. The study of soil geography is called Pedalogy. Soil is a dynamic layer because in the soil complex activities are going on. A soil is made up of three substances i.e solid, liquid and the gas. The physical properties of soil are-

a) Soil texture
b) Soil structure
c) Porosity and weight of soil
d) Soil colour
e) Soil temperature.

It is the **colour** we first notice. This colour is due to the mineral salts and humus present in the soil. The color varies from white to brown. This gradual changing is due to the increasing humus content in the soil.

The relative size of the soil particles is expressed by the term **texture**. If refer to the fineness or coarseness of the soil.

The term texture is used in reference to the size of soil particles (Fig. D.1) but when the arrangement of the particles is being considered, the term **structure** is used.

That portion of a given volume of soil which is unfilled with solid matter is termed **pore space**. The proportion of a soil occupied by pore space depends on both the texture and structure of the soil and on the shape of the particles. A high content of organic matter leads to much pore space.

The amount of pore space in a soil is expressed as a percentage of the total soils volume. The term **porosity** refers to the total pore space in a soil rather than to the size of the individual pores.

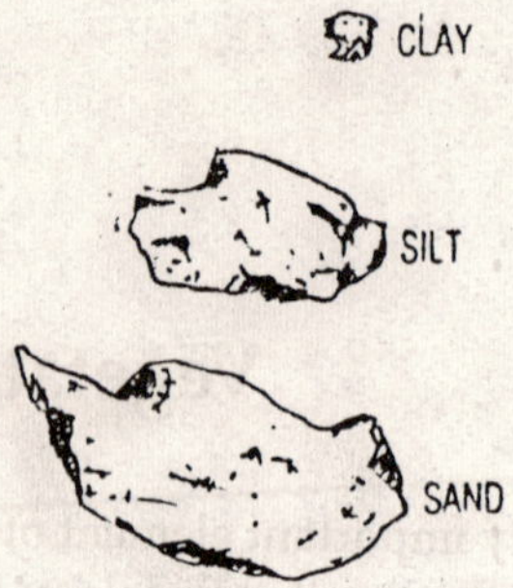

Fig. D.1 *Relative sizes of major soil particles*

The amount of pore space in a given volume of soil greatly influences its **weight**.

As **temperature** decrease, the life processes of both plants and animals are slowed down until finally they cease together. Man must depend, on the sun to warm the soil sufficiently to enable crops to grow.

Formation of Soil

There are five important factors for the development of soil formation. They are-

(a) Parent material
(b) Land form
(c) Time factor
(d) Climate
(e) Biological activity.

Parent Material or the parent rock is a passive former. The bulk of the soil is made up of the weathered materials of the parent rock. It is generally the parent rock along with climate which determines the type of soil. There were many variations in the original rocks from which soils were derived. Igneous, sedimentary and metamorphic rocks all served as sources, and within these broad groups there are, of course, many differences in composition, structure and ears of decomposition.

Land Form- Another passive former is *land form.* Wherever the slope is steep, run off and erosion is more rapaid, the soil will be thinner on the steep slope. Flat lowlands have thick deposition of soils but they are poorly drained. Here constant saturation retards decay of vegetation and allows organic matters to accumulate. Gentle slopes, where drainage is good but erosion is slow are the ideal places for soil formation.

Time- A question which has many interesting aspects, is, "How much time is required to form an inch of soil or for a soil to develop?" For development from hard rock, the time may be very great. On the other hand, development can proceed rapidly in permeable, unconsolidated parent material in a warm and humid climate. Aridity and the rapid removal of soil by erosion on steep slopes can delay or prevent the development of mature soils. It becomes clear than that the rate of development varies greatly from one soil to another. Conditions that hasten the rate of soil development are warm, humid climate; forest vegetation, permeable, unconsolidated parent material low in lime content; and flat or depressional topography. A soil is said to become mature when it has been acted upon by all soil forming processes for a sufficiently long time to have developed a profile that hardly changes with the passage of time. In young soils the horizons are absent or poorly developed. No age in terms of years can be given to all matured soils because its development depends on many factors.

Climate : *Climate* is the most important active soil former (Fig. D.2) Climate determines the relative rates of activity of the different forces of weathering and soil formation. It also limits the extent to which soil development proceeds. In arid regions, for example, the lack of water has prevented soil development from progressing much beyond the physical disintegration of the materials.

With icreasing moisture content, chemical changes assume a more important role. An excess of precipitation however tends to leach the soil. In warm climate where rainfall is extremely heavy, silica is largely removed from the soil and carried off in streams. This process is termed as **desilication** which makes the soil infertile. In dry climates ground water is brought to the surface by capillary action and evaporates leaving behind the salts that was dissolved in the water. Climate also plays a major role in determining the distribution of different kinds of vegetation.

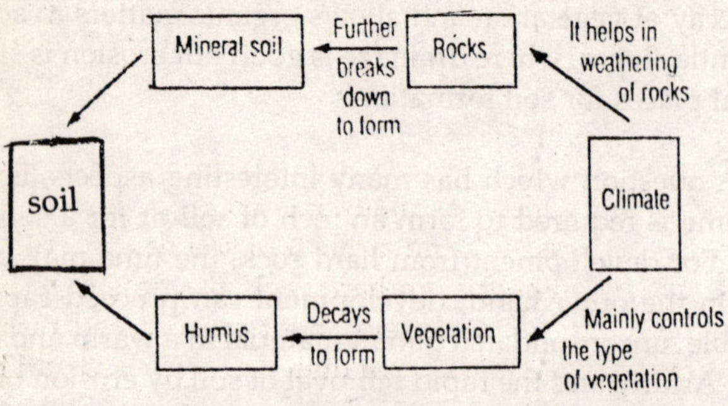

Fig. D.2 ***Effect of climate on soil formation***

Biological Activities and Soil Development:- Both plants and animals profoundly influence the formation of soil. In the very early stages of mineral decomposition and soil formation the lower forms of plant life, such as lichens, fungi, and bacteria, undoubtedly played a major role. The ability of certain bacterial forms to extract nitrogen from the air for their own body needs, unquestionably played a considerable part in the building up of nitrogenous organic material in the soil in the early stages of development. It is through the action of such organisms that plant and animal remains are decayed, thus liberating the nutrients contained for the use of the next plant generation and producing Co_2 and complex organic compounds which aid in mineral decomposition.

Higher plants, such as grass and trees also exert a great influence on soil development. The absorption of soluble nutrients from the soil and their return in plant parts, even the variation in chemical composition of leaves of different species, are important in their effects on soil development. Roots, particularly small ones, penetrate crevices in rock fragments, enlarging them and sometimes splitting the rock as growth continues. The number of pores in the soil is also increased as the result of root growth dead plants provide humus which is the organic matter of the soil.

Worms, insects and other small animals play a greater part also. The continuous burrowing of worms and insects establishes drainage channels in the soil and also brings large quantities of soil from the lower horizons to the surface. Many insects consume plant material both on the surface and within the soil. Worms are active in dragging fragments of leaves and grass into the soil to become a part of the soil organic matter. Rabits, moles, prairie dogs, ground squirrels, beavers, rats etc. are amongst the largest modifiers of the soils.

Soil Types

For a critical analysis of an agricultural conditions in India a study of soils in the country becomes essential.

Considering the process of formation, soils of India can be divided into two main kinds -

(a) Soils of Peninsular India

(b) Soils of Indo-gengetic lowland.

(a) Soils of peninsular India are the soils which have been formed by the decomposition of rocks in *Situ* (original place) and these soils through the action of rivers and rains have been transported and re-deposited only to a limited extent. These are also called residual soils. On the other hand (b) Soils of Indo-gangetic lowlands are entirely transported soils, brought down mostly from the Himalayas by great river, that drain them and have been deposited as sedimentary alluvium. A much smaller part is due to the rivers draining north form Peninsular.

The *residual soils* or *zonal soils* are black soil, red soil, laterite soil and saline and alkaline soils.

The *transported* or *azonal soil* include the alluvium soil, sandy soil and forest soils of the Himalayas. They are deep and very fertile.

Alluvial Soils:- It is by far the largest and the most important soil group of India contributing the largest share to the country's agricultural production. It covers about 24% of the total land surface. The entire great plain from Punjab to Assam in the valley's of Peninsular India in the eastern coastal plain and in Kerela the alluvium soil is found. Along the coast of Kerela it is known as coastal alluvium and in the deltas of eastern coastal plain as deltaic alluvium. Geologically it is divided into newer alluvium and older alluvium.

Newer alluvium is called (1) *Khadar*. It is finer and is sandy, loamy and clayey in texture and is acidic in reaction. The soil is deficient in lime, phosphoric acid and humus. It occurs in the deltas and flood plains. (2) *Bhangar* They are found in alluvium terraces of about 30 meters in height above the flood level. They are clayey in composition, coarse and dark in colour. The soil is full of lime nodules called 'Kankar'.

The foothills of the Himalayas is compsed of coarsed often pebbly soils called (3) *Bhabar*-This is made up of coarse alluvium soils and through the pebbles the water will percolate down. So the soil is unsuitable for cultivation.

To its south occurs the swampy lowland with silty soils known as (4) *Terai*- This soil has a poor drainge pattern and is marshy in nature. The alluvium soil from Bihar to Assam is to some extent leached due to heavy rainfall. Hence the lime content is low.

The fertility of the alluvium soil is due to its high mineral content rather than the presence of humus. *Secondly*, these soils are composed of minerals drawn from different rocks and therefore content a great variety of mineral salts. *Thirdly*, these soils are very fine grained, porous and light in nature. That is why they are easily tilt and are regarded as the best agricultural soils of the country.

Inspite of the positive aspects, these soils are also defective in few respects. They allow water to sink into the ground making it unsuitable for those crops which require retention of water. Secondly, they are *deficient* in *humus* and *nitrogen* contents. This needs heavy *fertilisation* particularly with nitrogenous fertilizers. These soils are suitable for the cultivation of all types of crops.

(ii) **Black Soils**:- These soils are black in *colour* and are ideal for cotton cultivation. They are also called as 'regur' soil. These soils are developed over deccan lavas. Granites and basaltic rocks have been weathered into black cotton soil under semi-arid conditions. They are found in Maharashtra and Gujrat, Parts of Madhya Pradesh, Andhra Pradesh, Tamil Nadu, Karnataka, Uttar Pradesh and Rajasthan. These soils vary in colour from deep black to light black to chestnut in colour. The black colour is due to the presence of compounds of iron and magnesium. These soils are deficient in nitrogen and humus but rich in lime and potash. The *texture* is fine grained. These soils are highly retentive of moisture. They become sticky when wet and develop deep white cracks on drying. The cracks are often 12 cm to 50 cm in width and upto a metre in depth. This helps in the process of self aeration and absorption of Nitrogen. These soils are endowed with inexustable *fertility* and have known to have supported agriculture for centuries. The crops grown here are cotton, wheat, sugarcane, jowar, tobacco, bajra, ground nut and ragi.

(iii) **Red Soils**:- It is found in the whole of Tamil Nadu, parts of Karnataka, Maharashtra, Andhra Pradesh, Orissa, Chota Nagpur, Western part of West Bengal and in parts of N.E. hilly states. The granite and gneiss on weathering has given rise to red soil. The *Colour* is due to the presence of iron. It lacks in lime, free of carbonate and has the presence of soluble salts in a very small quantity. The soil though *deficient* in *Nitrogen* and *organic matter* contains magnesium, iron and aluminium compounds. With the application of fertilizers in proper proportions it iron exceptionally productive soil from agricultural point of view. On the uplands it is thin and poor in quality, sandy or stony and are used for the *Cultivation* of millets. On lowlands they are deep in *colour* and fertile loams on which under irrigation excellent crops like cotton, wheat, linseed, pulses, millets and tobacco are produced.

(iv) **Laterite and Lateritic Soils**:- They are especially well developed on the *summits* of hills of the Deccan, Madhya Pradesh, Rajmahal Hills, Eastern ghats, certain parts of Orissa, Assam, Karnataka and Malabar. It is found in regins of more than 200 cm of *rainfall* which promotes leaching of soil and alternating dry and wet periods. Laterite is a perro-genous aluminous rock occasionally having titamium. It is deficient in Nitrogen, lime, potash, phosphoric acid, magnesium and humus. The distinguishing peculiarity of the soil is its acidity and the main agricultural problem is the correction of this acidity. Tea, Cinchona, rubber and coffee are groud on such soils. Though the soil has *low-fertility* but responds readily to manuring and good cultivation. With the help of irrigation and manuring this type of soil can be utilised for garden lands.

(v) **Desert Soils**: This soil is formed under arid and semiarid conditions. It covers the thar desert, south Haryana, south Punjab and Rann of Kutch. The sand is derived from the *weathering* of the *surface rocks* and is also largely blown in from the coastal regions and Indus valley. The soil is brown in *colour*, coarse and very porous. It cannot retain water. It contains *high percentage of soluble salts* and lacks in humus and nitrogen. This type of soil may be reclaimed if irrigation is available, Maize millets and cotton are cultivated with the help of irrigation.

(vi) **Forest Soils**: They occupy the Himalayas and other hill tracks of the country. They are young and immature in nature but coarse in *texture* and have shallow *depths*. The forest soils are very rich in humus and deficient in potash and lime. *Need fertilization* for good yield. Tea, Coffee, spices and tropical fruits are grown here. In western Himalayas temperate fruits, maize, wheat are barley are also raised.

(vii) **Saline and Alkaline Soils**: These soils are found in some parts of Uttar Pradesh, Bihar, Haryana, Punjab, Maharashtra, Sundarban region of West Bengal and coastal Orissa. In places of canal irrigation in Punjab, Haryana and Uttar Pradesh, due to *Capillary Transference* of salt solution of lower layers of under ground water has made the top soil saline. As the injurious soils are confined to the top layers of the soils it becomes *infertile* and unfit for cultivation. Such saline soils are called '*reah*', '*Kallar*' and '*Usar*' in Uttar Pradesh, Punjab and Haryana. These are actually cultivable waste lands in Sundarbans of west Bengal and in Mahanadi delta the tide washed coast has turned the soil saline in nature.

Alkaline soils are found all over the state of Maharashta around gulf of Kutch in Gujrat, some parts of estuaries of Narmada, Tapti, Mahi and Sabarmati, Portions of Dharwar district and Bijapur.

Soil Profile

A *Soil profile* is a display of vertical section from the ground surface down to the parent rocks. Thus a soil profile denotes the vertical distribution of soil components (e.g the living organisms-flora and fauna-and organic matter, the inorganic minerals, the soil solution and the attributes of soil atmosphere) and various associations of the properties of these components.

The *layers* in a soil profile characterized by distinctive characteristics of physical and chemical composition, organic content, structure, etc. are called soil horizons. The characteristics of one horizon differ from the characteristics of the other horizon of a given soil profile. Different *soil horizons* of a given soil profile having distinctive characteristics are developed vegetation, animals and reliefs of a particular area over a long period of time.

The soil horizons of soil profiles are basically divided into two broad categories e.g (i) **Organic Horizons** (indicated by letter O) and (ii) **Mineral Horizons**.

(i) **Organic Horizons** are the topmost layers of a soil profile and these contain organic matter whether dead or alive. The decomposed organic matter is called **Humus**.

(ii) **Mineral Horizons** Contain inorganic minerals. Besides, the upper layers also contain some limited amount of organic matter. This mineral horizon is again divided into three layer horizons and are designated by capital letters A, B, C and D. The A layer is composed of undercomposed litter of twigs and plant leaves. This layer show some degree of leaching or *eluviation.*

The layer of accumulation or *illuviation* is technically designated as the 'B' layer.

The parent material is referred to as the C layer and underlying strata (such as bed rock) are called the D horizon. The layers A and B together constitute the *solum.*

The horizon/layer A is again sub-divided into five divisons.

A_{00}-undecomposed litter of twigs and plant leaves.
A_0- partially decomposed organic matter
A_1- Predominance of mineral particles and organic residues.
A_2- Shows maximum effects of leaching.

The layer 'B' is sub-divided into B_1, B_2, and B_3 sections, depending on the degree of accumulation in evidence.

All these horizons are not present in every soil. **Horizons of a Generalised Soil** Pro.ile (D.3).

Podsol Soil is a very matured soil and is found in the temperate

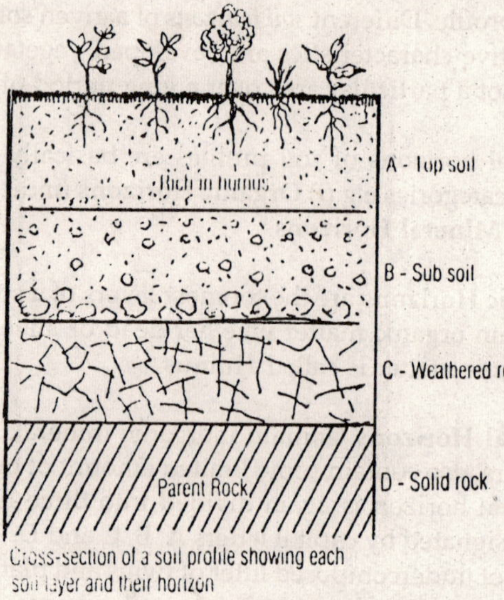

Fig. D.3 ***Soil Profile***

regions of the world . This soil exhibits acid humus and leaf mould. Below the A_0 horizon, A_1 is visible which is thin, compact and very fine in texture. The *Colour* ranges from grey to brown to reddish brown and is extremely *rich in humus* A_2 soil layer is heavily leached. Thus the materials are percolated down to B layer.

In this 'B' layer the leached minerals come and accumulate. This often forms the hard pan and the 'C' layer of podsol is the *Parent rock*.

Lateritic soil is the typical soil in the humid tropical and equatorial region of the world. The parent rock layer is mechanically weathered or it has undergones chemical decomposition.

The A_1 layer is yellowish-red to dark red sandy loam. It consists of moderate medium subangular blocky structure; slightly hard and very friable. It has a gradual smooth boundary.

B_1 is yellowish-red to dark red sandy loam. It is slightly hard, friable and slightly sricky in nature. Many fine and medium roots are there. B_2 has yellowish red to red sandy clay loam. Moderate medium subangular blocky structure, slightly hard, friable and slightly plastic in nature. It consists of many fine and medium roots.

B_3 has gravelly loam; massive; hard, friable, sticky and plastic. Iron-manganese concretions are present.

C layer has hard, gravelly laterite.

Alluvial soil is a transported soil. Thus it never gets the time for a soil profile to form.

Soil Erosion

Soil erosion is a comprehensive natural process of detachment and removal of loosened rock materials and soils by different processes such as running water, ground water, sea waves, wind, glacier etc. The eroded materials are then deposited in valleys and alluvial plains. Erosion caused by natural processes without being interfered by human activities is also called as **Geological Erosion. Acceleratcd Erosion** refers to the increased rate of erosion caused by various land use changes effected by man. Thus *soil Erosion* normally means accelerated erosion which is al called as *Man Induced Erosion* because of greater impact of h an activities than natural factors on soil erosion.

Causes of Soil Erosion

There are different causes of soil erosion. They are as follows:-

(a) **Splash erosion**: It is the scatkring of detached soil particles by the impact of raindrops. On sloping land, splash may cause considerable soil movement.

(b) **Sheet erosion** : (Fig. D.4) is the removal by rain of a very thin layer of soil from the entire surface of somewhat large area. Muddy runoff from the field is an indication of sheet erosion. It is found in Rajasthan region.

(c) **Gully erosion** : is the fromation of wide and deep channels from small channels all over the field along the water course. The gullies, usually V-shaped or U-shaped, are formed by channel erosion on sloping land. These may be seen in a roughly triangular

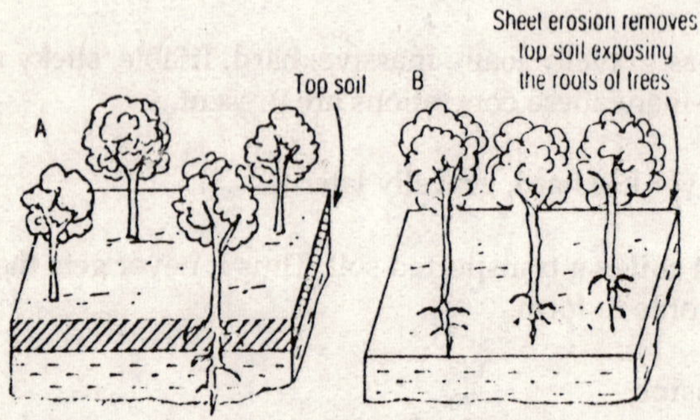

Fig. D.4 *Sheet erosion*

area formed by lives joining Mathura, Allahabad, Bhilwara, particularly along the Chambal, Jamuna, Betwa, Banas river.

(d) **Wind erosion** is the loss of soil by the action of wind. In the northern plains of India and the desert, there is a continuous period of strong dusty winds (locally called 'loo') from late March to later May or early June. These winds are most effective in soil erosion. Wind erosion is probably the highest in and around Rajasthan. The adjoining parts Punjab, Haryana, Malwa and Gujral come next.

(e) **Accelerated soil erosion** : takes place when the ecosystem is disturbed, the balance between soil development and soil removal is greatly upset and the rate of removal is faster than that of formation. In deforestation soil erosion is accelerated. There are other types of soil erosion, broadly termed as mass wasting, viz-landslides, landslip etc. Hilly parts of India faces the above problems.

Problems of Salination due to Irrigation

The soluble salts that accumulate in soil consist principally of sodium, calcium and magnesium. In the humid and perhumid regions with adequate rainfall, most of the soluble salts which are formed under the process of rock weathering and soil formation are leached down either at some depth below the surface or into the ground water. *Soil salination* is quite common in the arid and semi arid regions having an annual rainfall of less than 55 cms. Incrustation of salts on the land surface occur extensively in the northern parts of India.

Fluctuating depth of ground water or the water table leads to salinity in soil. With excessive irrigation on a particular land, soluble salts move upward along with rise in the water table. The salts are left behind when the water table recedes and accumulate at varying depths below the soil surface. Upward movement of soluble salts already accumulated at some depth of soil also takes place similarly. The process of salination is *accelerated* by rapid evaporation from the surface. The higher the depth of water table, the higher is the rate of evaporation.

Irrigation water containing a high concentration of soluble salts, particularly sodium leads to *soil salinity*, if proper drainage is not provided to leach the salts beyond the root zone. The soils which have salt accumulation at certain depths below the surface may also lead to salinity in the depth of irrigation water which is inadequate to leach down the salts. Seepage from canal or irrigation channel may cause salinity. Soluble salts move along the see page water and are accumulated at the water front.

Salination due to the irrigation is quite common in the Indo-Ganga plains of Uttar Pradesh, Haryana and the Punjab.

Soil Conservation

As men are so dependent on the soil for the study of food, fuel and fibre, it is vital that great care should be taken to conserve, protect, renew and maintain soil fertility. All possible measures must be taken to fight the twin evils of soil impoverishment which is the loss of soil fertility due to repeated cultivation i.e overcropping, mono culture and soil erosion. The following farming practices such as those described below are the most important for preserving soil and for improving crop yields.

(1) **Contour ploughing** : If ploughing is done at right angles to the hill slope, following the natural contour of the hill, the ridges and furrous break the flow of the water down the hill. This prevents excessive soil erosion, as gullies are less likely to develop and also reduce run-off so that plants receive more water (Fig. D.5).

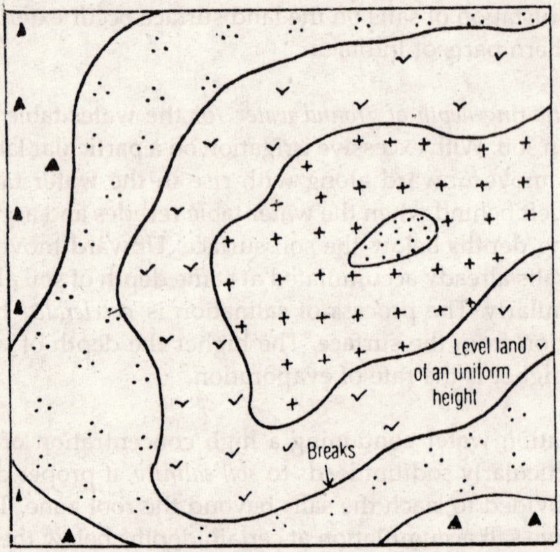

Fig. D.5 *Contour ploughing*

(2) **Terracing** : Slopes may be cut into a series of terraces with sufficient level ground on each terrace for cultivation, and an outer wall at the edge to retain the soil and to slow down the flow of rain-water down the slope (Fig. D.6) Terracing is widely used in Monsoon Asia for wet rice cultivation such as in West Bengal, Bihar, Orissa states of India, as the excess water and silt can be retained at each terrace to form flooded padi-fields.

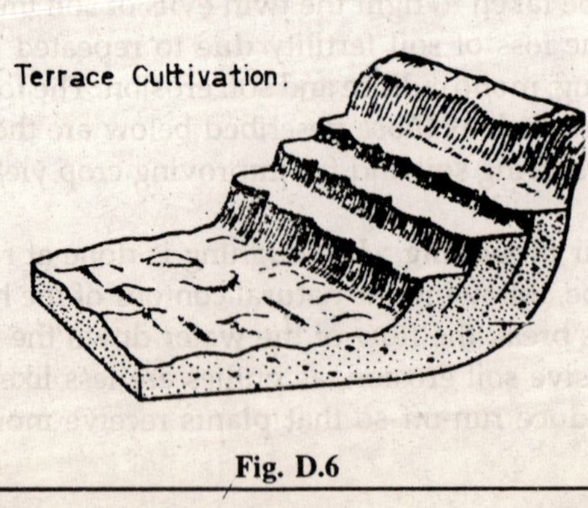

Fig. D.6

(3) **Strip Cropping** : Crops may be cultivated in alternate strips, parallel to one another. Some strips may be allowed to lie fallow while others are sown to different kinds of crops e.g grains, legumes, small tree crops. The various crops ripen at different times of the year and are harvested at intervals. (Fig. D.7).

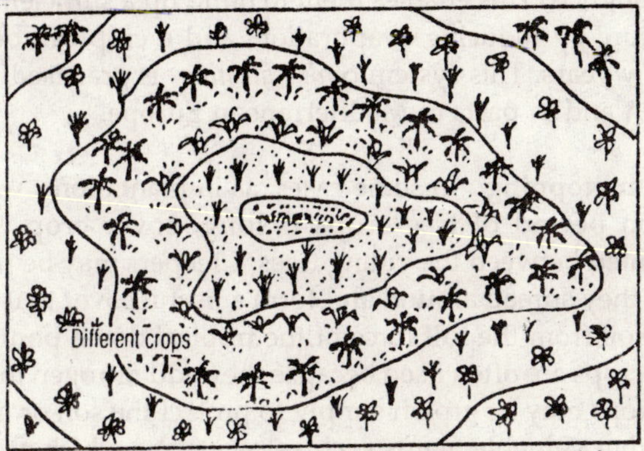

Different crops grown in the same contour belt, having varing growing time period

Fig. D.7 ***Strip cultivation***

(4) **Shelter belts** : Big trees which act as shelters to the crops from strong, gustly winds are planted to stop soil erosion. Winds getting obstructed by the big trees loose their capacity to erode fertile soils. (Fig. D.8).

Fig. D.8 ***Shelter belts***

(5) **Fallowing** : Sometimes it is important to allow much-used land to rest or lie fallow, so that the natural forces can act on the soil. The decayed natural vegetative matter helps to increase the

sub-soil moisture and improves the general structure of the soil. *Winter fallow* is commonly practised in temperate regions after the harvest, but cultivation is resumed in the spring after the snow and frost have weathered the top soil. In semi-arid areas fields may be allowed to lie fallow for several years, though they are often ploughed. This enables them to build up a sufficient supply of moisture by reducing evaporation, and a crop can be grown every few years. This system of *dry farming* is practised in Western U.S.A and in parts of Mediterranean Europe.

(6) **Cover cropping** : In some cases, as in plantations, where the gestation period of tree crops is long, cover crops may be interplanted between the young trees. Creepers may be preferred because they spread around and form a useful cover that protects the top soil from the full force of the tropical down pours. Leguminous crops are often used because they add nitrogen to the soil. Cover crops may be grown simply to protect the soil or may consist of other valuable plants such as vegetables which provide an income while the plantation crop matures.

(7) **Crop Rotation** : It is not advisable to grow the same crop in the same field for more than two years in succession as the crop will tend to exhaust one particular kind of mineral nutrient. Legumes such as peas, beans, clovers and many other plants, add nitrates to the soil by converting free nitrogen in the air into nitrogenous nodules on their roots. Crop rotation has several other advantages.

(a) **A varied range of crops** : is provided on the farm including cereals for bread-making, clover for animal feeding, barley for beer-making, and root crops as winter fodder for livestock.

(b) **Attack by insects and fungi is minimized** because different pests are associated with different crops.

(c) **Weeds are kept down** because there is no fallow period in a continuous four-year rotation of crops.

(d) **Many crops produce mineral residues at their root tips** which may be harmful to themselves but not to other crops. This is true of turnips, most cereals and even cloves. By varying the crops in the following year, this harmful effect can be eliminated and the next year's crops can be stimulated.

(8) **Crop Diversification** : This practice is often like crop rotation in that it helps to monitor soil fertility. Where annually-harvested crops are grown they can be alternated in the field. In particular it reduces the danger of depending on a single crop when world commodity prices are falling. Over-dependence on one crop can be disastrous to the national economy, as in the case of Malaysia's rubber, when prevailing prices for the major money-earning crop are low. Another great advantage of crop diversification is that all types of land can be used e.g rubber can be grown on hill slopes, oil palm on flat plains, coconuts on sandy soils.

(9) **Use of fertilizers** : Farmers all over the world have found that soils vary in their fertility and crop-bearing capability, because of the different proportions of mineral nutrients they contain. Continuous cultivation will exhaust some of the nutrients and soil fertility has to be maintained by the application of fertilizers. Organic manures such as animal dung, composed or decomposed vegetation usually provide a balanced supply of the major soil minerals. Chemical fertilizers e.g phosphates, potash, nitrates are among the common fertilizers in use today.

(10) **Water Management** : One of the major ways in which land can be improved for farming is by water management. By regulating the amount of water in the soil aeration can be improved, activity by useful bacteria can be stimulated and crop yield can be improved. In addition by draining or irrigating land, areas which are marginal or useles in their natural state, such as deserts or swamps, can be brought into agricultural production.

Natural Vegetation

Broadly speaking, the major climatic divisions have each their dominant type of vegetation. Within those divisions **rainfall** or more correctly available moisture is the first factor in the determination of major variations in the lowland vegetation; **soil**, which is iteslf largely a product of climatic conditions, determines local variations. (Fig. D.9). Even minor variations in rainfall are reflected so intimately in the vegetation that generalized descriptions are apt to convey entirely false impressions. For example, almost untouched ever green rain forests, actively exploited timber forests, dry scrublands and thorn-bush deserts are all equally characteristic of India alone.

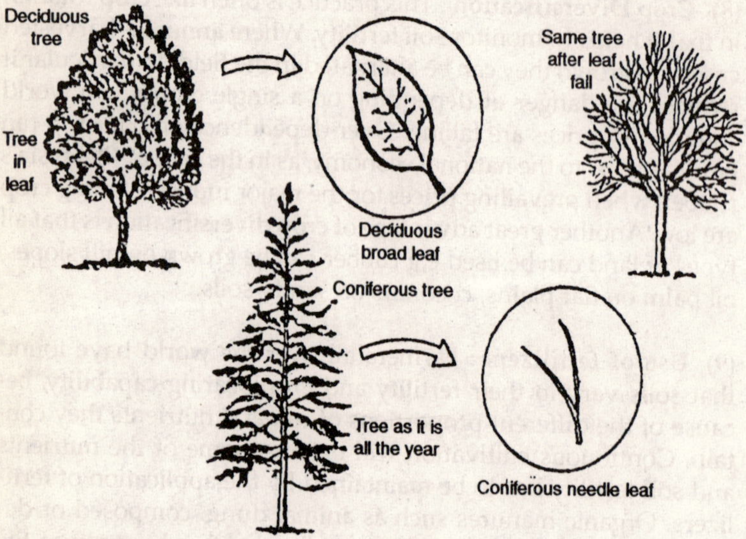

Fig. D.9 ***Comparison between Deciduous and coniferous Trees***

It will be convenient, therefore, to review briefly the natural vegetation of a country (Fig. D.10) Keeping in mind the climatic regions of that country. (Fig. D.11).

(1) **Tropical Rain Forest** : This vegetaion consists of lofty, evergreen forest mainly hardwood species. The canopy is dense, but sufficient light penetrates to the floor of the forest to permit the growth of a lower storey of trees, bamboos and canes, and often of a luxuriant ground vegetation. Many of the trees are furnished with 'Plank-buttresses' important supports for their great height. The trees are of mixed variety, thus creates difficulty for commercial exploitation. A feature of the forests of south-eastern Asia is the large proportion of the trees which have winged seeds. The species are mainly teak, sal, bamboo, iron wood. This type of forest occurs in Sumatra, Java, Borneo, Malaysia.

The factors which influence this dense forest are high temperature all the year round and is characterized by its very small variation. Rain falls at all seasons of the year and there is, typically, no 'dry season', except in a relative sense. The rain falls in torrential down pours, usually of short duration. The relative humidity in regions of Equatorial climate is uniformly high, being on an average over 80 percent, the year through.

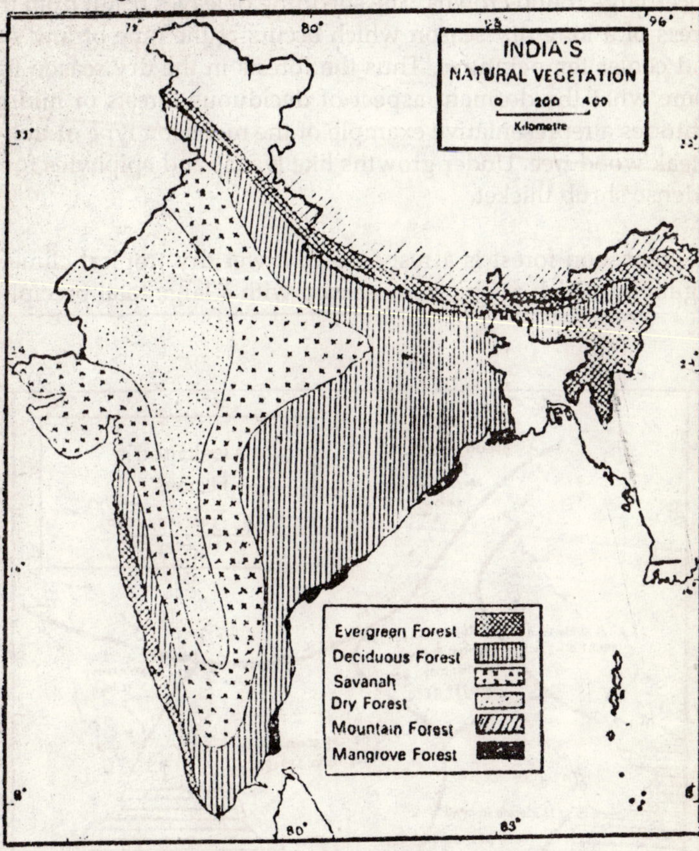

Fig. D.10

In Southern and South Eastern Asia tropical rainforests are extensive in coastal zones and highlands that have heavy monsoon rainfall and a very short dry season. The Western Ghats of India and the coastal zone of Myanmar have tropical rainforests supported by orographic rains of the south west monsoons. The Tropical rainforests are associated with a pedogenic regime of laterization under an equable climate.

Monsoon forests of South East Asia present a more open tree growth than the equatorial tropical forests. Consequently there is less competition among trees for light but greater development of vegetation in the lower layers. The trunks are massive, the barak is often thick and rough. Branching starts at a low level and produces large round crowns. The shedding of leaves result from the stress of a long dry season which occurs at the time of low sun and cooler temperatures. Thus the forests in the dry season has some what the dormant aspect of deciduous forests of middle latitudes a representative example of the monsoon type of tree is a teak wood tree. Under growths like lyanas and epiphytes form a dense shrub thicket.

Monsoon forest is a response to a wet dry tropical climatic regime in which a long rainy season with a large total precipita-

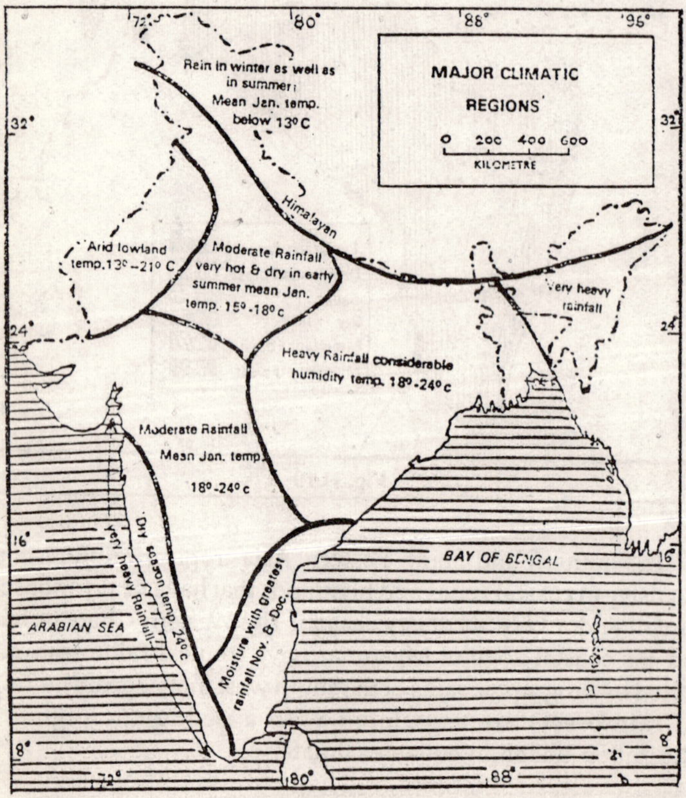

Fig. D.11

tion alternates with a dry rather cool season.

The prevailing pedogenic regime of monsoon forest areas is that of laterization. Despite water surplus is developed during the warm rainy season.

(2) **Tropical Grasslands** : As the rainfall drops below 100 cms or 75 cms it is, in general, too dry for the adequate growth of trees. The thick tropical rain forest gives place to Tropical Grassland type of vegetation separated by wide areas of ground-bare and brown for half the year, covered with green grass and herbs for the few months of the rainy season. Many of the species found as low bushes-such as Acacia catechu 'and 'Acacia luecophloea'. This type of grassland are found mostly in a continuous belt running through the Punjab, Haryana, Uttar Pradesh, Rajasthan and central part- of the Deccan.

Tropical Grasslands or 'savanas' are used as grazing ground for cattle. Some grasses are used for rope-making, thatching and oil fuel. Sabai grass is useful for paper-pulp making and rope-making and both 'kan' and 'ula' varieties of grasses are used for thatching huts. These grasses are not eaten by domestic animals.

The pedogenic process most closely associated with tropical savanas is laterization promoted by high temperature associated with the rainy season. Laterization gives way to calcification as the savana is tracked towards the higher latitudes where thorn bush and steppe grasslands are encountered.

(3) **Tropical desert vegetation**: The desert and semi-desert vegetation occur where the rainfall is less than 50 cm. Broadly it may be said that the vegetation in any given region is an impoverished representative of that found in neighbouring regions more favoured by nature in water supply. This is very much clear in case of a desert, Rajasthan, some parts of U.P, the Punjab and the Deccan have this type of forest. Desert plant have long roots and thorny leaves. Many consists of small hard leaved or sponge shrubs. Succulent plants or hard grasses. Many species of small annuals may be present but apparently after heavy rain has saturated the soil. Babul, Acacia and thorn trees are common. Various types of gum and resin are obtained from the desert plants.

A distinction may be made between true deserts, such as the heart of the Tarim Basin or the Ruba'el Khali in southern Arabia, which are virtually lifeless, and the tame deserts which support a measure of both animal and vegetable life, especially in good rainfall years. The dominant pedogenic process of dry desert is salinisation locally presenting areas of salt crust. Humus is lacking and soil are pale.

(4) **Vegetation in Tropical highlands** : With the change in altitude in the Himalayan region, there are conditions leading to a corresponding change in vegetative life. Again, the Eastern Himalayas are wetter than western and this also has some effect on the growth of different species of forests in these two areas.

(a) Vegetative zones in the western Himalayas:-

(i) Up to a height of about 900 m from the sea level, there occurs Scrub-Jungle and dry forests resembling the forests of the dry zone.

(ii) Forest of Chir-pine occur in altitude between 900 m. and 1800 m. They supply light timber and resin. Owing to transport difficulty the forests have not been fully utilized. Coniferous forests of spruce, pine, fir, cedar etc. Occur in altitude between 1800 m. and 3000 m. They supply soft timber, utilized in the manufacture of packing boxes, match-sticks, match boxes and high grade paper pulp. (iv) The Alpine vegetation is found in altitude between 3000 and 4000 m. The region is covered by sweet grasses, shrubs, rhododendrons and Junipers. The hill-pastures in Kashmir are used during summer months for sheep. On account of bad transport these forests are yet to be developed.

(b) Vegetation zones in the Eastern Himalayas.

(i) At the height of about 1200 m. from the sea-level occur the Terai forests, which contain both ever green and deciduous varieties, together with sal, tall grasses and bamboos.

(ii) The Evergreen forests of oak, magnolias, laurels, maples birches and alders occur in altitudes between 1200 m and 2400 m.

(iii) The coniferous forests of silver fir, yew, spruce and deodar occur in altitudes between 2400 m. and 3600 m. The trees supply soft timber.

(iv) The Alpine vegetation of rhododendrons and Junipers occur in altitude, between 3600 m. and 4800 m.

(5) **Vegetation in Tropical deltas** - In monsoon lands one finds tidal or mangrove forests as in the equatorial regions and fringing forests of Casuarina on sandy shores. The tidal forests of the great river deltas of the Ganga, the Mahanadi, the Godavari, the Krishna and the Cauvery contain evergeen trees of Sundari, Pussar, Byne, Keora, Garan, Gneo, Garjan, Hintal etc. and a large variety of creepers. Honey is collected from the forests. Timber for fuel and creepers and other products are obtained.

5

Field Work

Geography belongs to Earth Science, and enjoys a high position among Field Sciences. For proper understanding of the subject, observation of geographical facts in the field is absolutely essential. As a part of modern methodology comprising of three distinct categories:-

(i) Pre-field method
(ii) Field method
(iii) Post-field method.

The **Second one** is of particular geographical significance in a systematic study of terrain characteristics. Maps are one of the important tools of a geographer. They guide us to understand unseen lands along with geographical personalities of constituent regions. The study of a region through them without field checking is primarily theoritical. The first hand information is obtained only by visiting the spot. The knowledge of the surface features of the earth gained by maps may be truly visualised by sight-seeing and perfected by detailed comparison with actual facts in the field. Broadly speaking, we study in books the control and influence of natural forces over human developments. For an example, by closely analysing the topographic forms of a certain area personally, we may find a clue of human responses to the physical environment. It is for this reason that the study of geography in the field method becomes an essential despite the availability of various tools in recent years.

The field work involves the minute **observation** of landscape-both natural and cultural-in the field. The art of observation is not simple. A geographer may visualise the direct or indirect relationship between man and his environment. Regarding the nature of study to be made in a particular area certain points in connection. With the collection of data especially from primary sources in general may be explained in the following paragraphs. Primarily there are two kinds of elements in the topography:

(i) the fixed elements

(ii) the dynamic or movable elements.

On the **cultural side** primary fixed elements are buildings, fields and fences, means of communication, canals, pit-heads, mines, etc, and the main movable elements are crops, livestock, wagons, vehicles, machines and man. On **natural side**, the chief fixed elements are structure, slope and soil, etc; and main movable are drainage, climate, vegetation and animals

Besides statistical information computed by official and semi-official sources, some **geographical facts** of paramount importance about the people living in isolated corners can be obtained only by personal observation and interview with the local people. It is very likely that the people will utter many unscientific things, but patiently and sympathetically they have to be listened. Enquiry should not be confined to one individual or one locality. You must meet many people wisely selected from various sample villages within the area. Sometimes it may become essential to stay with them for long and develop close association by frequent visits. Thus some of the interesting aspects of their life may be revealed which can be correlated with the natural environment from a true perspective.

How to write the regional account?

After collecting the data according to the instructions discussed in a systematic geographical account of the region examined may be written indoors. Field specimens of rocks, minerals and soils can be pested in the note book. In writing the account help may be taken from other books and papers. For drawing climatic statistics, if available, may be used. Settlement and communication maps may be drawn by simply tracing those features from topographical sheets. Drainage map with changes in the course of the streams, noted in the field can be prepared.

Thus a report of anarea should be written under the following heads in general :

(i) Area and location (ii) Physical features with special reference to structure and landforms (iii) Drainage characteristics (iv) Climate (v) Natural Vegetation (vi) Soil (vii)Population and settlements (viii) Resources (viii) Land use agriculture, dairy farming, and forest (cultural) (ix) Economic Industries (x) Means of transport and communication and trade (xi) Suggestions for planned development (Land use Planning).

These headings may be modified according to the nature of investigation. For instance, if you are investigating and studying the land form of the area, then the heading will vary. Landform study will be made under:

(i) Geology and structure, (ii) Types of landform (iii) Evolution of landforms in relation of structure, process and stage; (iv) Influence of landforms on human activities.

In case the investigation is in the field of Human Geography the account will be under:
(i) Environmental setting, (ii) Distribution of population
(iii) Human Habitations (iv) Food (v) clothing (vi) Economic activities (vii) Social customs (viii) Stage of cultural Development (ix) Cultural Associations.

Problems and Patterns of Field Research

Before undertaking a field research programme, it is essential to be familiar with what others have discussed about the area selected for intensive observation. Such a familiarity with the existing knowledge of the area concerned is quite helpful in visualizing the objective and correct perspective of the problem pertaining to physical and/ or socio-cultural, economic and historical aspects.

For a successful research in geography, the following essential series of steps to be followed before the working programmes:

(1) **Formulation of the Field problem**: or the asking of a previously unanswed question in exact terms. This also includes the previous determination of the areal extent within which the research work will be conducted.

(2) **Determination of the type of data to be collected**: pertinent to the research problem. The specific nature of the research problem and the size areal extent of the matrix will determine the type

of data that must be obtained, the way the data will be classified, how the data will be collected and processed will depend on the problems.

(3) **Collection of data** : which involves the analysis of published materials and field survey through questionnaire method.

(4) **Analysing and processing the collected data**: which involves the selection of appropriate cartographic and statistical methods of analysis. Further, this final step includes stating the conclusion and determining if the proposed hypotheses are confirmed or rejected.

It is quite obvious from an examination of Fig E.1 that the approaches to field studies involve certain systematic steps. By

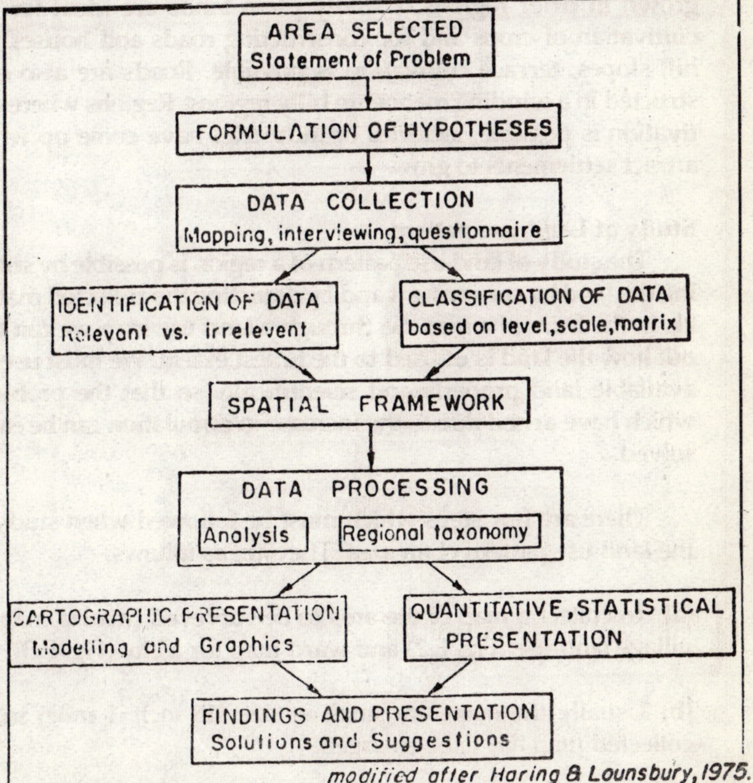

Fig. E.1

following such steps as shown in the model, one may be able to present quite clearly scientific analyis of the area selected for field study.

This model (Fig. E.1) has been constructed after Haring and Lounsbury (1975).

The Different uses of land

In geography to study the different utilites of land is an important aspect. We use land in different ways:-residential, roads, factories, agricultural use etc. Some lands are arable where agriculture is possible while some are non-arable which are left vacant. Crops which are grown along rivers and near any water body or in a region with high rainfall is different from those that are grown in drier regions. Usually plain lands are ideal for the cultivatian of crops and for constructing roads and houses. On hill slopes, terrace cultivation is possible. Roads are also constructed in a winding manner in hilly regions. Regions where cultivation is possible, factories or industries have come up which attract settlements to grow.

Study of Land use pattern

The study of land use pattern of a region is possible by studying the land by surveying it and by depicting the collected materials in the form of a map. So through a land use map we can find out how the land is utilised to the fullest extent. We must use the available land properly and scientifically so that the problems which have arised due to the increase in population can be easily solved.

There are few steps which must be followed when studying the land use pattern of an area. They are as follows:-

(a) To collect a map of the area to be surveyed (mauza map for village land use (Fig. E.2) and ward map for a city (Fig. E.3).

(b) Usually the maps are small in size (16 inch=1 mile) so the collected map has to be enlarged.

(b) The enlarged map must have proper scale and the north line must be shown. All the mauzas or the wards must have numbers.

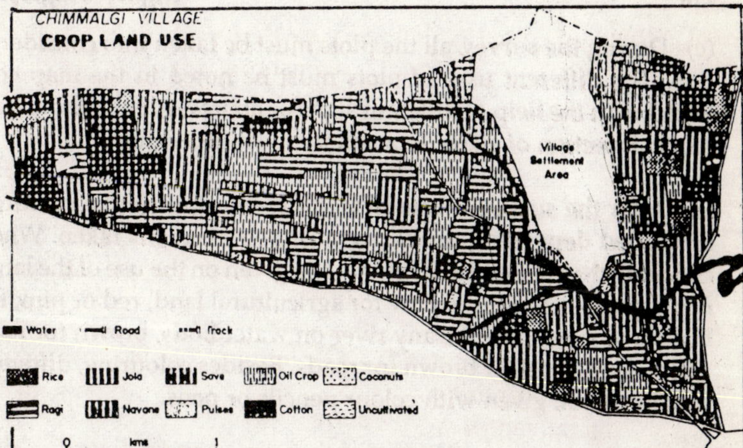
CHIMMALGI VILLAGE
CROP LAND USE
Village Settlement Area
Water
Road
Track
Rice
Jola
Save
Oil Crop
Coconuts
Ragi
Navane
Pulses
Cotton
Uncultivated
kms

Fig. E.2

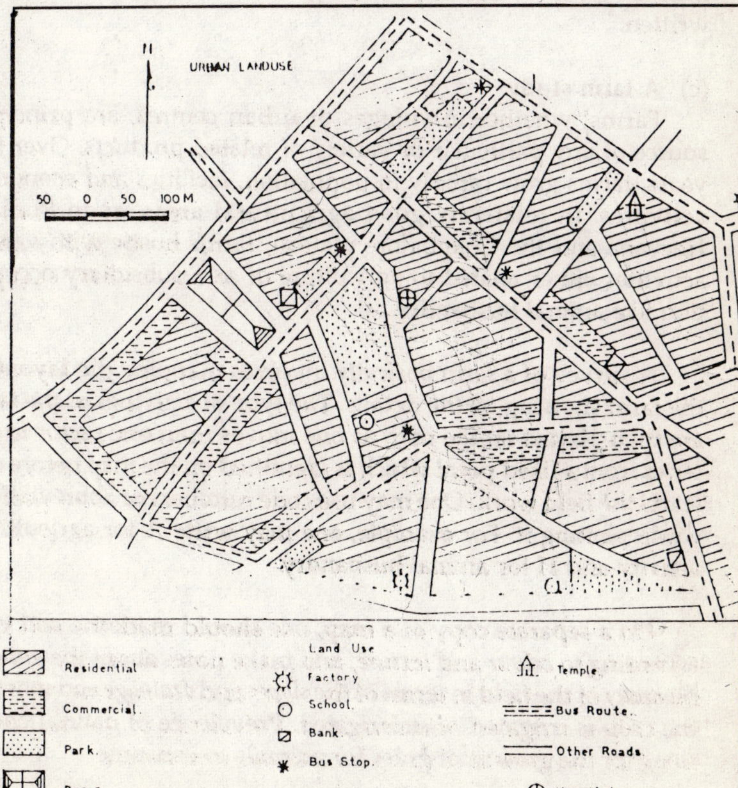
N
URBAN LANDUSE
50
0
50
100 M.
Land Use
Residential
Commercial.
Park.
Bazar
Factory
School.
Bank.
Bus Stop.
Temple.
Bus Route.
Other Roads.
Hospital.

Fig. E.3

(c) During the survey, all the plots must be taken into consideration. The different uses of plots must be noted in the map collected with the help of different signs or abbreviation of the actual name. Selection of signs depends upon an individual.

(d) After the survey is complete, different plots can be coloured or shaded depending on the signs or abbreviations taken. When choosing the colour attention must be given on the use of the land. For example green or yellow for agricultural land, red or pink for houses or huts, blue for any river on water body, brown for non-arable land, black or brown for roads. Besides colouring, different shades can be given with colour pencils or pens.

(e) After the land use map is complete, ward or mauza numbers must be given. The names of villages, towns local thane must be written.

(c) **A farm study**

Farms, whether in villages or urban centres, are principle source of any particular or variety of related products. Over the years, farms grow rapidly in population, facilities and economic activities. In relatively good agricultural areas, as in Punjab, Haryana and the Coimbatore plateau, farms bustle with varied activities either related to agriculture or as a subsidiary occupation like animal husbandry.

A survey of a farm basically involves mapping the **layout** of the farm showing all the details. The type of activities of the farm are then plotted on the map as one moves from one sector to the other from a fixed point which is identified on the map before one starts the field work. One may use code numbers or abbreviations while plotting it. For example, one may write A for agricultural activity and H for animal husbandry.

On a separate copy of a map, one should mark the **soil type** according to *colour* and *texture*, and make notes about the general *character* of the field in terms of the *slopes* and *drainage* and whether the crop is irrigated or unirrigated. Prevalence of natural conditions for the growth of grass for animals to consume.

Another copy of a map where the different products being made *sector-wise* are to be marked.

Next comes the *enquiry* with the farmers and other workers of the farm. For this purpose one will need a schedule and questionnaire in which the various columms are filled up by the gathered informations from the persons questionned.

The farmer is the person who takes decisions regarding the crop to be grown and the intensity of land use with irrigation and other inputs to raise the productivity of the land. The questionnaire is given below for convenience.

Table : 4

Farm Reconnaisence Survey :- No.1

Sl No.	Field No.	Name of farmer	Area of field in hectors	Type of Soil (red, black loamy etc)	Crops Grown[1]			Irrigation Kharif		
					Kharif	Rabi	Inter season	Kharif	Rabi	Inter season
1										
2										
3										
4										
5										
6										

1. Tabulation to be made on actually grown.
2. Farmers are to be asked about the number of times he irrigates the land in a given time, and his source of water for irrigates.

Other activities e.g raising of animals for milk and making different products out of milk are to be surveyed and reports to be made on them.

Table-5

Sl No.	Field No.	Area inhectares	Animals Kept (Number)	Goods Extracted	Products made out of them.
1					
2					
3					
4					

Transport plays a big role in sending the finished products to the markets to sale. Thus the mode of transportation is to be noted.

For the purposes of compiling the information one may have to form different groups of students. This will enable to cover a larger area in a short time.

The next stage of the work involves proper tabulation of the data gathered from the students and to prepare a map of land use, using colours or live-shading for different crops and other activities.

Another map may be prepared to show soil types. Having completed the mapping, interpretation is to be done on the pattern of land use and its variations.

The data collected on different products made and their related raw materials are to be correlated.

Analysis of the maps and tables is then presented as the final report of the field work, enclosing the maps and tables in appropriate sections of the report.

(d) A Study of Port

A port refers to a point which provides a connecting link between sea and land. A country's exportable surplus is brought from its surrounding areas to that place on the water route where ships can find accomodation during the period of loading and unloading of cargo.

To study a port, few surveys are to be made keeping in mind few important objectives.

Firstly of all whether the port concerned has a natural or an artificial harbour is to be found out. A natural harbour is generally an indentation in the coast line sufficiently enclosed or protected by its environment e.g Bombay.

An artificial harbour is constructed in those places where environmental and topographic features are not favourable. Where the water is shallow, dredges keep the outlet deep, e.g Madras.

Secondly the hinterland of the port has to be marked and can be plotted on a location map of the port. Actually, the trade of a port reflects the conditions of production, consumption and transport facilities of its hinterland. So all these aspects are to be studied.

Thirdly According to the location, a port has to be categorised:- (a) Ocean port, (b) River port, (c) canal port, (d) estuary port.

Fourthly The trade through a port consists of three kinds - (a) export, (b) import and (c) entrepot. These are to be studied through data collection and surveying. An entrepot is the procedure of importing commodities for the purpose of re-export. Entrepot goods should have a high value and good keeping quality so as to stand long journey and delay.

Fifthly: The importance of a port can be measured by considering the following points which are usually employed as standards of comparison :-

(i) The number of ships entered during a year (ii) the gross tonnage of ships entered in a year (iii) tonnage of goods handled by a port in a year; i.e, volume of imports into a port and exports through a port (iv) value of the goods handled by a port (v) earnings of a port.

After the collection of relevent data and informations, a final report is to made with maps and diagrams must be given wherever required and possible.

In conclusion, the future prospects of the port is to be made giving the surveyer's view to it should be added.

(e) A study of some land forms

To study some land forms of a particular region, the concerned toposheet printed by Survey of India has to be collected. The topographical sheet will help us to correlate the landforms with natural vegetation land form with the human habitation of the area under study.

Block diagram is a technique which may be utilized to show effectively different types of landforms and their evolution. Its chief advantages lies in the fact that it is diagrammatic and unlike maps it is three dimensional; thus it is possible to lay great emphasis on the prominent features.

Landforms of Nainital and Adjoining Region

The topo-sheet number 530/7 comprises mostly a part of Nainital District. At a glance, two sub-regions may be identified: (i) The Siwalik foot hill region, and (ii) the Terai region. The rugged topography of the hilly tract presents a keen contrast to the flat lowland topography of the Terai region. The streams emerging from the hills on the plain below are strikingly divided into numerous branches and channels. In the hilly region the main water parting may be marked distinctly, which runs from Nainital north-west ward, separating the south westerly drainage from the north-easterly drainage which is carried by Jokh nadi, Ghora gad and Mawani Gadhera etc. The extensive Tal around which the town of Nainital has grown up presents a remarkable feature at an average elevation of about 1829 meters above sea level. The main river of the basin may be easily marked along the line from which the drainage is flowing into the present Tal on the one hand and also going out wards in all directions on the other (see Fig. E.4a, 4b, and 4c).

Thus the bottom of the basin is occupied by water pouring into the present Tal and the remaining portion of the basin is studded with habitations. Students must note the narrow 'v' shaped gorges and the breaks in the longitudinal profile of the rivers in their hilly courses. The streams have steep gradients in their upper reaches and the moment they descend to the plain they become gentle and their capacity to carry loads decreases and the main channel is divided into numerous branches.

Forests mantle the plain and hill slopes in general. Settlements are thinly distributed. Linear settlements are found along streams and canals. The region is made conspicuous by the scarcity of modern means of communication. The circuitous nature of the metalled road that leads you form Kathgodam to Nainital will exhibit the true nature of terrain which stands in the way of constructing roads in the hill.

(f) **A study of mining complex**

Mines are the areas from where minerals are extracted. Mines

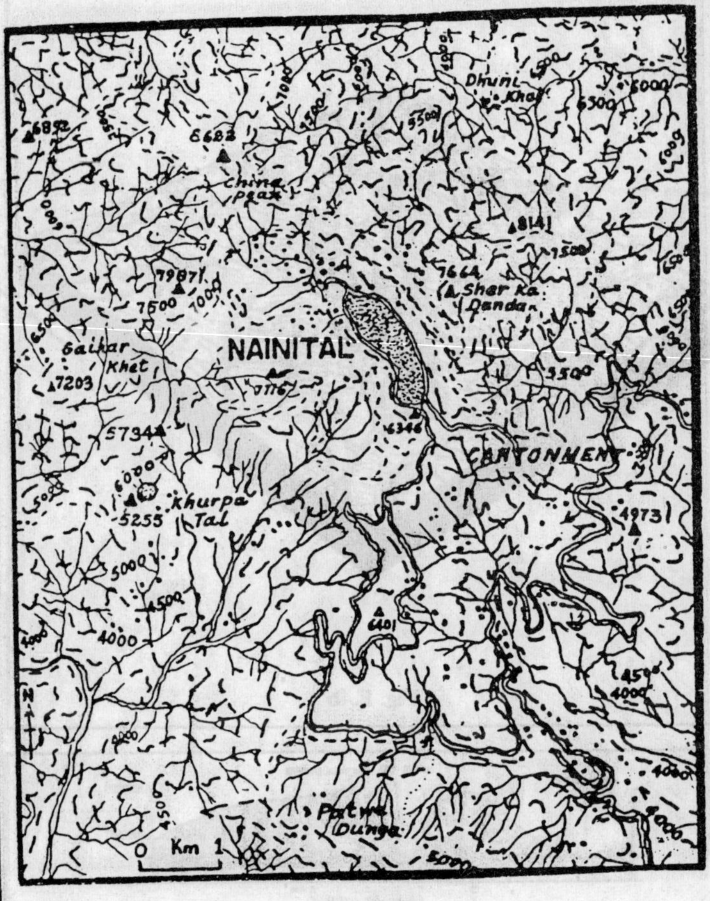

Fig. E.4a

can be open-cast (Fig. E.5a) or closed (Fig. E.5b) Over the years the techniques of extracting minerals have changed. The survey of a mining complex essentially involves field observation and local enquiry with the help of a questionnaire.

Objectives of the Survey

The survey of a mining complex could have several objectives, depending upon the purpose of the survey. A mine can be studied with a view to understand the mineral which is extracted and the different processes involved in it.

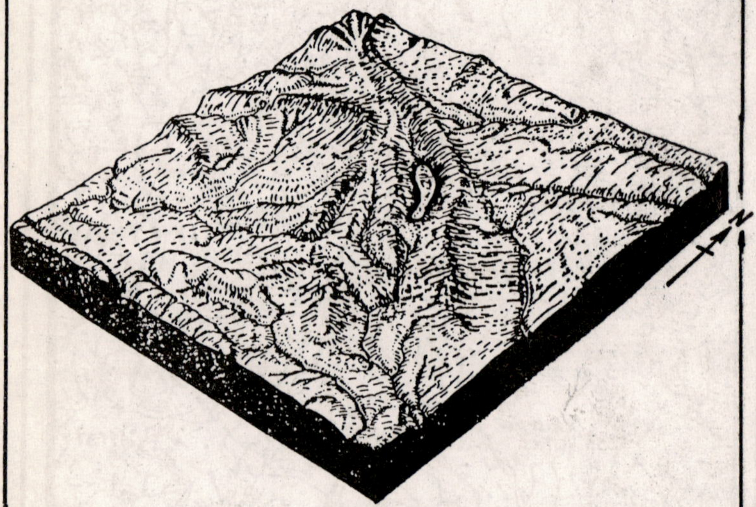

Fig. E.4b

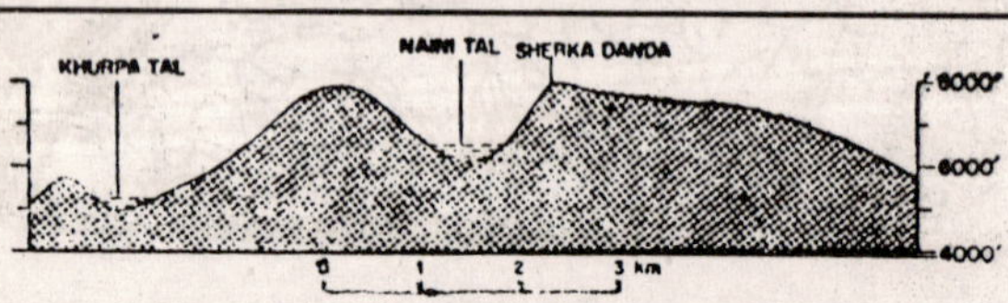

Profile section from Khurpa Tal to Sher Ka Danda Peak.

Fig. E.4c

Conducting the Survey

We shall now illustrate the various stages in the procedure for conducting a survey of the mine with the objective of analysing the type of mine and the workers involved.

A **Preliminary study** has to be made in choosing a mine keeping in view its safety and its accessibility. Once the selection of the

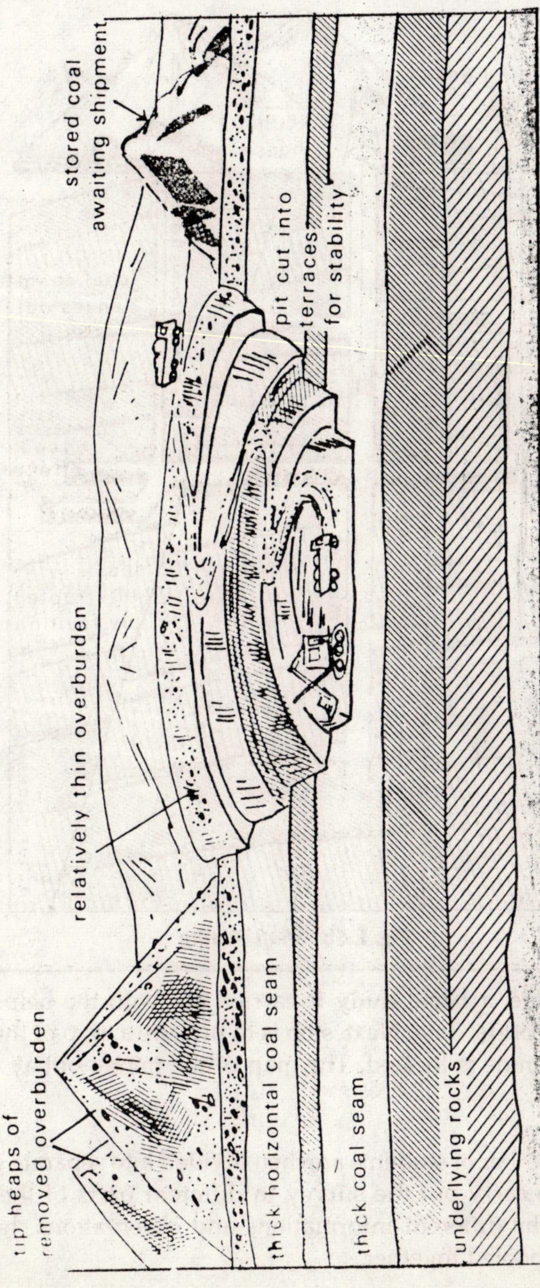

Fig. E.5a *Open-cast mining*

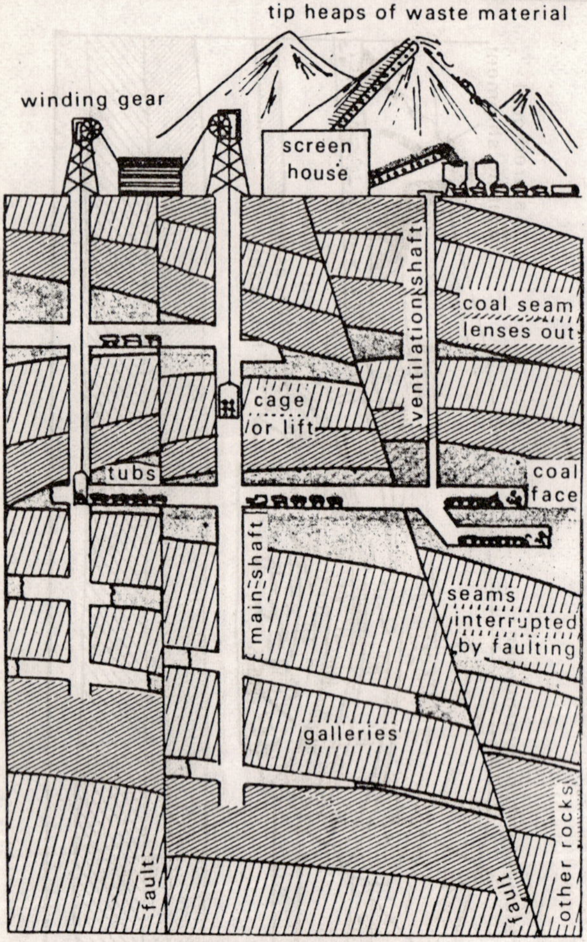

Fig. E.5b *Shaft mining*

mine is made, a **basic study** is carried out with the help of the available reports, data. **Next** step is to procure a map of the place where the mine is located. The map of the mine's outlay can be prepared.

The number of students are then divided into separate groups in order to carry out the survey in different parts of the mine. **Later** on, the different informations and observations thus collected are pooled together.

Questionnaire and Processing of the Data

The following questions should be asked from the proprietor, manager, public relations officer or other responsible persons of the organization. Wherever it is necessary, include a map or a sketch map along with the area given.

a) what do you mine?
b) Is it an open-cast or underground mine?
c) What is the average quantity of the minerals being extracted daily?
d) How are they processed?
e) What are the chief items of capital goods, machinery and the like?
d) What is the paid-up capital of the unit?
f) Labour

[Note : Try to understand the technology of extracting the mineral from its ore].

Please give the number of employees in the following categories and also indicate the residential addresses of all or on a sample basis (every fifth, tenth, fifteenth and so on) for each category. Include the information on report as diagram (numbers) and flow map with explanatory comments.

Number Residential address

(i) Manual
(ii) Semi-skilled
(iii) Skilled
(iv) Secretarial or clerical
(iv) Managerial or Executive

(g) **Markets**

Where are the minerals chiefly sold?

[Note : Mention the industries using the mineral as their raw material and their location with respect to the mine and also if the mineral is supplied directly to any specific market]

(h) **Land Use**

What is the land use of the area under the mine ?

[Note: Include access roads, car parks, mining area, outdoor storage of raw materials, space for gardens, recreation, etc.]

(i) **Power**

What source of power do you use?

(i) Electricity
(ii) Diesel
(iii) Steam
(iv) Others (Non- conventional energy)

[Note: Use horse power, hours per day, kilowatt hours or other appropriate units.]

(j) **Water**

(i) What is the source of water?
(ii) How much (in M^3)?
(iii) For what purpose?
(iv) What is the degree of pollution through discharge of waste materials?

(Include in report as text unless it is a main item for your unit; justifying a map or flow diagram).

(k) **Transport**

What are the modes of transport used for the extracted minerals?

Table-6

Mineral	Rail	Lorry	Tempo	Bullock cart	Human Labour	Other

(l) Extent of pollution and measures to minimise pollution (m)

(m) Accidents if any

[Note : The mode of accident, year, number of casualties]

(n) Stability or change

(i) Is the mine stable/growing/declining ?
(ii) Are the processes stable or changing (if changing state nature

of change?)
(Include a report as text)

(o) Conclusion:-Finalise your report with a short section on the objectives. Add any views you have found about the significance of the mine for the economy and society of its environs, or in some cases for the region and the nation.

(g) **A study of a manufacturing industry**

To a study a manufacturing industry special questionnaire for the survey of the industry is to be made.

The questionnaire are to be distributed among the workers of the industry. After the survey is complete, the collected data and informations are to be grouped and processed for the final report.

Reconnaisence Survey

1. Name
2. Name of the industry
3. Ward number (for Location purpose)
4. Address of the industry
5. Year of establishment
6. Nature of manufacturing goods
7. Total number of workers- (a) local (b) from out side
8. Number of workers directly related with the manufacturing unit (blue-colour factory staff)
9. Number of workers of the administrative unit (white colour office staff)
10. Other (driver, gate-keeper, sweeper etc.)
11. Monthly income:-

	Group (in rupees)	Total number
a.	500	a.
b.	500 to 750	b.
c.	751 to 1000	c.
d.	1001 to 1500	d.
e.	1501 to 2000	e.
f.	2001 and above	f.

12. What are the products that are manufactured in the industry?
13. Source of raw materials
14. Yearly rate of production
15. Markets of the products

a) Local e) Different parts of India
b) Calcutta d) Outside India.

16. Means of transportation of the products to the concerned markets.
17. Facilities of stay of the workers, if any:-
    a) All the workers c) None
    b) Group of workers
18. Total working hours/day of the industry
    a) 24 hours c) 8 hours
    b) 12 hours d) Any other working nature of the industry
19. Any information not related to above questions of the industry.
20. Surveyor's view.